# INTROI
# POPULAᴋ ᴄᴜᴌᴛᴜᴋᴇ

## THEORIES, APPLICATIONS AND
## GLOBAL PERSPECTIVES

J. RANDALL GROVES | JOHN SCOTT GRAY | ROBERT QUIST

*Ferris State University*

**Kendall Hunt**
publishing company

Cover and chapter opener images supplied by Yue Min Jun Studio

**Kendall Hunt**
publishing company

www.kendallhunt.com
*Send all inquiries to:*
4050 Westmark Drive
Dubuque, IA 52004-1840

Copyright © 2012 by J. Randall Groves, John Scott Gray, Robert Quist

ISBN 978-1-4652-2346-3

Kendall Hunt Publishing Company has the exclusive rights to reproduce this work, to prepare derivative works from this work, to publicly distribute this work, to publicly perform this work and to publicly display this work.

All rights reserved. No part of this publication may be reproduced, stored in a retrieval system, or transmitted, in any form or by any means, electronic, mechanical, photocopying, recording, or otherwise, without the prior written permission of the copyright owner.

Printed in the United States of America
10 9 8 7 6 5 4

# CONTENTS

# ACKNOWLEDGMENTS

I would like to thank Ferris State University for the sabbatical they gave me to write the first chapter. I would also like to thank my wife, Lynette Vought, for her decades of support for my projects. Her advice, suggestions and corrections were invaluable to me in the writing of this book.

*John Groves*

I would like to thank my two co-authors, Professors Groves and Gray for their helpful support. I would also like to thank my wife Melanie for her continued support.

*Robert Quist*

I would like to offer a few words of thanks to my mentors who started me on the road to a life of the mind. In particular, Thomas Buford at Furman University, Elmer Duncan at Baylor University, and George Schedler at Southern Illinois University in Carbondale have served as great inspirations and role-models that I have unsuccessfully tried to emulate in my own career. I also want to thank my students throughout the years, whose creativity and desire to ask questions make my job as fulfilling as it is. In addition, thank you Kirsten Johnston and Ella Shaw, the two secretaries in the Department of Humanities, for their constant assistance and for helping to keep an absent minded professor on the straight and narrow, as well as my colleagues in the department, both past and present, whose constant hallway conversations push me to be a better scholar. Lastly, I would most like to thank my wife, Jo Anna Meyer, for her continued support, inspiration, and collaboration. Any good ideas that might be found in my writing probably had their origin in her mind.

*John Scott Gray*

# INTRODUCTION: A NOTE TO EDUCATORS

This book was written to fill a need for a textbook on Popular Culture at the beginner's level. After teaching the course for years using textbooks unsuited to our students, the authors decided to create a basic text that covers the core theories as well as a range of issues typical of cultural studies. We also thought that adding a global perspective would be beneficial since the cultural arena is increasingly global in nature. The result is the book before you.

The authors have tried to represent a comprehensive range of cultural theories used the most by theorists of popular culture. It is our view that restricting this range any further would undermine the claim to a general overview of cultural studies. We believe teachers and students of cultural studies will appreciate the broad range of theories presented here. Teachers may very well choose to ignore one or more theories covered because of their own interests or the type of class being taught. These teachers will find, however, that the theories they actually want will be there. Readers may also find that they like using all the theories, as the authors do. The same is true of the rest of the chapters in this book. They can be read largely independent of each other. So the instructor may pick and choose which ones to use in the course. The book's modularity makes this sort of adjustment rather easy. One might skip any particular chapter, but use the rest of the book without having to look up things in the chapter that was skipped. The exception to this rule might be the theory chapters, which provide students with the toolbox they will need to tackle the topics of the other chapters; but the rest of the chapters are meant to be largely independent of each other. Although one chapter may reference another, the full explanation of any point is always within a given chapter. Because of this chapter independence, the professor can pick and choose those closest to his or her interests and expertise.

The authors have a multitheoretic approach to popular culture, which is reflected in the number of theories covered in the first two chapters. The idea is that human experience is by its nature open-ended. No single theory can capture all the dimensions of human experience. A purely economic analysis, for example, will probably neglect the psychological or structural aspects of a text. A religious interpretation may neglect the economic dimension of a text. So cultural interpretation, by necessity, uses many theories. We call the group of theories covered our "toolbox." The toolbox can be applied to more than popular culture texts. The toolbox can be used to interpret all cultural texts of whatever sort. It is in this sense that the book asserts the aesthetic continuity between high culture and popular culture. While we acknowledge the aesthetic greatness of high art, that does not keep us from an appreciation of popular culture. Not only is popular culture interesting from a social scientific point of view, it also deserves a place in the aesthetic conversation. We will make this case in a number of places in the book.

The theoretical foundations and the canon of cultural theory are intimately related in this book. The cultural theories and topics covered are intended not only to function as a theoretical foundation for cultural studies, but also as a canonical statement of the dominant theories. It is both hermeneutics and social science; and ultimately, it is philosophy. Only philosophy has the generality to appreciate the complexity of popular culture. One can read this book as a proposed statement of the core theories and topics that should be covered by the field of popular culture. Any treatment of popular culture should begin with theories. After the theoretical foundations are laid, any general treatment of popular culture should address some of the dominant genres. We picked horror, science fiction, superheroes, and comedy since together these constitute a large percentage of the overall market in film and television. The same is true of the sports market. Any general analysis of popular culture that neglects these genres or the sports market is missing much of the phenomena they are treating.

Technology holds a special place in popular culture. Technology is not a genre, theory, or sport, but it has come to play such an important role in the way people consume popular culture that it merits serious treatment. The significance of technology goes deep. This "depth analysis" of technology as more than the mere history of artifacts but as a constitutive part of human being goes back to Heidegger and Marx. The analysis of particular technologies (printing press, the steam engine) also has a long pedigree. The computer, the internet, Facebook, etc., are rapidly changing our world, and we try to analyze the issues raised by these changes.

While we have been fairly successful at providing a synoptic view of the theories in cultural studies, no book could cover every major topic. Are there still gaps in our treatment? Yes. We neglect, for example, romance and reality television. These are important genres to understand, but this book does very little with these topics and many others. However, a conscientious effort to work through what is in this book would prepare someone to tackle those genres. Of greater significance is the absence of a section on popular music. Music, however, requires more in the way of theoretical understanding than we could give in a textbook of this type. It is also unlikely that we could assume students had ever had a course in music appreciation, so we would have to cover a significant amount of basic theory to even get started with an analysis of popular music. There are complete texts and courses on popular music that would be a better venue for an analysis of popular music.

A common flaw among textbooks on cultural studies is the lack of political impartiality. There is a strong tendency for textbooks in cultural studies toward a left-leaning perspective. While we cover each of the theories of interpretation, we do not take a stand on the politics of each theory. That is left up to the student to decide. It is our view that these theories are useful even to those who might disagree with the politics of those espousing the theory. One can use Marxist economic interpretation on texts without agreeing to the dictatorship of the proletariat. One does not need to be a feminist to use theories developed by feminists to analyze sex and gender in texts. The grouping of the theories according to academic discipline (economics, religion, sociology, etc.) helps to break free of some of the ideological bias typical of cultural studies. Instead of just treating Marxism, for example, we look at the more general economic dimension of texts. While we give Marxist theories, for example, the lion's share of the space on economic interpretation, we also raise the possibility of other approaches. In this time of political polarization it is important to present cultural studies as neutrally as possible.

This is a book for a broad range of undergraduate students, from nonmajors to majors in the humanities at the beginning of their education. It is written so that any competent college-level student can understand the reading. Cultural theory is difficult enough without the additional burden of overly opaque readings and specialized vocabularies, so we have tried to present the theories and issues in as plain a language as we can. Some terminology is necessary, of course, but it is best kept to a minimum for a textbook like this.

It is important to note that we have made a vigorous effort to have up-to-date examples. We try to make sure the student could easily find a way to view any example we give. We also reference important classics when doing so contributes to the students' understanding or is some sort of canonical need (everyone needs to know about the shower scene in *Psycho*). But we try to keep our examples very current. We are well aware that our students are not experiencing the same culture in which the authors grew up.

The role of popular culture in universities' general education mission bears comment. The reality of undergraduate education at most universities is that students get nothing near a synoptic view of the world of high culture. It is not uncommon for students to only have to take three courses in the cultural areas (Humanities, English, Philosophy, History). This means there are going to be wide swaths of ignorance remaining after an undergraduate education. Given this situation, it is important that students get some understanding that human life, like art, is an interpretive exercise. This book's first two chapters offer a basic treatment of the standard theories one would end up with after extensive study of cultural theory. These theories give a student a good foundation for approaching many different kinds of texts, including their own lives. The other topics are defensible in their own right. Students need to think very seriously about technology, for example, given the effect it will most certainly have on their lives. We are living in a science-fiction world, so understanding the future shock it may bring is important. It is true that the genres we chose are not uniquely essential, but they are certainly as good as any others we might have chosen. And it is true that a life that only consumed pop culture would be culturally impoverished. Harry Potter is not King Lear; that much is certainly true. But a student who studied this book will know how to interpret his or her world and would even be better prepared to interpret any high culture they happened to come across.

Why study popular culture at all? Why not confine ourselves to high culture? We need to study and understand popular culture because it is the cultural sea in which we swim. Most of our students are going to consume much more popular culture than high culture after graduation. But each of those students will still have to engage the world interpretively. Their world of interpretation, to a significant extent, is going to be the realm of popular culture. Popular culture will be important to people's lives; it will be the jungle in which they need to survive. It will affect how they see the world, but it is largely outside their control. This book is an attempt to foster student autonomy, to help them avoid the unthinking acceptance of a culture produced by a culture industry.

Culture will not take care of itself. We must tend to it, and to tend to it we must first understand it. We cannot rely on the producers of popular culture to consider the effects of popular culture on our way of life or cultural autonomy. The producers of popular culture have no real interest in the betterment of their customers. That is not their job. They want to sell books, movies, and music. To maximize their profits, they simply produce what will become most popular. What will become most popular constitutes a distinct category of texts that is not necessarily the same as what a person should consume if they wish to maintain their autonomy. That is why a book like this can provide a great service for our students; it provides needed skills in cultural self-defense.

There is a civic aspect to the study of popular culture. Autonomous citizens make for a more genuine public sphere in a democracy. A public sphere inhabited by college graduates with a thorough knowledge of the great books, social sciences, and other relevant disciplines would be even better than one which only had a single treatment of many theories like this book gives. But the latter is a good consolation prize if our students cannot get a full treatment of cultural study because their general education requirements do not require it.

The chapters can be grouped into the theory chapters (chapters one and two), the global perspective chapter (chapter seven), the genre chapters (chapters three and four), and the sports and the technology chapters. The theory chapters, as we have indicated, are meant to provide the "toolbox" of theories that students can use to interpret texts. The treatments of each theory are brief and aimed directly at that part of each theory conducive to interpreting texts. The idea was to give the student "handles" for interpretation. These brief treatments, of course, are no replacement for a full-semester course on cultural theory, but they do give the student something fairly clear and solid to apply to textual interpretation. One of the difficulties students face in tackling cultural theory is coming away with a clear sense of how the theory can be applied to cases. The two theory chapters try to do that. The chapters also use contemporary examples to make sure the student is on familiar ground, but there is also occasional reference to the texts to high art to remind the student of the ultimate continuity of popular and high culture. The topic of aesthetics was given its own chapter to indicate that although the authors think that the theories discussed in chapter one are crucial to a complete understanding of texts, aesthetics remains at the core of textual analysis.

Chapter three covers Horror, Science Fiction, and Super Heroes—three of the most popular genres in film and print. Seven of the top ten blockbusters of all time fall into one of these genres. Because of this popularity the authors decided to spend a complete chapter on these three related genres. Given that students will probably see more films and read more books in these genres than any other, it makes sense to concentrate our examples of interpretation in these genres. The centerpiece of the chapter is the interpretation of the *Alien* films, all of which are still available in most video rental stores. These films have been a constant subject of interpretation by cultural theorists since they came out, and for good reason: In addition to being aesthetically defensible films, they are excellent vehicles for using the theories laid out in the first chapter. The chapter also contains extensive treatments of vampires and zombies, both of which turn out to be quite amenable to cultural analysis.

Comedy is also an extremely popular genre, and it too receives a full-chapter treatment. We begin with the theories of comedy, and then turn to a description of several types of comedy. The authors believe that any genre is capable of greatness, and this includes comedy. Because of market imperatives comedy tends to the lowest common denominator, but there is nothing inherently unsophisticated or unworthy about comedy. Comedy can achieve high art even if it fails to do so most of the time. But that is true of all genres. This book operates on the assumption of qualitative neutrality about the inherent aesthetic value of genres. It is no aesthetic mark against a text that it falls into a certain genre.

The role of technology in affecting popular culture cannot be overstated. The digital revolution is in full swing as we connect ever more closely with iPhones, Facebook, iTunes, and games. This closeness is a central topic of chapter five. Our consumption patterns of music and video are becoming very different. At what point do changes in our consumption patterns mark a change in our identity? Recent changes in our technological lives have raised the possibility that we are becoming different kinds of people. We seem to be becoming more open with our thoughts and feelings. This has meant a corresponding loss in privacy, and many people find this problematic, but the trend continues nonetheless.

Sports is a major industry and merits a chapter-length treatment. Most people follow at least one sport, and the economy of sports is extremely large. Sports stars are the new heroes. Americans participate in sports in large numbers, and they watch in equally large numbers. The Super Bowl has become almost an American holiday. But sports, like all cultural phenomena, is deeply affected by the market and the rationalization process that comes with it. It is also the arena for the standard questions of race and gender. The first woman or non-white person in a sport is always news. So while sport may seem to be a very different kind of thing than films or songs, it is subject to many of the same fissures.

The chapter on global popular culture is meant as a corrective to U.S.-centered treatments of popular culture. We had considered making the whole book completely international, with examples throughout from all over the world, but we felt it would actually hinder comprehension rather than aid it since no student from any given culture would get a majority of the references. Having a chapter that goes through the next three most important cultural markets—India, China, and Japan—seemed to be the best way of adding the international perspective in a general book on popular culture. While it is nothing like a comprehensive examination of any of these popular cultures, all of which have been the subject of full book-length treatments, it nevertheless gives the student a solid start in approaching the popular culture of other countries. We try to get the key historical and cultural facts about these countries that will best inform the analysis of their popular cultures. This knowledge will provide a nice bridge for any other international education students receive during their college careers. Students should find the background material presented on India, China, and Japan to be not only consistent with what they would learn in a history, political science, language, or literature course on these countries, but to supplement it and enrich it as well. Understanding Chinese popular culture, for example, will give students in a history class on China a better understanding of the long-term significance of Confucius, Mao, Deng Xiaoping, the cultural revolution, and economic reform.

This book constitutes an attempt to provide the student with a basic understanding of popular culture. It provides them with a greater ability to interpret texts of all types, which, in turn, makes them more informed citizens and autonomous agents. We believe students and educators alike will find the book readable and fun as well as educational and transformative. We hope you enjoy our book.

# CHAPTER 1

# The Concept of the Text and Theories of Interpretation

The study of popular culture is wide-ranging. Cultural theorists examine everything from films to television to video games and popular music. What is it about these things that they can all be fruitfully studied by an academic field? They can all be seen as "texts." You probably are not used to the term "text" used in this way. A text, in cultural studies, is anything that can be interpreted. The most common use of the term is in reference to books, but the meaning has been extended to many other things. Films, comic books, iPods, cars, television and video games are just some of the texts that can be "read." When cultural theorists use the term "read" we mean *interpret*. In other words, we use the term "read" as a metaphor for "interpret." In fact, one can think of this whole book as a series of lessons in interpretation. This book will teach you aesthetic, economic, ideological, moral, religious, memetic and feminist forms of interpretation. These tools will give you a start in understanding the more important aspects of your cultural reality. They will also enrich you as you learn to apply the theories to your own life.

Interpretive ability is probably the most important skill one can have. It is the ability to apply multiple frameworks of understanding and different sets of assumptions. Learning new models of interpretation from one's own and other cultures is absolutely crucial in today's globalized planet. We all live in cultures populated by texts infused with meanings, but these texts do not interpret themselves. They must be given interpretations, must be given meaning, in order for us to function in the cultural world.

The first thing to understand about interpretation is that it comes from somewhere because *we* come from somewhere. We all have a "point of view." This point of view for the Chinese is different from the cultural world Indians or Americans inhabit, but there is overlap between these cultural worlds, so we are able to understand them. Indeed, it is imperative that we do so since the world is increasingly more intertwined than the world of the past. So we must pay attention to both local and non-local identities.

We all grow up in cultures. Our identities are formed in interaction with these cultures. This gives everyone a sense of "place." The "place" from which we interpret the world is elusive. On the one hand, it is easy to describe our culture. We can just say "American" or "Peruvian" or "Russian." But each of these societies is heterogeneous, which means, for example, that the cultural experience of an American from rural Mississippi is quite different from that of an American from New York. In fact, in some ways, the world views of urban Parisians and urban New Yorkers could be more similar than the views of the New Yorker and that of a Wyoming rancher. So we must be careful with the notion of identity. We all carry multiple identities. Let's assume, for example, that we are from Calcutta. That will give us a local identity. But we are also Indian, which would be our national identity. Identity is more than a function of place, however. Religion, gender and race also play significant roles in determining who we are. Our Calcutta resident might be either Hindu or Muslim. It matters whether the resident is male or female. So does the resident's caste. Our New Yorker might be a member of any number of religions or races. Our identity is also historical. It makes a great deal of difference whether one is living in Berlin of the 2030's or in the Berlin of the 1930's. It makes a difference whether it is the Berlin of 1945 or 1989.

Living in a changing and multicultural world requires that we constantly reassess our mode of life to make sure we aren't being irrational in our choices. Rationality in regard to pop culture requires that we assess it with all the tools of all the relevant sciences and methods. And since we live in popular culture, we have an interest beyond understanding; we need this information to make informed choices and to decide who we are. A critical attitude toward popular culture increases our autonomy. Much of popular culture is meant to persuade us to do something. Advertising is explicit in its attempt to influence us to buy things. But media and political culture besides advertising also influence us. Understanding popular culture is therefore a form of cultural self-defense against manipulation. One needs to be able to perceive attempts at persuasion, which are sometimes very subtle, in order to engage this persuasion critically. Otherwise we will never be sure that our preferences or opinions are really our own rather than the result of commercial or political manipulation. Being who you want to be necessarily requires that you resist the efforts of those who wish you to think in ways they prefer.

Humans in mass society operate in a number of cultural contexts or arenas. Humans are moral beings, so there is always a question of the morality of an example of popular culture. Humans are economic beings, so the economic arrangements implied by a given sample of popular culture are of interest to us. Humans are gendered, so we should be aware of this aspect of texts. Interpretation basically maps theory onto reality, but this is what we do in living anyway. It is what we must do. There is no "pure cultural reality" out there that is distinct from our reading of that reality. There is most likely *a physical reality* outside of our perceptions, but *cultural reality* is infused with meaning, and meaning always requires interpretation.

We may be unaware of it, but we are always employing theories. Even perception itself is somewhat theory-laden. So there is no avoiding the use of theories in interpretation; there is only the refusal to acknowledge that you are using them. The theories we cover consist of the most popular theories among academics. However, when we think about popular culture, it probably fits within the framework of theories used in cultural theory.

Cultural Studies is a combination of several approaches to culture. It is very common in cultural studies to use Freudian, Marxian, Feminist and other theories to interpret texts. Such an eclectic field of study could easily become a hodge podge of ideas unless each of the parts is put into context with the others in such a way that amounts to a coherent field of study. In this book, we divide the field into two basic but complementary analytics: Aesthetics and Social Theory. Aesthetics looks at culture as art and applies the standard categories of aesthetic analysis to whatever example of popular culture brought before it. For example, we might analyze the visual form of a car or political advertisement and decide that it does or does not display an aesthetically fruitful way to present an image. The other part of Cultural Studies is social theory. Social theory adds to the aesthetic question various other questions, such as "What, if anything, does a given film say about economic arrangements between worker and employer? Is it suggesting a certain kind of alienation?" or "What does a set of lyrics to a rap say about gender?"

These sorts of questions are the domain of social theory, and so we employ the theories and techniques of the social sciences and the humanities that are usefully applied to popular culture. For example, there are many ways to measure the popularity of a phenomenon that utilize mathematical models. Such a model might compare two singers, Taylor Swift and Beyonce, in popularity by simply adding up the number of compact discs or downloads sold by each. But one might also be interested in the meaning of the lyrics to their songs. Or one might be interested in the changes in the technical production of songs like those of these singers. Or one might be interested in the overall music industry that produces music of these kinds. Or we might do a music theoretical analysis of their songs and make an aesthetic evaluation. Or we might note the political relevance of a certain song or the political relevance of the structure of the music industry. Cultural theory does all this, but in spite of the wide variety of scholarship involved, all cultural theorists are committed to "popular culture" as a unit of academic investigation.

For the purposes of this book we divide cultural interpretation into "micro" and "macro" levels. At the micro level we look at particular advertisements, books, iPods etc. From the macro point of view we look at society as a whole. Microcultural analysis might look at the different interpretations one can give to a film. Macrocultural analysis looks at larger questions about the structure of society, its political culture, and how popular culture factors into the quest for autonomy and self-realization. This way of dividing the subject mirrors what we find in other social sciences. Economics, for example, divides into microeconomics, the economics of the firm, and macroeconomics, the economics of the economy as a whole. Interestingly, the same thinkers whose theories apply microculturally, also apply macroculturally. Freud uses his theory not only to analyze particular dreams; he also uses it to analyze civilization. Freud wrote *The Interpretation of Dreams,* but he also wrote *Civilization and its Discontents.* The reason this occurs is that the methodology works at both levels.

## ☐ CULTURAL STUDIES: THE BEGINNINGS

What is cultural theory and how did it get started? Most surveys of the field begin with Matthew Arnold and F.R. Leavis. In succeeding years, social theory from Marx, Freud and others was brought in to approach popular culture more systematically. And now, in a third phase, cultural theory is described and carried out using the terminology and theories of the social sciences and humanities. Cultural theory is therefore inherently interdisciplinary. It draws on several fields in order to present a more complete picture of popular culture. But cultural studies originally grew out of literary criticism, particularly the literary criticism of Matthew Arnold and F.R. Leavis.

Matthew Arnold (1822–88) and F.R. Leavis (1895–1978) inaugurated the discussion of macroculturology in the early 19th century. It was at this time that consciousness of the rise of mass society led people to think about the state of culture it would bring. Arnold began with literary criticism, but later in his career he turned to social criticism, what we call, macroculturology. Concern with the state of popular culture as a whole—macroculturology— goes all the way back to Plato's *Republic*, but Arnold and Leavis were the first thinkers to recognize—and lament, the looming dominance of popular culture, what Leavis calls "mass civilization."

Matthew Arnold identifies popular culture with anarchy. In his 1867 book, *Culture and Anarchy*, Arnold argues that with democratization comes a debasement of culture as the uneducated masses make their demographic presence felt in the marketplace of culture. Although Arnold feared the diseased culture of the masses, he has little faith in the aristocracy or the middle class either. It was the job of the state to educate the masses; indeed, it was necessary for the state to civilize them first and then to educate them. Arnold is writing just when the modern popular culture of mass society was beginning to develop, and he did not like the looks of it. If he were alive today he would certainly be appalled by popular culture, for the vast majority of it is appalling indeed, at least from an aesthetic point of view. Arnold would appreciate our modern school system, but he would be distressed at its failure to raise the aesthetic consciousness of ordinary people. Arnold is wrestling

Matthew Arnold

© Bettmann/CORBIS

© Hulton–Deutsch Collection/CORBIS

F.R. Leavis

with a basic truth about popular culture: most of it is not very good. On the other hand, our interest in popular culture does not end with this realization; it begins with it. First, even though the percentages are low, the market for popular culture is so large that a certain amount does turn out to be excellent. Part of the task of this book is to teach you how to find this small percentage of good work in the midst of the mostly bad work. Second, the popularity of even bad work (and lack of popularity of good work) requires explanation. Third, popular culture exists in social contexts, and so understanding the inter-connections between popular culture and the workings of society is important regardless of the quality of popular culture.

For Leavis, real culture is the domain of a cultured minority, whose proper role is to lead and inform the masses. Leavis felt that the masses were simply incapable of making sound aesthetic choices and that they required the tutelage and authority of the cultured minority to keep them from consuming inferior works. Leavis writes, "The minority capable of appreciating Dante, Shakespeare, Donne, Baudelaire, Hardy (to take major instances), but of recognizing their latest successors constitutes the consciousness of the race (or of a branch of it) at a given time … Upon this minority depends our power of profiting by the finest human experience of the past; they keep alive the subtlest and most perishable parts of tradition. Upon them depend the implicit standards that order the finer living of an age, the sense that this is worth more than that …" (Leavis and Thompson, 1977: 3) Leavis believes that only an elite minority can appreciate culture from the past and recognize those rare instances of good art in the present. The masses are incapable of this sort of discrimination. Leavis and Arnold inaugurate the study of popular culture and conclude that popular culture is a problem that society needs to address. But neither thinker developed a method for understanding popular culture. This method began to be developed with the application of social theory to popular culture. However, Arnold and Leavis are still important because they call our attention to the important changes in culture that occur in the transition to mass civilization.

It is worth pausing over this idea of mass civilization. The distinction between mass civilization and high culture is a historical phenomenon. There was a recognizable time before the rise of mass civilization. When did it happen? It arose in the late nineteenth and early twentieth century with the increasing popularity and influence of newspapers, the book industry, national magazines, advertising, the recording industry and films. All this was possible because of the increasing buying power and leisure time of the middle class. Before that time it is better to oppose high culture with folk culture, which is a very different phenomenon. Folk culture arises spontaneously, without regard to the market and unsystematically since the market for it is too small; not enough people had disposable income or the leisure time for the consumption of popular culture. We will see that the market for popular culture is absolutely crucial for understanding its content. Once the popular culture market reaches a certain threshold it turns folk culture into popular culture. Popular culture operates to a great extent according to the dictates of the market, which means that producers will become increasingly more responsive to market forces. This creates a system that produces not great art, but art that is aimed to capture the largest market share. Arnold and Leavis saw this, but they were not in a position to really understand it because they were operating with only the tools of literary criticism. To understand popular culture we need to draw on social theory.

The most famous social theorists were Marx, Freud and Darwin, but there are many others that we will be using throughout this book. If we look at them as a group we see that they actually cover a fairly large area of academic study. If we think about Marx, Freud, Simone DeBeauvoir, Darwin and others as a group, we see that a large part of the human condition is addressed. These thinkers' contributions have led us to consider economics, biology, psychology, religion, sexuality, literary theory and memetics in our examination of texts. But that tells us that the thinker's actual theories are secondary to the approaches they have opened up to us. So instead of sections on Marx, Freud, Darwin et al, we will have sections on economic interpretations of popular culture, psychological interpretations of popular culture, and so on. This book will also attempt ideological neutrality in each of these areas. Like all moral sciences, the study of popular culture impacts current policy debates. That cannot be avoided. But it is not the place of a theory text to judge the outcomes of these debates.

Cultural studies should not be partisan, but it should be critical. We no longer read Marx, Darwin, Freud, Weber or Nietzsche as authoritative; rather, thinkers like these lead us to think about economics, psychology, religion, sociology, sexuality and the like in systematic application to popular culture. We may not agree with Marx's critique of capitalism, but we should agree that some topics he raised, such as class struggle and alienation, are often implicated in texts. And we should certainly agree that the economic perspective is relevant to understanding texts. We may not agree with a Freudian interpretation of the film, *Psycho,* but one would be remiss in thinking psychology irrelevant to the interpretation of the film. We may have quibbles with a particular feminist interpretation of the film, *Thelma and Louise,* but gender is certainly part of any good interpretation of the film. We therefore turn to each of these perspectives in turn, beginning with psychology.

## ☐ PSYCHOLOGY

In the film, *Psycho,* the character of Norman Bates kills people while dressed in his mother's clothes. The abnormality of the action leads us directly to psychological analysis. Freud's theory of psychosexual development has an explanation for this kind of behavior. In general, texts that raise psychological issues are open to psychological analysis. However, one should refrain from using psychological analysis when interpreting parts of texts that do not raise any psychological issues. It is sometimes unclear whether a text is

Paramount Pictures/Photofest

Stills from the shower scene in *Psycho*

raising psychological issues, and in these borderline cases one should be careful in the application of psychological theories. Nevertheless, a large amount of popular culture does raise psychological issues. This is not surprising since culture is to a large extent the result of the workings of the mind.

While one could use any psychological theory to analyze texts that raise psychological issues, the ideas of psychoanalytic thinkers such as Freud, Jung and Lacan are ones most often used to interpret texts. These psychoanalysts have notions of the mind that have been very influential for both the interpreters of texts as well as the creators of texts. From Freud we use several key ideas from his work. We use the tripartite conception of the mind into id, ego and superego, the theory of psychosexual development, and his conception of the relation of mind to civilization to interpret texts. From Jung we use his theory of the collective unconscious, and from Lacan we use his concept of "lack."

Freud is best known for his theory of psychological development, and many scholars have used it to interpret texts. And since Freud wrote his ideas have become part of the culture as well, and so they have influenced the creators of culture.

We begin with Freud's division of the soul or mind into three parts: Ego, Id and Superego. Our mental life is, at its core, a function of our desires, and these desires collectively constitute our Id. The Id operates, therefore, according to the *pleasure principle*, which seeks pleasure and avoids pain. The Ego, on the other hand, operates according to the *reality principle*. The ego represents the person's core "self," It is the organizer of thought and the locus of consciousness. It directs the desires of the Id into a coherent set of actions. The superego is formed in the process of psychosexual develop-

Sigmund Freud

© CORBIS

ment. It is ultimately the result of internalizing the father figure in one's life into the unconscious where it works to discipline the Ego by making it feel guilt or shame in the same way an actual father disciplines a child.

Freud believes all humans go through key stages of psychological development. The first stage is the oral stage, in which all consciousness is focused on the mouth. There are personality characteristics associated with this stage, depending on how one handles the frustration from the end of nursing. If nursed too long one becomes optimistic, but gullible. If not nursed long enough, then one becomes pessimistic and envious. The anal stage works through the problem of toilet training and determines whether a person might be anal retentive (meticulous, careful and stingy) or anal expulsive (messy, reckless and defiant). The main character in the film, *American Psycho*, is a serial killer, and he is anal retentive. He is extremely meticulous and tidy, and this characteristic deepens our understanding of the methods the serial killer displayed. The Phallic stage is the most important for textual analysis. It involves the very influential Oedipus complex. In the Phallic stage the person wants to possess the opposite sex parent and expel the same sex parent. For the boy, the father stands in the way of the boy's desire for his mother, but he fears his father's power, which is manifested in the castration complex (fear of castration). Eventually this fear overcomes the desire for the mother and the boy takes to identifying with his father instead, and in the process internalizes the father figure so that a superego is formed. For girls, they notice that they do not have penises and blame their mother for their apparent castration. Girls begin to have penis envy, which only abates, to the extent that it does, by identifying with the mother, and having a child to replace the missing penis. Just as with the other stages, fixation at this stage causes various personality characteristics. A phallic fixation can lead to narcissism, failure to be able to love, or, as Freud thought, homosexuality. (Needless to say, this theory of homosexuality is controversial). The last two stages are the latency stage, when the sexual impulse is submerged and turned into productive activity, and the genital stage, when the attention returns to the genitalia and people turn to members of the opposite sex for gratification. These last two stages are rarely referred to in textual analysis, so we can move on without exploring them further.

Dream analysis was the first application of psychosexual development to textual analysis, and Freud's *Interpretation of Dreams* remains a classic of interpretation. In dreams the normal barriers between the conscious and unconscious are broken down and we can get glimpses of a person's inner life. Many films, songs, artworks and television have been concerned with dreams. In the film, *What Dreams May Come*, Robin Williams plays a man attempting

Lon Chaney as *The Wolfman*

to come to terms with the death of his family. Stories often utilize a dream sequence in order to reveal the inner feelings of a character.

For Freud, art sometimes performed the same function of moving across the barrier between the conscious and unconscious. Freud felt artists had a greater ability to tap into the unconscious. Freud himself applied his theory to literature and art. Freud, for example, argued that Leonardo's fascination with the *Mona Lisa*'s smile was connected to his relationship to his mother, who Freud conjectured to probably have

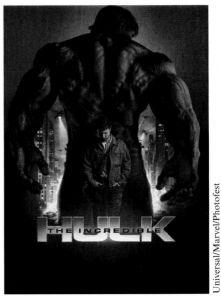

The Incredible Hulk

Universal/Marvel/Photofest

a similar smile. Freudian analysis has been applied to all kinds of text ever since. One of the tasks of this book is to get you started at employing the theory on your own.

Two popular characters, the werewolf and the Hulk can be interpreted in Freudian terms. The werewolf can be read as a story of mismanaged adolescence. The werewolf represents the Id that is trying to break free in adolescence. As hormones rage, the adolescent boy struggles to maintain control of his desires, the animal in him. The werewolf represents a failure in this struggle that leads to social dysfunction. Social control of desire is reasserted with the death of the werewolf, often caused by a father figure reasserting his authority, thus showing the necessity of staying within social norms. In the film, *The Wolfman*, the werewolf is about to kill (a stand-in for rape in this case) the love interest, but the father kills the werewolf with a walking stick (phallic symbol). Werewolf stories are thus Freudian morality plays in which the punishment for transgressing society's sexual boundaries is death.

The Hulk is similar to the werewolf in that he represents a dysfunctional id. The Hulk story emphasizes the dangers of losing control. Again, adolescence is a time when people sometimes lose control and need to be restrained, and when restraint fails, suffering results. When the character, Bruce Banner, gets angry or upset he turns into a rampaging monster. The harm he causes is thus attributed to the inability to control himself.

The structure of families and the transition to adolescence are the most fruitful psychological dramas to be interpreted. So even if we reject a Freudian analysis, it is certainly true that growing up in families gives the growing child a framework to which he or she reacts and develops. And even if one has doubts about the Oedipus complex it is certainly true that the transition to adolescence is probably the most significant for textual interpretation.

In two highly influential books, *Civilization and its Discontents*, and *The Future of an Illusion*, Freud extends his psychological theories to the study of civilization in general, what we call macroculture. In Civilization and its Discontents Freud sees Civilization functioning as a collective superego. Civilization produces unhappiness precisely by denying us the complete satisfaction of our desires. The reality principle has extended from nature, which also put limits on our desire for satisfaction into society. Society will always impose a restriction on our liberty as the individual gives way to the needs of the collective. But that is the cost of civilization and the security it brings.

Freud argues that there are two main forces operating in civilization: Eros and Thanatos. Eros is the life instinct, while Thanatos is the aggressive part of our nature, our death instinct. Civilization arises out of the conflict of the two. Just as the superego is generated by the internalization of a person's instincts, civilization is generated by the repression of our aggressive instincts and obedience to law. Society plays the role of father to the individual, and just as father-son relationships involve conflict, so does the relationship between the society and individual. In both cases an outside entity is preventing the unrestricted satisfaction of our desires. Thus we see that there is a deep connection between psychic and cultural structures. In *Future of an Illusion*, Freud argues that God is an extension of the individual's father figure to everyone's father figure. As we grow up and leave our father's protection we replace it by creating a God who protects us after our fathers are no longer able to. Heaven is the result of wish fulfillment. We do not wish to die, so we create an afterlife in which we live forever. Freud's macrocultural views are a logical extension of his psychological theories. He simply extends them from the individual to societies in general.

Jung reverses the order of causation between mind and culture that Freud postulated. Rather than the mind conditioning culture into certain structures of ideas, cultural conditions inform the structure of mental life. For Jung, all mental life taps into a collective unconscious shared by us all. This shared consciousness is shown by the existence of persistent sets of symbols we find in all cultures.

Jung's theory gave rise to another, the theory of myth propounded by Joseph Campbell. Campbell revolutionized our thinking about the hero myth, showing how the key elements of hero characters are similar across cultures. For example, Campbell lists the following elements of the hero that are found in most hero stories:

1. Begins in the ordinary world
2. A sign of destiny or fate
3. Loss of parents
4. Lives with another family
5. Traumatic event early in life
6. A calling to quest or adventure
7. A special weapon
8. Supernatural help
9. Unhealable wound

Mark Hamill as Luke Skywalker

© Sunset Boulevard/CORBIS

*Harry Potter*

Photofest/Warner Bros. Pictures

Let's compare two heroes from popular culture, Luke Skywalker and Harry Potter. Notice that both characters lose their parents, get adopted by another family, encounter tragedy, are called to a quest, enter a new and strange world (Hogwarts and outer space), have special weapons (light saber and wand) and have supernatural help (the force, magic). Harry has the scar on his forehead, and Luke loses his hand. Both writers, George Lucas and J.K. Rowling, were conscious of the work of Joseph Campbell, but it is not the case that the creator of a text must be thinking of a certain theory to exemplify it in her text. In fact, the key idea in Campbell's theory is that all writers will tend to give heroes these characteristics because of the nature of our inner mental life whether or not they are aware of the theory. Thus it is perfectly legitimate to utilize these theories to illuminate the meaning of a text even when the creator may not have been thinking this way when she created the text. We would not necessarily expect an author or painter to consciously employ Jungian theory; it is rather that Jungian theory applies in such a way that our interpretation is enhanced. If we find that the symbols in a film of one culture are related to those in the films of another culture, we may be able to illuminate the meaning of both more fully.

Lacanian psychoanalysis has become the dominant theory used by film criticism. Lacan rethinks Freudian psychology and focuses on his notion of "lack," which is the sense all people have of being removed from *the Real* that they inhabit as newborns. This lack leaves us in a state of wanting to return to *the Real*, which as babies means the pre-differentiated union with the mother. Desire is ultimately the desire for completion, the desire to be whole as we were in *the Real*. But such a return is impossible and the desire is repressed and becomes part of the unconscious.

As newborns, babies make little differentiation between themselves and the world. They are one with *the Real*, with everything. It is only when they encounter a mirror that they become aware of disparity between their bodies and their ability to control them, which indicates the boundary between self and world. The *Mirror Stage* involves repeated attempts to control the body, which requires engagement with the world, and this engagement requires in turn that we see ourselves as both subject (something that looks at the world) and object (something looked at). The ego is formed as we become conscious of our differences with other objects, and to do this requires that we constitute objects.

We continue our developmental path with the *fort-da* game, where the child throws an object with a string attached and then pulls it back. For Lacan, this is a symbolic representation of the process of losing the mother and bringing her back. The child exerts control in this way, and creates the symbolic order at the same time. The symbolic order structures what Lacan calls the *Imaginary*. The Imaginary is articulated within language, which Lacan sees as accomplishing the final separation of the child from the Real. Language differentiates *the Real* and creates a distinction between being and meaning. Prior to entering the Imaginary we are pure being, but once we become part of the symbolic order of language we become both subject and object. For Lacan, this alienation from *the Real,* by becoming a distinct object and a self, is a form of castration and functions in a way similar to Freud's castration complex. Our alienation from *the Real* is a loss of our pure being. It is important to note that Lacan's *Real* is not the same as "reality." Reality is actually only constituted in the realm of the Symbolic. There is no reality outside of us until we create it. Thus our imagination creates reality.

The third stage is that of the Oedipus Complex in which the child encounters sex differences and the relation to the mother becomes problematic with the introduction of the father, just as it does with Freud. The child comes to terms with the notion that the mother will never be regained, and thus the child is forever banished from the Real. The narrative of our lives is then finding substitutes for the lost love object.

The application of Lacanian psychology to the interpretation of texts works well with "road" or "journey" films, especially journeys that are attempts to return home. The return home is then read as a struggle to regain the plenitude of the Real, to regain oneness with one's mother. The Japanese novel, *Kafka on the Shore* by Haruki Murakami, fits well with Lacanian analysis. A young teen grows up without a mother and with a distant father. He feels the need to leave home in some general way, and so he takes off on an adventure where he joins the ambiguous quest of an illiterate man with special abilities. During the quest the teen finds out that his father has been killed, and he is unsure at first whether he is the killer. Eventually the quest returns him to his lost mother, and while a sort of union takes place, she is again lost to him, which accomplishes the Oedipal lesson. From just this much plot summary we can see the applicability of Lacan to textual interpretation, and a thorough reading of the novel would yield a fairly large amount of material that fits Lacanian interpretation.

It should not be surprising that psychological theories would have wide applicability to the interpretation of texts. Texts typically involve people, and most interesting characters are shown to have psychological issues to work out. Further, we have seen that psychoanalytic theory is a theory of interpretation itself. Applying it to all kinds of texts is a natural extension of the theory.

## ☐ ECONOMICS

Like psychology, economics plays a significant role in interpretation. Just as our mental life figures in the interpretation of texts, so does economics play a role. We are all embedded in a economic structures, and they cannothelp but influence our interpretations of texts. Karl Marx developed the first economic theory to be applied totextual interpretation. Theorists not only used Marx's theory, they also started using other theories, such as those of Antonio Gramsci, to apply to textual interpretation. This book will suggest that other economic theories can beused for textual interpretation as well.

Karl Marx was not primarily concerned with texts in general; rather, he was interested in one particular text: the economy. Marx argued that capitalist economy had been misunderstood by the early economists. Economists such as Adam Smith had argued that there was an "invisible hand" that made the economy run in an orderly, efficiency-maximizing fashion. Supply and demand interact in such a way that people end up getting the best products for the lowest prices. Further, the overall economy would run best if just left alone. More people

Karl Marx

© Bettmann/CORBIS

would stay employed and the standard of living would continue to rise over the long term. By Marx's time, however, there had already been a series of economic crises that caused doubts to form in his mind about this story. Instead of the steady workings of an invisible hand Marx saw a pattern of increasing crises ending in the fall of capitalism.

Marx tried to put economics in historical context and developed a theory of history to explain the state of the economy at any given point in time. For Marx, history progresses because of the conflict between different economic classes. The classes in question are determined by the stage of history. During Feudalism, for example, the contending classes were the lords and serfs. Under capitalism, the contending classes are the workers (the "proletariat") and the owners of businesses (the bourgeoisie). In each case this conflict is caused by what Marx thought were "contradictions" in the system. In Marx's view, capitalism contained the seeds of its own destruction. In its never-ending attempt to increase profits, capitalists squeezed workers to the point where they started to work together to fight against their class enemies, the owners of production. This produced a "class consciousness" that enabled the workers to think through their predicament and formulate plans to change the system. The plan they should follow, according to Marx, was revolution. The workers should take over the government, eliminate private property and establish a dictatorship of the proletariat until it was no longer needed and faded away. Thus communism becomes the new form of government at the end of history. Communism is the end of history because history was fueled by class struggle. Communism only allowed for a single class, so there would be no conflict, hence no more history.

The critique of capitalism that Marx formulated made two key claims. First, capitalism was exploitative. The workers didn't get their fair share of the proceeds from their labor. Second, capitalism is alienating. Workers fail to achieve self-realization when they are exploited. This is where we come to the part of Marx's theory that lends itself to the interpretation of texts. Any economic injustice portrayed in a pop culture text, such as a film, song, or television show can be given a Marxian interpretation. This is not to say that all texts present a Marxist critique of capitalism. Far from it. Marxists believe that most texts reflect the views of the ruling classes, and so Marxian interpretation often becomes a criticism of the text in question. The reason texts reflect the interests and views of the ruling classes is explained by Marx's theory of "base and superstructure." For Marx, the structure of society is determined by its level of technological and economic development. Societies change from the bottom up. First there is a technological revolution like the steam engine. Then it is applied to the production process like the factory system. The production process, in turn, creates an overall economy, capitalism, that is conducive to the factory system. The factory system, in turn, produces a set of institutions and ideas that tend to support this economic structure. These ideas and institutions are called the "superstructure." This superstructure produces an "ideology" that serves to keep this base-superstructure combination in place. Thus, under capitalism the ideology produces ideas like: "Those who work hard will prosper," or "If you are poor it is because you are lazy." These ideas find their way into texts because they become very deeply entrenched in ways of thinking.

Ideology and ideology critique are crucial to the interpretation of texts. Not only do we use Marx's theory to interpret texts, we use it to criticize them. We also take it one step further and use the text to criticize the society in which it was composed. Take, for example, a text that involves an ill-fated couple in love, but destined to be forever apart because they are from "different sides of the tracks," which means they are from different classes. A Marxist analysis would not only point out the role of class conflict in the story, it would also note that class conflict is the source of their troubles. The implicit argument would then be that until we change the system this sort of injustice will continue to occur.

Sigourney Weaver as Ripley with the monster from *Alien*

But we need not agree with Marxist views of society to use Marxist textual analysis. We can note the tragedy of our ill-fated couple from different sides of the tracks without implying that there is any way to eliminate the problem. We might simply note the perennial existence of "haves" and "have-nots" without also agreeing with the view that there is a way to eliminate this class division. We do not have to be Marxists to use Marxist tools for textual analysis. In fact, we need not even regard such analysis as Marxist at all since it is really just looking at texts through an economic lens. One could even give an anti-Marxist but economic analysis of our ill-fated lovers that focuses on the bad economic decisions of one of them (usually the one on the side of the tracks with lower income).

An example of class conflict in popular film comes from the 1979 movie, *Alien* (still available in video stores). As we will see at greater length in horror section of this book, the film is about a mining ship in space in which the workers are regarded as expendable for the sake of company profits. The corporation that owns the ship decides to bring back a dangerous alien even if it costs the lives of the workers. The workers also exhibit class consciousness by complaining constantly about their pay and working conditions. Thus a film about humans defending themselves from a murderous alien has a subtext that is economic. In fact, throughout the Alien series of films the economic factors—the company's quest to obtain and weaponize the alien, seem to constitute the ultimate cause of the troubles the humans must endure.

Antonio Gramsci looks at culture a bit differently than Marx. We have seen how Marx's model is one in which the ruling class is able to impose its world view upon the lower classes in order to foster acquiescence with its exploitative character. But Gramsci thinks the process is a bit more complicated. He sees the attempt to impose ideological interpretations as only partially successful. In fact, the popular culture that results is one that is a function of competing interpretations. The lower classes do not accept popular culture uncritically; they bring their own views to the interpretive table as well. The result is something of an un-negotiated compromise between the classes. Gramsci calls this "hegemony," and hegemony is often a better lens through which to interpret a text than a full-blown Marxist ideological imposition of the viewpoint of the oppressors.

Applying economic analysis to films is fairly simple. Begin by looking for the class status of primary characters. In the film, *Titanic,* the two main characters, played by Kate Winslet and Leonard DiCaprio, are from very different social classes. Kate Winslet, who plays the character of Rose, travels first class, while Leonard DiCaprio, a drifter, travels third class. Rose attempts suicide because she is being forced into a marriage for economic rather than romantic reasons. Jack and Rose forge a relationship, but it is a difficult one because of their relative economic status.

Sometimes economic structures become part of genres. Stories in the Western genre are often set in a context of the modernizing economy of the American West. Conflicts between farmers, ranchers and railroads are the expression of a changing economy in the western U.S. In the 1953 film, *Shane*, a farmer is besieged by a cattleman, but Shane saves the day for the farmer. One can take this as an individual case of feuding between individuals, but one can also step back and look at this conflict in historical and economic terms. As time went on cattlemen had to give way to the farmers as they fenced in the land to protect their farms. If this is the case, then Shane represents the inevitable economic change in the American West from the cowboy way of life of the cattle herder to the more civilized and law-abiding—existence of the farmer.

Leonardo DiCaprio and Kate Winslet in *Titanic*

More recent films, such as *Clerks* (1994) focus more on the alienation of the worker. At the micro level we can say that for the convenience store clerks, life is one silly, meaningless episode after another. At the macro level we might point out how the service economy provides the kind of jobs most people would regard as meaningless and alienating. Or one might take a completely different perspective and decry the laziness of the workers in the film and even say this represents a decline in the values of the American worker.

The film *Wallstreet* looks at the finance industry, which makes it a good candidate for economic analysis. In this film we see economically rapacious Wall Street traders engaging in all kinds of illegal and immoral behavior that helps the traders but ruins the lives of ordinary people. Thecentral storyline concerning a young man's (played by Charlie Sheen) decision whether to become crooked like his mentor (played by Michael Douglas) is therefore "thickened" by the back story of an economic system that permits and even encourages immoral behavior. What we see with this example is the way a story is deepened by the addition of the economic element. We can better understand the story of the individuals portrayed by considering the economic forces at work on the character's decision making.

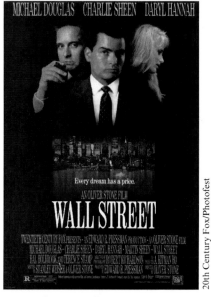

Poster from *Wallstreet*

20th Century Fox/Photofest

## ☐ SOCIOLOGY

Max Weber was one of the founders of the discipline of sociology, and he has contributed a key theory that is used in popular culture studies: the theory of Rationalization. The theory of rationalization is meant to help us understand the logic of development in the cultural arena. For Weber and sociology generally, rationalization does not mean "make excuses for something" as it does in common parlance. Rather, it means a process in which a practice is increasingly shaped to respond to a framework of authority or rules. Such frameworks are the economic, legal, religious and other systems that govern how we live. An example of rationalization is the ordering of the music industry to maximize profit by producing music and music videos that appeal to basic desires and a simple aesthetic with broad appeal. Thus we see the music market increasingly characterized by simple melodies and harmonies with certain kinds of rhythms that appeal in an almost biological fashion. That is why videos featuring sexy young girls such as Britney Spears singing songs with relatively few chord changes and repetitive and catchy melodies are so popular. This is because the producers in the music industry are profit-oriented and as certain types of music are found to be reliably profitable, the industry focuses its efforts on those types of music. The theory of rationalization also explains other aspects of popular culture, such as the tendency toward films that fit easily within standard conceptions of genre. Thus a film that is clearly a Western or a Science Fiction film will be typically more popular than a film that does not easily fit within these categories. The film industry is therefore "rationalized" into groups of films linked by genre.

Weber's theory of rationalization also helps to explain the globalization of popular culture. Rationalized popular culture tends to spread because rationalized culture will generally overwhelm non-rationalized indigenous cultures. That is why we see the music of both India and China increasingly replaced by Western music. Western music rationalized its tuning and notation system and developed a systematic music theory that enabled the use of harmony of a higher order of magnitude than that possible in Chinese or Indian music. Western music's use of standard progressions makes its melodies, which are in turn rationalized to fit the harmonies, much more appealing than those in Indian and Chinese music traditions. This is not to say that Western music is better; it is simply to say that Western music is likely to win a popularity contest with music from (traditional) India and China, even in China or India.

Globalization is one of the most important developments of the modern era. Globalization has been going on for thousands of years via the Silk Road and other trade routes, but the rate has increased to a point where it has significant and pervasive effects on almost every place in the world. Plane travel, television and the internet have created a new kind of world, a world in which a song or film can travel in mere seconds to any part of the world, a world where all nations' economies are closely linked, a world in which products transcend national borders. One type of globalization is particularly significant, namely, what is called "McDonaldization." George Ritzer first coined the term, and his book, *McWorld*, argued that we live in a world in which the McDonalds' business and sales model has been adopted nearly everywhere and in most businesses. Ritzer is correct to highlight the role of McDonalds in propagating its method of operation, but it is really just a specific manifestation of the more general Weberian notion of rationalization that we have already discussed. McDonalds has simply made certain kinds of rationalization more popular. Ritzer lists four key elements of McDonaldization:

1. Efficiency: the optimization of all production methods and services. If there is a more profitable way of doing something, including transition costs, then the switch is made. For example, if McDonald's can redesign their cash registers so that the cashier can serve more customers per hour, then the redesign is adopted.

2. Calculability: the quantification of all aspects of a business so that they may become subject to calculation. For example, how much ketchup do most customers prefer on their hamburgers? If you do not measure the amount put on hamburgers you cannot make this determination. Once you make this determination one must be able to calculate how to get employees or a machine to put on exactly that amount.

3. Predictability: designing processes so that they yield exactly what you intend to produce. McDonald's hamburgers are almost exactly the same no matter which restaurant you visit. McDonalds would not be anywhere as popular if people did not know they could expect this kind of uniformity. People also know that the employees will communicate in the same way at all McDonalds restaurants.

4. Control: this term is not as helpful, but we will stick with it in deference to Ritzer. What he actually means is that McDonalds attempts to replace humans with machines as much as possible in order to reduce human error and unpredictability.

McDonalds' branding with the arches and Ronald McDonald has become a model for all other businesses and has, in turn, produced other models, such as Disneyization. Alan Bryman, the originator of the idea, defines Disneyization as "the process by which *the principles* of the Disney theme parks are coming to dominate more and more sectors of American society as well as the rest of the world" (Bryman, 1999, p. 26). The practices of the Disney company have become a model for many other businesses. The first method is *theming*, which is creating or borrowing a story or character around which the product is centered. Secondly, *Merchandizing* employs theming to unify a group of different products (toys, cups, comics etc.) according to a set of characters and stories. Hence we have Mickey Mouse cups, action figures, wrist watches and so on. The third method is the addition to *emotional labor* to the physical labor required of employees. Not only must employees carry out certain physical actions, they must also pretend to be happy about it. And fourth, *De-differentiation of consumption* is the practice of combining the sale of different kinds of products in the same consumer experience. For example, upon leaving a ride at Disney World one is shuffled into a restaurant where one might decide to eat. And one might also be led past a toy story selling toys based on the ride. The idea is to maximize the profit from every consumer contact. To these four methods we add the general idea of "sanitizing." Sanitizing is the attempt to eliminate or diminish any negative appearances associated with the product. Disney World, for example, has put as much of the ugly workings of the park underground. There is also a tendency for any company to hide the less than palatable aspects of their business. Grocery stores would prefer that we not witness the production process involved in sausages. Meat production generally can be a gruesome affair about which most meat eaters would prefer to remain ignorant, and the meat industry is quite willing to accommodate.

© Pascal Della Zuana/Sygma/CORBIS

Mickey Mouse

Both McDonaldization and Disneyization point to an even deeper phenomenon, what Jurgen Habermas calls the "Colonization of the Lifeworld." The colonization of the lifeworld refers to the rationalization of all aspects of life, even those which lie close to the center of our being. Thus living patterns such as waking, sleeping, religious and emotional life are all becoming increasingly rationalized. Just as working life became rationalized with the development of the factory system, so does religious life become rationalized by television evangelists who employ the techniques of modern marketing to increase their flocks. Internet dating services rationalize courtship. This notion in one form or another has been a concern of a group of scholars known as the Frankfurt School, of which Habermas is an important member.

The Frankfurt School is known for its deep critique of modern society, and popular culture is subjected to serious criticism. Thinkers such as Theodor Adorno and Herbert Marcuse were very critical of the culture industry. Both Adorno and Marcuse saw popular culture as the expression of a "culture industry" whose effect was to dumb down culture in order to better manipulate the masses. Marcuse thought that culture tends toward "one-dimensionality." What that means is that thought in modern society tends toward a false consensus of support for the social and political systems. Critical thinking is

Herbert Marcuse

undermined as people are increasingly conditioned to believe in views that support the system. But worse, modern society has developed a pattern of absorbing and emasculating criticism so that change becomes increasingly difficult to bring about. Long hair and blue jeans were expressions of protest in the 1960's, but they were quickly incorporated into the system and turned into mere fashions. Products are advertised as "revolutionary." "Thinking outside the box" has increasingly come from inside the box. Political protest movements are often funded by political insiders, corporate interests and other well-financed groups.

Adorno was very critical of the pop culture, particularly pop music, of his day. His criticism of jazz, the popular music of his time, was that it was so standardized that it eliminated any real possibility for creativity. A key part of Adorno's criticism is that standardization necessarily limits the possibility of complete creativity that comes with the attempt to make every part of a piece of music relate to every other part. Jazz cannot do this because key aspects are limited to the characteristics of the genre, the swing beat, the 32 bar form et al. Adorno was not even impressed with improvisation in jazz, which he regarded as the recitation of a set of clichés assigned to certain harmonic changes. Adorno thought jazz to be mere dance music with no real potential for greatness. Adorno writes: *Considered as a whole, the perennial sameness of jazz consists not in a basic organization of the material within which the imagination can roam freely and without inhabitation, as within an articulate language, but rather in the utilization of certain well-defined tricks, formulas, and clichés to the exclusion of everything else* (*Prisms*, 123). Adorno even postulated the cause of the standardization of pop music in its competitive and imitative responses to the "marketization" of music. As songs compete with each other, the business leaders of the music industry note which sorts of musical composition tend to become popular. Further, if something becomes popular, it gets imitated. Over time popular music settles into standardized forms. Adorno is correct that something very like this process occurs with all forms of popular music, and it often causes the production of weak art, but it is interesting that as the years went by jazz came to be considered very creative and a genre generally considered "high art." It turned out that there was much more room for creativity than Adorno imagined. The primary mistake in his analysis was to infer a lack of creativity from standardization and genre. Jazz musicians keep finding ways to be creative with standard forms. Improvisation in jazz, especially, has reached a high level of aesthetic sophistication in spite of a standardization of harmonic progressions. This provides us with a good lesson in the critical analysis of popular culture. Sometimes an art form or genre may begin as the expression of the marketplace, but there may be a logic of development that is hard to discern in the beginning yet ends up turning the genre into something very creative. This is what happened with jazz. From simple beginnings it became a very sophisticated art form that is held in universal high regard. Adorno simply did not see jazz's potential. What this shows us is that the concept of rationalization must be used with care for the interpretation and assessment of microcultural texts. Adorno and the other members of the Frankfurt School were right to point to the often debilitating effects of the market on art and culture, but they did not realize that sometimes something delightful can arise out of the generally weak culture produced by the market.

## ☐ RELIGIOUS STUDIES

Religion provides a set of concepts and narratives that are often put to use interpreting popular culture. A Hindu interpretation might draw on the story of Sita in the *Ramayana* to interpret a love story involving a kidnapping. In the *Ramayana*, Sita, the wife of Rama, is kidnapped by Ravana, the demon king. Rama succeeds in securing her return, but the relationship is still doomed as mistrust between Rama and Sita is never overcome. Any story that involves the abduction of a woman or the unjust treatment of a woman can use the story of Sita as a model for interpretation. This is particularly true of Bollywood films since Indian writers operate within a tradition that gives the Ramayana a prominent place. A Christian interpretation might draw on the Book of Job to interpret film that involves an innocent person afflicted by one tragedy after another. Any story of traveling suggests the *Odyssey* or *Journey to the West* as possible interpretive frameworks. The key to religious interpretation is noting narrative parallels between stories in the sacred text and stories in popular culture. For example, the character of Neo in *the Matrix* might be compared to the Buddha because he "wakes up" and sees the deeper truth of existence. When zombies or vampires come back to life they can be seen as a perversion of Christ coming back to life. In fact, these films rely partly on this connection to create a greater sense of abomination. The source material for religious interpretation is quite large, so one can give a religious interpretation to just about any text. Whatever the story is, it is bound to match up with some religious story from some religious tradition. Religion can also provide us with general theories about various aspects of life. For example, Hindu symbolism presents an alternate interpretation of sexual life from that of modern psychology or feminism. The character of Shiva is a set of interpretations of the spectrum of sexual involvement from asceticism to extreme hedonism. The symbols of lingam and yoni are alternatives to Freudian ideas about the phallus. Jung, of course, would say that Freudian and Hindu differences about the meaning of the phallus betray a deeper underlying agreement.

## ☐ EXISTENTIAL INTERPRETATION

Existentialism originates with the work of Friedrich Nietzsche, who famously said "God is Dead," and Kierkegaard, who famously said that to be authentically religious one needed to make a "leap of faith," to set aside all reason and embrace the terror of rationally ungrounded decision. Nietzsche's view is that values are a human creation, so the only foundation for ethics is ourselves. Humans create all value out of nothing. There is no objective foundation for morality. Sartre takes this notion and argues that it is "bad faith" to fail to acknowledge it. When we fail to take responsibility for our actions by claiming a lack of free will in the matter, then we are committing bad faith. It is bad faith to say "it is just human nature" or "that is just how women act" or "blondes are bad at math." Such statements are inauthentic. To be authentic one must make choices according to one's freely chosen values rather than because something is traditional or because it would please others to choose in a certain way. Many films have the premise of the young girl whose awakening into adolescence involves learning to dress in ways more pleasing to men. Any film in which someone rejects doing what their family, tradition or society expects in favor of something they prefer for themselves has an existential dimension. In the film, *Legally Blonde*, Reese Witherspoon starts out entering law school in order to entice a man, who rejected her because she was a "dumb blonde," into becoming her husband. She thinks that by succeeding in law school she can convince him she is worthy. But as the film plays out she finds that she is a good lawyer, a better lawyer, in fact, than the man who rejected her. After she succeeds at law the man is finally ready to accept her, but she turns the tables and rejects him. She thus breaks out of the category of "dumb blonde," out of the stereotype, and recreates herself as a more authentic individual who makes choices for herself rather than for someone else. There is also a nihilist strain of thought in existentialism although there does not need to be. Some conclude that because there are no objective values there are no values at all. This is the view that life is ultimately meaningless and even absurd. Films such as *Clerks* (1994) and *Office Space* (1999) bemoan the meaninglessness of an existence working as a clerk. In one sense, working at a convenience store or in an office may seem completely unremarkable, just something we have to do until we get a real job. But what if we never get a real job? What if all jobs are ultimately meaningless? If all our jobs are ultimately meaningless, then life would seem to be absurd. It is important to distinguish existential absurdity with surreal absurdity. Surrealist texts often contrast widely disparate and unrelated elements in a seemingly absurd manner, but surrealist absurdity generally has some meaning, maybe contradictory meanings, but meanings nonetheless. *Donnie Darko* (2001) is absurd and surrealist, but it is not existential (in the sense of being meaningless) since it contains lots of meaning. In fact, the best way to interpret surrealist texts is probably psychoanalysis since surrealisms focus on dreams and dream-like experiences, which are the forte of psychoanalysis. Existential texts, on the other hand, try to resist our attempts to make sense of the story. There is often no ending at all. There is a whole sub-genre of "slice of life" stories, which simply recount an hour, a day or even a whole series of events in a person's life in a way that makes it difficult to draw it together into a coherent narrative. There is another kind of existential film that does not end in meaningless, but rather focuses on the idea of self-creation. Such texts may not be as bleak as films like *Clerks*, and they can even be highly uplifting, such as *Eat, Pray, Love* (2010). The idea of such films is to show the self-creation of someone into the person they want to be. This often involves a rejection of an identity or mode of life prescribed by family, tradition or society. In this scenario, life is not meaningless. Life can have meaning, but we must provide that meaning. It is not predetermined what our lives will mean, but we may give our lives meaning with our choice of interpretation. According to existentialists, this is the only kind of meaning there is anyway.

## ☐ FEMINISM: SEXUALITY AND GENDER

The Feminist movement has produced a large literature that looks at culture through the lens of gender and sexuality. Whatever one's position on or in the feminist movement, one needs to be aware of the various kinds of interpretive frameworks it has developed. The first point to note is that there are many different kinds of "feminist" interpretation, and each of these frameworks arises out of different feminist positions. It would be impossible to do justice to all the different forms of feminism, so we will restrict ourselves to the more popular forms, particularly those most useful for interpreting texts. First, we have liberal feminism.

**Liberal Feminism** argues that feminists should work to achieve equality in all aspects of life. Thus women should be paid the same as men for equal work. They should also be treated equally by the law and suffer no discrimination on the basis of being female. This perspective is useful for

Demi Moore as *G.I. Jane*

interpreting films such as *9 to 5*, *Working Girl*, *A League of Their Own*, *Erin Brockovich*, *GI Jane* and many others. Any film in which a woman has to fight to be treated equally with men is open to a liberal feminist interpretation.

**Radical Feminism** argues that the problem goes much deeper than mere equality, as liberal feminism asserts. For the radical feminist the problem is the gender biased *system* of patriarchy. Male dominance is built into our whole way of thinking. It lies so deep we may even be as yet unaware of how much of the way we think is due to gender. Radical feminism looks at general concepts such as hierarchy or contract as rooted in male group dynamics. For many radical feminists, the fact that patriarchy runs so deep in the order of things means that the methods

Geena Davis and Susan Sarandon in *Thelma and Louise*

used to uproot may need to be radical as well, even up to the call for an extreme separation from men. Both the theory and the tactics of radical feminism can be a basis of an interpretation. The film, *Thelma and Louise,* presents us with a world that is so thoroughly patriarchic that a woman who rejects the patriarchy has no hope of a happy ending. There is thus a tragic element to radical feminism. Even if patriarchy can be mitigated in the long run, it will still cause great pain and injustice in the meantime. Radical feminism's great contributions are its call to look into the deep structure of patriarchy and its suggestion that radical action may be required to change the deep structure. This contribution becomes a premise for the rest of our feminist theories. They will simply differ on how they characterize this deep structure.

All feminists seek to define what makes women subordinate to men, and **Marxist Feminists** think that the capitalist system is the culprit. They think that gender oppression can be likened to the oppression of the proletariat by the bourgeoisie in that men command the services of women. Their subordination to men serves the interests of the ruling class (men). In their traditional roles as wives and mothers, women have not even earned a wage for their work. As wage earners, women have been exploited at higher levels than men. The "mommy track" is a good example of this. Essentially, women are oppressed workers subject to the ruling class, both in the private and public sector, just as the proletariat is subject to the bourgeoisie. This has taken many forms throughout history. It was not until 1900 that all states had some law in place that granted women the right to own or inherit property. Women have not enjoyed equal status in the professional world, and while it is weakening, the glass ceiling still exists in many areas of corporate America. Marxist feminists believe that the only way to create gender equality is to eliminate the Capitalist system and embrace a socialist society.

The Marxist Feminist interpretation schema focuses on the economic aspects of the male-female relationship. The relationship between men and women becomes a monetary relationship, with marriage matches decided for economic reasons, women being singled out for lower pay, and even straightforward prostitution, all demonstrating the important economic dimensions of feminism. With most Indian marriages, for example, the choice of the partner is left to the parents, who arrange the marriage, so this is a theme that resonates very deeply in the female Hindu psyche whether it ends well or badly. In India, most marriages are arranged; so many Bollywood films lament the fate of the girl sent into a loveless marriage to establish an economic partnership between two families, such as *Dilwale Dulhania Le Jayenge* (There Goes the Bride). In other Bollywood films the result is that after several early conflicts the arranged couple will fall in love, thus validating the system in the manner of an Indian conservative feminism. We see this in the film, *Rahul's Arranged Marriage*. Prostitution films are ideal for this kind of interpretation since women are reduced to purely sexual commodities. *Pretty Woman*, *Striptease*, and the Korean film, *Chaser* are all very open to Marxist Feminist readings.

**Conservative Feminism** argues that liberal, radical and Marxist feminists are forgetting women's biological and social roles. While agreeing with liberal feminists in the justice of equal pay for equal work, and while agreeing with the radical feminist that gender runs very deep in human experience, conservative feminism asserts that men and women are inherently different and that certain roles, duties and privileges follow from the differences. Conservative feminism applauds women in the workplace, but it allows for a significant percentage of women deciding to be "stay-at-home" moms as well. For Conservative feminism, the roles of wife and mother, and the biological realities of pregnancy, dictate that certain duties are simply part of female reality. According to conservative feminism this reality should be embraced, or at least respected.

**Psychoanalytic Feminism:** From what we have said about psychoanalysis, it should be clear there is significant overlap between gender and psychosexual development. Just as men have their Oedipus Complex, women have a corresponding Electra Complex. The castration complex is central to the psychological differences between men and women. Men fear castration, and women feel penis envy, which is a sort of castration complex in itself. But many feminists have argued against simply appropriating Freud. In fact, some feminists suggest that Freudian psychology and more of a product of patriarchy than an explanation of it.

Nancy Chodorow argues that the female self is a self-in-relation-to-others and the male self is an autonomous and independent self. Chodorow works through and rewrites Freud's account of the female Oedipus Complex. For Chodorow, gender identity acquisition for women works in such a way that the primary relationship of the daughter with the mother is established differently than with sons and mothers since mothers and daughters are of the same sex. Both boys and girls first "other" is their mother. But since the mother is a different sex than the boy, the boy more quickly forms an identity separate from others. Girls stay linked to the mother; they never really reject the mother the way a boy must reject the father. Texts that involve mothers and daughters lend themselves to Psychoanalytic feminist readings, films such as *Joy Luck Club, Freaky Friday, Hannah and Her Sisters*, and *Little Women.* But Chodorow would also have us pay attention to mother and son relationships, such as we see in films like *Kuch Naa Kaho*, a Bollywood film about a mother intent on having her son marry, or the Chinese film, *Mother Loves Me Once Again* (1989).

**Black Feminism, Lesbian ethics and Womanism:** Other subgroups of women such as black or chicana women, lesbians, the transgendered and the disabled have provided perspectives that significantly alter and deepen other kinds of feminist thinking. Black women and Chicanas have analyzed the multiple identities faced by women of color, and they have criticized liberal feminists for their lack of attention to the special circumstances of non-white women. Lesbians and the transgendered have added a recognition of the importance of considering sexual preferences and sexual identity in relation to femininity and the legal framework governing men, women and the transgendered. Disability activists have argued that the liberal feminist defense of abortion may lead to discrimination against the disabled. Some of these subgroups have become so disenchanted with liberal feminism that they have come to prefer another term without the connotations the term "feminist" has come to have, namely "womanist." They point out that women of different ethnicities have distinct problems. Asian women, for example, are regarded as cunning "dragon ladies," exotic sexual adepts, or "China dolls," the submissive, fragile and weak woman

Lucy Liu as Ling Woo in *Ally McBeal*

ever ready to please her male partner. One particularly popular storyline is of the Asian woman eagerly awaiting for the Western male's return from the West to rescue her from her inferior Asian existence, as in the musical, "Miss Saigon". Tracey Owens Patton (2001) has shown how the television series, *Ally McBeal,* reinforced the stereotype of the Asian woman as a cunning and sexually adept dragon lady. Lucy Liu played the character of Ling Woo. As a watcher of that series earlier in life, the writer of this chapter can reassure readers of the powerful effect Lucy Liu's character had on American culture's conception of Asian women at that time. But we should not see merely the negative aspect of the Ling Woo character. While Ling Woo had many negative characteristics, people, both men and women, were attracted to her strength and realism, and frankly, her eroticism.

This is a good occasion to mention the crucial role of identity in interpretation, and how we should think about social criticism related to the concept of identity. People often criticize a film or another form of popular culture for its negative portrayal of some character or set of characters from an ethnic group, and conclude that the work is sexist or racist. One should never be too quick to level such a morally charged accusation, so one must be careful with this kind of criticism. What is the ideal portrayal of an ethnicity, race or gender after all? To be an ethnicity, for example, there must be shared characteristics. If there were no shared characteristics then we would have mistakenly created a term that has no reference. So if there are categories like "male," "African-American," "Chicana," etc., then it must be the case that there are shared characteristics. The characteristics that make up an identity are of numerous types. We can distinguish essential or objective characteristics from arbitrary subjective characteristics if we wish, but the truth of the matter is that such a distinction is also arbitrary. The philosopher, Hegel, established long ago that our identities are essentially social, so other people will always have a role in determining ethnicities, races etc. Sometimes, however, an identity is produced almost entirely from the outside and constitutes a negative and oppressive portrayal.

We can think of stereotypes as a subgroup of the list of characteristics we associate with an identity. We most often concern ourselves with negative stereotypes, which can be pernicious for various reasons including the origin of the characteristic's inclusion on the list of all characteristics associated with a certain identity. Did the idea get on the list because it was an observed phenomenon linked to the concept of the ethnicity, such as a physical characteristic or a behavior pattern, or was it the result of some misunderstanding, misperception or outright slander of the ethnicity? Thus portraying a character in a negative fashion while indicating that this is a shared characteristic among members of that ethnicity is a reason for criticizing that portrayal. On the other hand, portraying an objectively observed characteristic cannot be a reason for criticism. One can criticize a film if its overall message about a certain character or set of characters is meant to imply a shared characteristic among members of that group that is unfairly and inaccurately applied. Merely portraying a Spanish-speaking American woman, for example, as a thief cannot be in itself objectionable. It can only be objectionable if the portrayal can be construed as saying or indirectly implying that a negative attribute unfairly applies to a group of people. A film that is about racism, for example, might contain many racist stereotypes about Asian women, such as we see in Clint Eastwood's *Gran Torino*, but yet be an overall argument against this type of behavior. Complaining that the film is racist would be simply missing the point.

**Eco-feminism** holds that the women's issues and environmental issues are intimately related. Eco-feminists suggest that the source of the problems with women is the same source of our problems with the environment. Male need to control women is related to the human tendency to try to control nature. The *femme fatale* provides us with a very interesting character to analyze from an eco-feminist perspective. Beauty in nature is a tool to facilitate reproduction. It is the most natural thing in the world for a man to be mesmerized by a woman's beauty. This gives women a certain natural power over men. A *femme fatale* is a beautiful woman who uses her beauty and sex appeal to entice, control or destroy men. A feminist might rightfully wonder why men are so fearful of women when men have been in a position of power over women throughout history. Men have greater strength, a dominant economic position and social arrangements that favor them, so why do we see so many femme fatales in movies, television, music and books? One theory is that men transfer their fear of nature to women because women are associated with nature. This theory begins with the idea that men are associated (rightly or wrongly) with culture while women are associated (rightly or wrongly) with nature. These associations are built on the facts that men have traditionally been outside the home and in society working, while women have traditionally been inside the home. Men in society create culture while women carry out the biological (natural) function of bearing children, breast feeding, etc. Women's fertility is associated with agriculture and therefore nature, and a woman's monthly menstrual cycle also connects women to nature. But nature is fearsome. It holds many dangers that have ingrained themselves into men's psyche from time immemorial. So when men are shown fearing women it is really a transfer of this fear from nature to women.

**Existential Feminism** argues that what woman will be is not a matter of discovery; finding out what it means to be women is not simply a matter of subtracting male influence; rather, women will decide what it is to be a woman.

Poster from *Body Heat* with William Hurt and Kathleen Turner

Simone DeBeauvoir developed this line of thought in her *Second Sex.* The Woody Allen film, *Annie Hall,* presents us with such a woman-in-progress. **Postmodern Feminism** takes us one step beyond Existential Feminism. While Existential Feminism argues that it is a matter of choice what it means to be a woman, Postmodern Feminism argues that one need not choose a single femininity; one can also embrace more than one identity simultaneously. Even contradictory identities are viable choices. Further, one's decision can change over time. The film, *A Long Kiss Goodnight*, has its female lead, Geena Davis, exemplify two contradictory identities, and then later in the film the two identities mesh as she integrates both of them into a single, new identity.

## Anti-Feminism

In an interesting twist, feminism has also given rise to what we may call "Feminist Backlash" films, such as *Disclosure* (1994), a film starring Demi Moore as an aggressive executive who sexually harasses a male executive (Michael Douglas) under her authority and then falsely accuses him of sexual harassment. In another film from 1994, *Oleanna,* a professor is unjustly accused of sexual harassment by a female student who is angry at him for other reasons. These movies clearly drew on the zeitgeist of the time in which men

Demi Moore and Michael Douglas in *Disclosure*

were becoming afraid of inadvertently transgressing a moral boundary they did not understand, or of being falsely accused of transgressing the boundary.

Feminism will continue to be a fruitful category of interpretive analysis for the foreseeable future. We are far from having worked out the proper way for men and women to interact. It may that there is no single proper way for men and women to interact. Whatever the case, it is clear that feminist interpretation is a very useful tool for the analysis of texts.

## ☐ RACE AND QUEER THEORY

Race and sexual preference are basic parts of our social fabric and texts reflect this social reality. The portrayal of characters of different races can be positive, negative or neutral. Among the things texts do, one of them is to present identities. Any portrayal contributes to these identities, and thus the portrayals can be a subject of evaluation. One obvious criterion is equality. Are races presented as equals? Another criterion is essentialism: does the text commit the "essentialist fallacy" of attributing certain characteristics of identity as essential attributes that are not actually applicable to all members of that race? These questions arise from **Liberal Race theory**. Liberal race theory, like liberal feminism, focuses on the concept of equality. Liberal Race Theory asks that we approach social relationships from a "color blind" perspective, and that we treat and understand people as individuals rather than as members of a particular race.

**Critical Race theory** argues that Liberal Race Theory errs with its notion that the key to understanding race is through methodological color blindness; rather, a better approach is "color consciousness." The idea is to critically engage our world views in order to ferret out racial assumptions of which we may be unaware. Critical Race theory thus has certain affinities with the Frankfurt School of social criticism and Radical Feminism. Like the Frankfurt School, Critical Race Theory asks that we engage in a deeper questioning of our assumptions, in this case, assumptions about race or ethnicity. And just as Radical Feminism argues that patriarchy permeates our whole world view, Critical Race Theory argues that race permeates a good deal of our thinking as well. In order to carry out the project Critical Race Theory developed a methodology that can be applied to the interpretation of texts. This method employs what we call a "Counter-narrative." We create "counter-readings" from the text that reveal any hidden assumptions about race. What is a "counter-reading"? A counter-reading carries out a skeptical interrogation of the text by postulating a reading counter to the more standard readings. For example, a story or film may present a story with "good guys" and "bad guys," as well as a more general valence of positive and negative. A counter-reading will attempt to flip these characterizations. A Critical Race Theorist will attempt to write a counter-narrative in which the bad guy is either the good guy or at least a victim of circumstance. For example, early American Western films often portray whites as good and Native Americans as bad. This is the standard "Cowboys Indians" structure. But we can construct a counter-narrative that presents the Native Americans as the good guys and the white European settlers as the bad guys. The Western could then be rewritten as a story of foreign invasion, occupation and oppression. Another example might be war films. American World War II films often portray the Japanese very negatively. A counter-narrative would attempt to rehabilitate the Japanese perspective of the 1930's and 40's. Viet Nam War films are also very open to counter-readings. Instead of seeing the Viet Nam war as a war between communism and capitalism, Viet Nam War films could be reconstructed as stories of American foreign invasion and imperialism. The method does more than "turn things upside down," rather, the counter-reading is the beginning of a process of interrogation in which it is possible to make explicit the racial assumptions that are previously only implicit. Thus a counter-narrative asks for an experiential appropriation of the counter-narrative.

Not all texts are about race, of course, but this kind of analysis applies anytime there is a narrative structure of "us and them." When this structure is a component of a text then it is crucial to have a theoretical framework we can apply. There are also limitations to the practice of counter-narratives, however. The creation of a counter-narrative has few boundary limits in the range of construction. Within proper limits counter-readings can open our eyes to aspects of the text we had previously missed; beyond those limits it is simply creating new texts that have little to do with the original texts.

**Queer Theory** is similar to racial and feminist theories in that there is a liberal approach as well as a more radical approach. A liberal approach will focus on the unequal treatment society given to heterosexuals and homosexuals. The more radical queer theory is comparable to Radical Feminism and Critical Race Theory in that it asks us to forego certain basic assumptions about a text. Queer Theory looks at the way majoritarian heterosexuality structures our ideas of sex, gender, social relations and so on. Queer theorists argue that there is a "compulsory heterosexuality" underlying the way we think about these topics. Queer theory sees sex and gender as performatives rather than essences, so Queer theory correspondingly looks for the construction of gender roles in texts. For example, a story about a boy becoming a man, or a girl becoming a woman typically contains elements of males and females engaging in modeling behaviors that are largely unexamined. Queer theory interrogates these behaviors and asks how gender and sex are being constructed by the performance of these behaviors.

## ☐ MEMETICS

Richard Dawkins coined the term "meme," in his *Selfish Gene*, where he conjectured about the possibility that genes might not be the only replicator that evolves because of differential selection in an environment. Dawkins thought that ideas might fit the bill of being differential replicators and chose "meme" for the term to indicate ideas could be conceived in this way. Dawkins drew on the Greek term *mimeme*, meaning "that which is imitated." Since there are many things that can be imitated in many different ways, memes can be found in many places and in many forms. Susan Blackmore writes,

> I shall use the term 'meme' indiscriminately to refer to memetic information in its many forms; including ideas, the brain structures that instantiate those ideas, the behaviors these brain structures produce, and their versions in books, recipes, maps and written music.

A meme can take many forms, but for our purposes, a meme is any non-genetic element of culture that is transmitted by imitation. Memes are replicators in that they are "capable of sustaining the evolutionary process of heredity, variation and selection." Memes are thus analogous to genes in that they function as differential replicators. In the case of memes, what are replicating are ideas rather than genes. But memetics is not genetics. Memetics is not an attempt to reduce cultural life to biology. Quite the opposite. Memetics argues that there is another replicator in town. Memetics is not sociobiology. There is no attempt to reduce behavior to genetics. A memeticist can consistently be an anti-reductionist.

In relation to humans, a meme can be beneficial to the organism it inhabits, neutral to the organism or harmful to the organism. They can be consistent with reason or inconsistent with reason. They simply do what they do, replicate, and while replication in a given case may have something to do with reason, it is not necessarily the case. Reason operates at the level of the organism. We use reason to pursue our self-interests, and sometimes, when morality requires, acting against our interests. But how we act is often determined by memes, which are not looking out for our interests. Their business is their own replication, not the survivability of the organism they inhabit. Like genes, memes are selfish.

If the theory of memetics is true we should therefore expect discourse to reflect the power of simple replication as much or more than the power of reason. In other words, those ideas will become dominant that tend to replicate more than others. Ideas replicate for lots of reasons, all having to do with whether they are more consistent with the discourse environment than their competitors, just as genes replicate if they are more consistent with the ecological environment than their competitors. This is not to say that reason has no memetic power. Reason is part of the discourse environment, and so we should expect it to have some influence. Some memeticists are highly skeptical of the memetic power of reason. Richard Brodie, for example, believes that a memes' truthfulness is of little aid in causing replication. He writes, "Truth is not one of the strong selectors for memes." Instead, memes replicate according to more basic drives, such as the desire for sex, food and danger-avoidance. Although there is much truth in Brodie's position, it is more likely that the power of reason in a discourse environment depends on the environment. The history of philosophy is a highly rational discourse environment in which the cogency of ideas is paramount. Public discourse about a topic such as gay marriage will be less so. Popular culture and entertainment have little to do with reason and much more to do with memetic replication.

The harmful memes are often the most interesting—hence book titles such as "Virus of the Mind" or "Thought Contagion"—but not always. Music is a largely neutral meme, but how and why it spreads is often quite interesting. We will look at the spread of Western music to India and China and give some memetic reasons this might have happened.

Music provides us with an interesting subject for the memetics approach. Music probably does not make much contribution to the genetic fitness of people who participate in music, but if we look at music memetically, its survival and thriving become more understandable. Daniel Dennett has developed a plausible memetic interpretation of the development of rhythm. Dennett writes:

> When one hominid starts drumming, soon others start drumming along in imitation. This could happen. A perfectly pointless practice, of no utility or fitness-enhancing benefit at all, could become established in a community. It might be positively detrimental: the drumming scares away the food, or uses up lots of precious energy. It would then be just like a disease, spreading simply because it *could* spread, and lasting as long as it could find hosts to infect. If it was detrimental in this way, variant habits that were less detrimental—less virulent—would tend to evolve to replace it, other things being equal, for they would tend to find more available healthy hosts to migrate to. And of course such a habit *might* even provide a positive benefit to its hosts (enhancing their reproductive chances—a familiar dream of musicians everywhere, and it might be true, or have been

true in the past). But providing a genetic benefit of this sort is only one of the paths such a habit might pursue in its mindless quest for immortality. Habits—good, bad and indifferent— could persist and replicate, unappreciated and unrecognized, for an indefinite period of time, provided only that the replicative and dispersal machinery is provided for them. The drumming virus is born.

Dennett's "just-so" story is helpful as a theory of the origins of music, but it is also a good example of memetic explanation. Now that we have a memetic theory of rhythm on the table, we can turn to the evolution and spread of music. It is not hard to imagine our hominid drummer stumbling into catchy and repetitive beats. Nor is it difficult to imagine an early hominid humming and thus creating melody. Or we can imagine humans learning (imitating) melody from birds in order to lure birds into hunting range. Now let's jump ahead to the present. Music develops on independent paths in different parts of the world. Music in the West gets caught up in the rationalization process explained by Max Weber and develops harmony and a certain conception of rhythm. India focuses on the development of complex melodies called ragas and rhythmic patterns called talas. India's music, while incredibly sophisticated, does not make use of harmony beyond the drone, and its rhythm develops into very complex patterns that are difficult for the layman to discern. China's music also neglects to utilize harmony and often restricts its scales to pentatonic scales. We find both China and India, when presented with Western music, find it beguiling. China even develops an attitude of inferiority about its indigenous music. India's indigenous classical musical tradition keeps its national respect and continues to thrive, but the larger popular arena of music in India has adopted Western harmony and rhythms. In this scenario, as in the case of the origin of music, memetics is a useful tool of explanation.

## ☐ STRUCTURALISM

**Structuralist Analysis** derives from the work of Claude Levi Strauss, who had a theory of signification that rethought the relationship between signs, signifiers and the signified. The typical view of language is that it is a set of signs that represent things in the world. But the connection between any set of signs and objects or ideas in the world is arbitrary. We could decide to call bikes "fikes" from now on. There is nothing necessary about the connection between the word "bike" and a bike out in the world. If there is no necessary connection between signifier and signified, then reference is ultimately accomplished by a negotiation of signifiers. Structuralism therefore considers how signifiers are related to each other, rather than how they are related to the world. Any structures governing the relations are given special note. Structuralists distinguish surface and deep structure and argue that the deep structure is binary. Strauss believes this is because he believes the mind itself organizes meaning in a binary fashion.

Structuralist analysis of texts builds on this idea and interprets texts in terms of the binary oppositions present in a work. The idea is that there is a structure of signification that we need to capture if we are to understand the text and that the structure is a binary one. Thus if you want to understand a story, you need to know who the good guys are, and you need to know who the bad guys are. Good guys and bad guys is an opposition. But these oppositions are not just moral. They can be literary, pictorial, historical et al. One might have a color binary in which colors are referenced and used in a work. One might have a contrast of old and new. One might contrast ideas like hate and love. Or the work may create binaries from its narrative. A work may present two characters opposed in their style of walking, speaking, thinking, etc. A work may present themes that are opposed. Structuralists also want us to look for mediation of the binaries. Does the flow of the narrative tend to mediate the opposed binaries? Or is the point of the work that the binary is unbridgeable? In either case, the process of mediation is an important part of understanding the text.

## ☐ POST-STRUCTURALISM

**Poststructuralism** is a theory–or better–a set of theories that attempts to "decenter" the practice of interpretation. Roland Barthes announced "the Death of the Author," and what he meant by this is that meaning of a text is not reducible to the author's intention. The meaning of the text is as much about the reader, if not more, than it is about the author. In fact, the author is herself a fiction, for on this view the self is a construct rather than an essence. Meaning therefore becomes highly ambiguous, and there is no guarantee of consistency of meaning between any two individuals. Emmanuel Levinas writes that words "signify from the 'world' and from the position of one who is looking." In relation to structuralism, this means that the structures we uncover may be ones that we supply rather than being inherent in the text. Further, these structures may be ultimately incoherent. Meaning, in this conception, becomes a matter of "play." The post-structuralist rejects the notion of a single meaning, and therefore any structures we isolate would only be the structures from one point of view, and there could be others. We must also note that the process of determining meaning is fraught with power struggles. The method known as "Deconstruction" is meant to break down the logic of binary opposition. A binary structure falsely indicates a more determinate and consistent meaning than actually exists. Deconstruction asks us to look for ruptures in the text and for the role of power in attempting to smooth over these ruptures. Systems of knowledge, which are also systems of power, determine meaning historically and constitute a cloak over the more realistic play of meaning which is always at work.

Using deconstruction is a matter of first doing a structuralist analysis, and then breaking down the binaries or reversing their relationship. Instead of employing the principle of charity in interpretation, in which the critic reads a text in such a way that it is the best work of art among the various readings, deconstruction asks us to look for contradictions in the text.

## ☐ POSTMODERNISM

**Postmodernism** is a name for a time period, roughly contemporaneous with the information age, but it has also come to designate certain beliefs and attitudes. The idea of Postmodernism is initially problematic. After all, Modernism was supposed to be the view that "anything goes." How do we go farther than that? Modernism does say that anything goes, but it adheres to stylistic consistency and what are called "metanarratives." Postmodernism jettisons even stylistic consistency with mixed technique and genre. Films like *Run, Lola, Run* and *Natural Born Killers* employ various kinds of media, from live action to animation rather than sticking to one

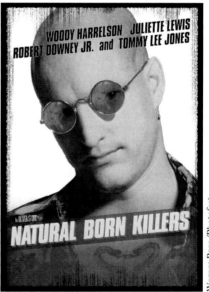

Woody Harrelson in *Natural Born Killers*

or the other. The music from the film is of a variety of styles, and the video itself is sometimes made to look antiquated, at other times perfectly contemporary. *Run, Lola, Run* also dislodges the temporal sequence and thus the narrative flow by telling the story backwards. *Natural Born Killers* displaces the perspective in several ways and moves in the mode of irony. There is an intense self-reflectivity in postmodern texts. NBK is a violent film that critiques violence, and NBK wears this contradiction proudly. The text is always expressing a hint at self-awareness about its perspectives and thus expresses a skepticism about narrative closure. In postmodernist culture there can be no heroes without nuance, without flaws.

Postmoderns will reject the idea that pop culture and high culture can be differentiated in any meaningful sense. Postmodernists claim that privileging high culture implies a "metanarratives" they are unprepared to accept. A "metanarrative" is a story that brings together the world of facts and orders them according to a perspective. For example, the belief in progress is a metanarrative. It looks at trends in facts and discerns a pattern of increasing goodness or efficiency. Marxist theory is a metanarrative because it is a "totalizing" theory that tries to bring together facts into a theory of history. Religions are also metanarratives. They give order to otherwise discrete facts and beliefs about the world. Postmodernism claims that metanarratives no longer have the force they once had. Today's cynical people just cannot put their arms around any such totalizing view. Postmoderns only claim allegiance to "little facts."

## ☐ POSTHUMANISM

**Posthumanism** is a speculative position that argues that humans are changing in such fundamental ways that we will eventually become something beyond human. The computer, cellphones, the internet, and many other technologies have already changed a great deal about modern living, and as it continues to change so will humanity. Humanity may possibly give birth to artificial intelligence, which will have a profound impact on culture. What will robot music be like? But humans themselves will change as biological engineering and prosthesis techniques progress and computers or computer-like devices become connected directly to the brain. This vision of humanity is quite common in current science fiction. What if we all had large (capacity wise, not physical size) hard drives installed in our brains so that we no longer forgot anything? Would we become more or less traditional? What would this do to education?

What if we could communicate with others via a wireless connection inserted into our bodies? Science fiction authors often imagine people sending their thoughts instantaneously to others. What if, as a result, the thoughts of people became less and less individualized? Is it possible to generate a collective consciousness in this way? It may all turn out to be a false dream, but even if it does, posthuman culture is forcing us to reconsider what it means to be human.

All the different kinds of popular culture implicate a wide range of topics and issues, and our theories help to illuminate these issues. The theories covered in this chapter should be kept in mind for the rest of the book. They can also be used to help you direct your life. These theories should help you to make your own decisions. They should help you understand your world better. Finally, they should make your life richer with your new ability to give deeper interpretations.

## BIBLIOGRAPHY AND FURTHER READING

Adorno, Theodor, *Prisms,* MIT Press, 1955/1983.

Arnold, Matthew, *Culture and Anarchy, and Other Writings*, Cambridge Univ. P, 1869/1993.

Blackmore, Susan, *The Meme Machine*, Oxford Univ. Press, 1999, 66.

Brody, Richard, *Virus of the Mind*, Seattle: Integral Press, 1996, 168.

Bryman, Alan, "The Disneyization of Society," http://fasnafan.tripod.com/disneyization.pdf, 1999.

Collins, Patricia Hill, *Black Feminist Thought,* New York: Routledge, 2000.

Dawkins, Richard, *The Selfish Gene*, Oxford Univ. Press, 1976.

De Beauvoir, Simone, *The Second Sex*, New York: Vintage, 1989/1953.

Degado, Richard and Stefancic, Jean, eds. *Critical Race Theory: the Cutting Edge*, Philadelphia: Temple Univ. Press, 2000.

Dennett, Daniel, "The Evolution of Culture," *The Charles Simonyi Lecture* Oxford University, (http://www.edge.org/3rd_culture/dennett/dennett _p1.html), Feb. 17, 1999.

Eagleton, Terry, *Literary Theory: An Introduction*, Minneapolis, Univ. of Minnesota Press, 2008.

Freud, Sigmund, *The Interpretation of Dreams*, Harmondsworth: Pelican, 1889/1976.

Freud, Sigmund, *The Future of an Illusion*, New York: Norton, 1927/1989.

Freud, Sigmund, *Civilization and its Discontents*, New York: Norton, 1930/2005.

Gramsci, Antonio, *The Antonio Gramsci Reader: Selected Writings 1916–1935,* David Forgats ed., NYU Press, 2000.

Habermas, Jurgen, *The Theory of Communicative Action Vol. 1,* Boston: Beacon Press, 1984.

Hooks, Bell, *Feminist Theory: From Margins to Center,* New York: South End Press, 1984.

Jung, Carl, *The Archetypes and The Collective Unconscious* (Collected Works of C.G. Jung Vol. 9 Part 1) Princeton Univ. Press, 1981.

Kierkegaard, Soren, *The Concept of Anxiety: A Simple Psychologically Orienting Deliberation on the Dogmatic Issue of Hereditary Sin* (Kierkegaard's Writings, VIII) (v. 8), Princeton University Press, 1981.

Leavis, F. R. and Denys Thompson, *Culture and Environment,* Westport, Connecticut: Greenwood Press, 1977.

Lévinas, Emmanuel, (2003) *Humanism of the Other,* Chicago: Univ. of Illinois Press, 2003, 11–12.

Lynch, Aaron, *Thought Contagion,* Basic Books, 1996.

Marcuse, Herbert, *One Dimensional Man.* Routledge, 1964/2002.

Marx, Karl and Friedrich Engels, *The Communist Manifesto,* Oxford Univ. Press, 2008.

Nietzsche, Friedrich. *The Gay Science*, Vintage, 1974.

Patton, Tracey Owens, ""Ally McBeal" and Her Homies: The Reification of White Stereotypes of the Other" *Journal of Black Studies* (Sage Publications, Inc.) 32(2): 229–260, Nov. 2001.

Ritzer, George, *The McDonaldization of Society 6,* Pine Forge Press, 2010.

Rojas, Maythee, *Women of Color and Feminism,* Berkeley: Seal Press, 2009.

Storey, John, *Cultural Theory and Popular Culture: An Introduction,* 5th ed. London: Pearson/Longman, 2009.

Tong, Rosemarie, *Feminine and Feminist Ethics,* Belmont: Wadsworth, 1993.

Weber, Max, *General Economic History,* Dover Publications, 2003.

Max Weber, Peter R. Baehr, Gordon C. Wells, *The Protestant ethic and the "spirit" of capitalism and other writings,* Penguin Classics, 2002.

# CHAPTER 2

# Aesthetics

A good portion of popular culture can be understood better when one understands theories of art. Films, television, advertisements, novels, and music are works of art. Even bad films and songs are art because they involve a form of human expression and organization in order to convey sensations or provoke emotions. Everything that employs design or style can be interpreted as a work of art. Style, design, and expression are evident even in documentary films and television news programs that endeavor to place their messages above art. Photography and cinematography, while showing an unbiased, realistic element are both art forms. This does not mean that everything created by human agency qualifies as art. Intention plays an important role. If one goes to a hardware store and looks at a piece of pipe, it is not considered art because the intention of the pipe makers is not artistic. However, if a person buys the pipe and mounts it to a base or hangs it on the wall with the intention that it should be looked at as a work of art, it becomes art. The most important question is not whether or not something is art, but whether or not that something is good art or effective art. Aesthetics is the key to discovering the qualities and failings of art, especially in popular culture.

The word "aesthetics" simply means the philosophy of art. It derives from the Greek word "aisthetikos" and refers to the senses. Although it encompasses a large subject, the specific meaning of aesthetics centers around beauty and its sensory effect on the individual. The broader implications of aesthetics move into other areas of study, such as psychology. For example, a small painting of flowers has a different psychological effect on the individual than a colossal statue of a warrior. The flowers may appear more beautiful to some because they feel less threatened. Others may appreciate the powerful effect the warrior has on the public more than the intimate flowers.

Size is only one of several areas within the aesthetic realm of study. During this chapter, we will examine other important areas, including realism, expressionism, formalism, and contextualism. We will also look at some of the more specific issues with loaded terms, such as the "sublime." The terms "kitsch" and "camp" will provide the reader with critical tools more applicable to popular culture. Included in this chapter is a discussion on "genre" or the way in which aesthetics has been classified over the years. Genres tend to differ from medium to medium, especially in comparing music to the visual arts. It is also one of the most misunderstood and debated areas of aesthetics. Therefore, it requires a good deal of our attention.

## ☐ REALISM

This area of aesthetics examines the ability of art to recreate an accurate depiction of the physical world. For the average filmgoer, the most important ingredient in movies is credulity. The worst thing a film can do for the layman is break with reality. If the acting is not convincing, if the dialogue is stale or pretentious, if the scenery is artificial then the film tends to fail audience appreciation. Similarly in painting, when artists abstract the imagery, they often run into realist criticism. However, realism has its fair share of critics even within popular culture. The invention of photography has made accurate realism easy and has raised moral implications within the popular arena.

Realism is one of the oldest and most conservative areas of aesthetics. In many ways, it was a major criterion for "good" art. The ancient Greek philosopher Plato criticized art for not being real enough to conform to his ideal theories. Pliny the Elder wrote about the painter Zuexis's ability to paint grapes so life-like that birds would try to eat them. The general theory that the history of art represents a drive to realism, culminating with the invention of the camera, has been a main issue of discussion especially in film circles. However, the drive to greater realism in the history of the visual arts is not without paradoxes and contradictions.

One of the major advances of realism arose with the invention of linear perspective during the Renaissance period and the whole concept of "Renaissance Space." Linear perspective was invented by the architect-genius

Brunelleschi during the early fifteenth century. Brunelleschi realized that by combining lines in just the right, geometrical manner, an illusion of depth appears on an otherwise flat surface. His invention was quickly adopted by art schools and workshops all over Europe. By the sixteenth century, linear perspective was a standard technique, which all artists were expected to master. Modern art theorists use the term "Renaissance Space" to refer to this use of linear perspective and also the well-defined spaces that Renaissance art tends to exhibit.

One of the most often cited examples of Renaissance Space is Raphael's *School of Athens*. Raphael's classical fantasy shows many of the great philosophers of ancient times discussing their theories in their own circles. If one looks closely at the lines on the floor and the coffers in the arches, the eyes and brain are tricked into thinking that there is depth. Images on this grid of space appear to be positioned back into the picture rather than simply painted smaller. The space is also well-defined and organized. The philosophers appear balanced and seem to conform to the notion of Renaissance Space. Although Renaissance Space was new during Raphael's time, it has been used so often in the visual arts ever since that we look at the painting without the amazement that people during the Renaissance must have felt.

However, artists and critics noticed a paradox with the use of linear perspective because the technique uses illusion to create realistic paintings. During the early modern period, many artists, such as Picasso, drew attention to this contradiction of using illusion to create realism. Picasso's famous saying, "art is a lie used to help us realize the truth" was meant to attack the monolithic belief that visual realism was the only truth in art. Consequently, Picasso and others shattered Renaissance Space and re-assembled it into Cubist Space. Yet, even Picasso never completely abandoned illusory depth. There remains depth in many of the Cubist works. Some artists such as Mondrian struggled to remove the spatial relationship between figure and ground. Complete flatness became not only an aesthetic choice for Clement Greenberg and the Abstract Expressionists during the 1940s and 1950s, it became an ethical issue. Illusion of depth, for Greenberg, was an illusion of art. True, real art avoided any such fantasy. To a larger extent, the Abstract Expressionist reacted against the Social Realists of the United States and the Soviet Union during the 1930s. The pop-culture revolution in the following decades (1960s and 1970s) moved away from Greenberg and illusory depth was used again.

© The Gallery Collection/Corbis

Raphael's *School of Athens*

**Realism in Pop Culture**

In popular culture, realism is the most used and adhered-to aesthetic theory. Realism is immediate, in other words, it does not require a high level of recognition. The so-called "suspension of disbelief" in film relies on the immediacy of realism. In order to create realism in a fantasy, blockbuster-type film, filmmakers provide detail and familiar surroundings. Film as an art form relies on the illusion of movement produced by the quick succession of still frames and the flicker of light, caused by the projection shutter. Thus it represent another illusion of realism.

Courtesy of the author

*Kanweiler*

A few fantasy films provide examples of realism. In the film *Edward Scissorhands* for example, the familiar surroundings of the suburb lends an element of realism. The Gothic castle and the scissor-hand star are placed within a more recognizable context, and the spectator tends to accept these more unbelievable elements. The suburb context also lends credibility to the time-travel blockbuster *Back to the Future*. The audience recognizes the familiar surroundings and is more liable to accept the dubious premise of going back in time several decades.

Fantasy films that lack the recognizable context often use realism with the large amount of detail given to the settings, costumes, and props. One has only to watch the behind-the-scenes features to *The Lord of the Rings* or *Star Wars* to see how much detail is involved. Detail, no matter how minute, distracts the audience from the superficial aspects of hobbits, light-sabers, and outer-space laser warfare. Of course, audiences want to be fooled in order to be more easily transported to Middle Earth or the "far, far away" galaxy.

The credibility of realism in film offers a powerful rhetorical tool for documentaries. In the early and mid-twentieth century, Sergei Eisenstein and Leni Riefenstahl made propaganda films using the realistic techniques that documentary filmmakers continue to use today. Riefenstahl provides an interesting case study. When she made the notorious *Triumph of the Will*, U.S. censorship organizations during World War II were alarmed, and they banned the film from American audiences. When one views this film even today, one can appreciate their sense of alarm. Riefenstahl shows several Nazi rallies and edits the swelling waves of adoring masses in an emotional manner that she learned from Eisenstein. Hardly anything in the film shows the dark side of Nazism; only one speaker mentions a passing sentence on racial purity; all of the speakers focus on issues of national pride. German audiences watching this film must have felt the ground-swelling sense of unity and a love for their leaders that reached a religious level. The Nazis were selling a product, and they knew the power of realism to push their agendas.

Realism, as a rhetorical tool, is also used to sell products in advertisements. Photographers show products in extreme close up in order to highlight the detail. Fast food companies show the detail of their food in order to promote desire in the spectator. Sometimes happy, attractive faces are added in order to associate an emotion of pleasure with the food product. In television commercials for restaurants or children's toys, the attractive, smiling faces become friends associating companionship with the product. The association depends on the immediate recognition, and the realism functions as a stamp of authority for the consumer.

## ☐ EXPRESSIONISM

Realism is often pitted against expressionism as an art theory. Many theorists in art consider art's primary purpose as a vehicle for expression. For the expressionist, realism lacks human emotions, being instead a lifeless re-creation of the physical world.

As with realism, expressionism has its roots in the ancient world. In the ancient Greek tragedies of Aeschylus, Sophocles, and especially Euripides we hear actors relate scenes of graphic violence. Characters, such as Oedipus who blinds himself with pins, Medea who kills her two sons, and Hippolytus who is torn apart by a monstrous bull sent by his grandfather Poseidon, convey strong emotions. Plato, as an idealist, objected to tragedies because of the emphasis on emotionalism. Aristotle, however, devoted much of his *Poetics* on tragedy. Tragedies affect a catharsis of pity and fear.[1] While it is not completely clear what Aristotle means by catharsis, it is generally assumed to mean a purging or cleansing. The term is used rather loosely today to describe the emotional workout that a tragic play, film, symphony, etc. can have on its audience. Even though Aristotle mentions "catharsis" in passing, later in *Poetics* he is very clear that tragedies must have a sense of the "marvelous" (Aristotle, 121). It is through the marvelous that we find pleasure in a tragedy or other works of art. Regardless of what is exactly meant by catharsis or the marvelous, Aristotle makes it plain that the expression of emotion is an important component in poetry, and one could easily extend this to the other arts.

Expressionism in drama gained more ground in Imperial Rome. Living under the nightmarish reign of Nero, the moralist Seneca wrote some of the most grotesque tragedies ever written. His Oedipus does not simply blind himself with pins, but rips out his eyes with his own hands. The Romans not only lifted the Greek ban on staged violence, but exhibited real staged violence done to slaves.

In the visual arts, expressionism also can be traced to ancient Greece. Shortly following the death of Alexander the Great, artists were especially influenced by the disturbing tragedies of Euripides. One of the best examples of sculpture during this time that reveals expressionism is the *Laocoön Group*. This work shows Laocoön, who had tried to warn his fellow Trojans about the wooden horse, in the coils a serpent with his two sons. As the serpent bites Laocoön on the side, he tenses every muscle in his body and turns his head up to heaven to cry his anguish up to the gods who sent the serpent. This sculpture was uncovered during the Renaissance and had an influence on Michelangelo and other artists. Expressive images of Christ on the cross, turning his head up to heaven, are drawn from this sculpture.

During the Middle Ages and Renaissance (476–1600), expressionism was primarily seen in the visual arts, and tragedies became dormant until Shakespeare's time. The sculptures on many Romanesque and Gothic churches display the Last Judgment with all of its horrors. Demonic monsters and images of torture were common visual aids for the sermons. Attending church during the Middle Ages was similar to watching a "torture-porn" film today as all the horrors of hells were exposed in graphic detail. Works of literature also contain hellish imagery such as in Dante's *Inferno.* However, hell is not the only realm to produce expressionistic works. The Passion of Christ was often rendered in graphic detail, especially in Germany. Artists, like Mathias Grünewald, emphasized the suffering of Christ on the cross with dislocated joints and gangrenous skin.

Baroque (1600–1750) artist went further with the expressionistic imagery than previous artists. Caravaggio in Italy was fascinated with decapitation and painted bloody images of David and Golaith and Medusa. Rubens and Rembrandt in Northern Europe showed similar expressive imagery of violence and terror. Although the Neoclassical period (1750–1800) revived the emotional restraint of ancient and Renaissance artists, it was only fifty years at most until Romantic (1800–1850) artists returned to expressionism with a vengeance.

© Araldo de Luca/CORBIS

Expressionism during the Romantic period reaches a high point that would not be reached again until the early 20<sup>th</sup> century. Artists during this time were quick to paint works of protest against the carnage of the Napoleonic wars and other related events. The *Laocoön Group*

Spanish artist Goya showed graphic imagery of mass executions and atrocities. During the later-part of his career (1820s), he produced a series of dark murals on the bare walls of his villa, now called the "Black Paintings." Even by today's looser standards, these Black Paintings are disturbing and grotesque.

Closely related to the Romantic theme of horror is the notion of the "sublime." Sublime is a loaded term in aesthetics that dates back to ancient Greece. However, it is through the works of the Enlightenment philosophers Immanuel Kant and Edmund Burke that made the theme influential on Romantic artists, poets, and composers. Burke devoted an entire book to the term's meanings. He describes the sublime as a type of horror: "Indeed terror is in all cases whatsoever, either more openly or latently, the ruling principle of the sublime."[2] Terror or horror results, Burke continues, when our reason is obscured or darkened. Thus, dark places such as old churches and in the woods at night are agents of the sublime. Kant, however describes the sublime as a form of beauty mixed with horror, an overwhelming beauty not to be mistaken for beauty that does not threaten. For example, a bouquet of flowers is a type of beauty that does not threaten us by virtue of its scale and harmless nature. A massive, black oncoming storm, however threatens us, but can also be thought of as beautiful. Standing at the edge of the Grand Canyon evokes similar emotions of awesome beauty.[3]

Expressionism becomes a movement during the late 19th and early 20th century. Although Expressionism proper does not occur until the early decades of the 20th century, its birth is noted in the works of Vincent Van Gogh and Edvard Munch. Both of these artists subjected line and color for emotional rather than descriptive effects. Munch's *The Scream* influenced popular culture to a high degree. The masked figure in Wes Craven's *Scream* movies as well as the *Home Alone* poster reveal re-workings of the distorted bald screaming figure in Munch's painting. During the early 20th century, artists in Germany, such as Wassily Kandinsky took expressionism to the level of pure abstraction. Kandinsky wanted to bring a musical element to his works and, thus, concentrated on the emotional or spiritual aspects of line, color, and composition.

After the Second World War, artists in the United States experimented with the idea of pure expression. Like Kandinsky, they eschewed descriptive representation. However, unlike Kandinsky and the other German Expressionists, the Abstract Expressionists wanted to throw out rational or conscious faculties as well. Although Kandinsky was an abstractionist, he made several sketches before completing a work. The Abstract Expressionists in the U.S. desired more intuitive elements. Thus, artists like Jackson Pollock and William De Kooning started "actionism" in which the work became a dramatic process rather than a finished product. Other Abstract Expressionists like Mark Rothko and Barnett Newman created huge canvases of color.

The emotional nature of expressionism in art became the main target for the popular culture revolution of the 1960s. Yet, expressionism was never completely abandoned by popular culture. We see it in films and video games, and we hear it in the counter-cultural alternative styles of hard rock and heavy metal.

## Expressionism in Popular Culture

Expressionism in film began as more of an art form than entertainment. Even though the German Expressionist painting style had died out by the 1920s, it was still alive in the operas of Alban Berg and the silent films of F.W. Murnau and Fritz Lang. Murnau was the first filmmaker to shoot a full-length feature based on Bram Stoker's novel *Dracula*. The film was titled *Nosferatu* partly because Murnau did not get the rights from the Stoker estate. Murnau felt that changing the name would help avoid legal issues. He was wrong as the film was shelved following its production. The expressionistic elements in *Nosferatu* are noticed in the distorted effects of the vampire and the melodramatic elements common in silent films.

© Erich Lessing/Art Resource, NY.

Munch's *The Scream*

Expressionism is the perfect style for horror films. The distortions of the vampire in *Nosferatu* reflect Bram Stoker's description of Dracula:

> His face was a strong, a very strong, aquiline, with high bridge of the thin nose and peculiarly arched nostrils, with lofty domed forehead, and hair growing scantily round the temples but profusely elsewhere. His eyebrows were very massive, almost meeting over the nose, and with bushy hair that seemed to curl in its own profusion. The mouth, so far as I could see it under the heavy moustache, was fixed and rather cruel-looking, with peculiarly sharp white teeth. These protruded over the lips, whose remarkable ruddiness showed astonishing vitality in a man of his years. For the rest, his ears were pale, and at the tops extremely pointed. . .[4]

Stoker and Murnau's show a grotesque form of expressionism that exploits the popular interest in abnormal reality or freak-show entertainment. In film, German Expressionism was more exploitative than its earlier counterpart in painting. In more ways, the cinematic form of German Expressionism resembled the Dadaists and Surrealists who were active at the same time. *Nosferatu* and other German Expressionistic cinema made an impact on the early Universal horror film classics like *Dracula* and *Frankenstein*.

The expressionism that is more common in today's cinema owes its existence to Alfred Hitchcock. *Psycho* stands as one of the most influential films ever, and part of its influence results from its expressive style. For the two murder scenes in the film, Hitchcock applies a dramatic form of expressionism through the use of montage (the editing of short, successive clips together) sharp camera angles, and dramatic lighting. Montage is noticed in the famous "shower scene" where the leading character, Janet Leigh, gets stabbed to death. The quick, short clips both parallel the stabbing gestures and give an emotional shock that would not occur had the scene been shot more naturally. When the private investigator gets stabbed in the head, Hitchcock shows the scene from an extreme high angle. Then the camera moves with the victim as he falls backward down the stairs. And when Norman enters the cellar to kill Leigh's sister, she swings her hand backward, knocking the lamp in motion. The swinging lamp then throws dramatic shadows over the cellar and its skeleton occupant. A realistic style would not have made *Psycho* as effective as these expressionistic elements.

Martin Scorsese, like many other living filmmakers, has inherited Hitchcock's expressionistic style. More than any other film-school-generation figure, Scorsese uses an expressive style to expose social problems. Robert De Niro's character in *Taxi Driver* resembles the internally troubled Norman Bates. In addition, the ending murder scene emphasizes the shocking brutality, only now with the graphic violence more direct. The fight sequences in *Raging Bull* use similar expressive montages as *Psycho*. It should be noted, however, that cinematic expressionism is not always used for radical or subversive purposes. The expressive montage is used frequently in popular action films in order to create tension and keep attention.

Expressionism in music is more difficult to recognize as the very medium implies expression. However, the darker styles of popular music can be thought to take on the expressionism mantle. Rock music has always expressed rebellious behavior since its beginnings with Elvis's suggestive pelvic moves. But what happens when rock becomes domesticated and accepted in mainstream popular culture? Well, it gets more expressive. When the supposed "hard rock" bands Kiss and ACDC are sold at Walmart and bought by soccer moms, then rebellious society demands more expression. Thus metal splinters into edgier sub-genres: black metal, death metal, and Viking metal to name a few.

"Screamo" is the result of the taming of rock music. In this case, screamo refers to the guttural vocal style of certain punk and metal bands. It is also one of the few examples of a noticeable style in popular music based almost entirely on expression. On one hand, screamo metal bands subvert the kitschy popular styles through chronic screaming. And it works because rarely will one hear an In Flames song on the radio. However, death metal is a text-book example of expressionism as it is a distortion of styles that are considered "natural." The Austrian Expressionist Arnold Schoenberg also distorted vocal styles with "Sprechstimme."[5] Schoenberg's music, although over 100 years old, is still ignored by radio stations. The expressive distortions of vocal styles tend to move in contrary motion to mass popularity.

Expressionism in popular culture brings up the issue of value and taste. On one hand, the works that express pain and tragedy tend to win the most awards. On the other hand, when works become expressionistic they tend to invite criticism. Horror films rarely win Academy Awards, and the Grammy Awards are notorious for ignoring metal bands. However, a musicologist could find more talent and artistic creativity in death metal than country. Yet, because death metal expresses styles outside of popular comfort, it is ridiculed or ignored. Thus, expressionism exposes a fallacy in taste. If the purpose of art is to express human emotions, then a horror film would be greater than a Shakespearean comedy because the horror film has more shocking and disturbing content.

## ☐ FORMALISM

However, as the philosopher David Hume pointed out, we pay money to see tragedy not to feel the emotions so much as to see the beauty of a good play.[6] Beauty arises from how well the work in question is put together. If one sees a horror film that has poor acting, editing, script writing etc., then it does not matter how much one is scared or affected, it gets deserved criticism. A Shakespearean play can suffer the same fate as a bad horror film if the acting or staging is poor. The issue of form and style, in other words how a work is put together, takes us to the next aesthetic theory: Formalism. The formalist theory asserts that art is "significant form" first and everything else second. Formalism is at odds with both expressionism and realism because they do not address the central question of artistic value. If realism is the central value of art, then a common photograph is a greater work of art than a Michelangelo painting; if expressionism is central, then a death-metal album is greater than a Schubert song cycle. The formalist would probably point out that Michelangelo and Schubert are greater because their works display significant form, or at least more so than the death-metal album and photograph.

Take, for example, Raphael's *School of Athens* again. A formalist theory regards the line and color and how these basic components are used and combined more than the realism or philosophy that the work contains. One can be ignorant of who the figures are and still appreciate the beauty. *School of Athens* is great and has passed the test of time because Raphael assembled the basic components in a significant manner, not because he shows people in a realistic manner, or because he expresses his admiration for the love of wisdom. Take, again, the example of Leni Riefenstahl's *Triumph of the Will*. The film is still watched and studied today because of its quality of formal elements and style despite its function and revulsion as Nazi propaganda.

Although formalism may seem more of a conservative or traditionalist theory, it is newer as a theory than both realism and expressionism, and it has been applied to radical and avant-garde works. Even though some scholars have noted formalism in the writings of Thomas Aquinas, the theory appears more substantially among Enlightenment (1700–1800) philosophers.[7] Despite the fact that David Hume showed little interest in art and disliked music, he understood the human tendency to prejudge works of art (Barrett, 109). Hume believed that taste was something to work at and acquire. Beauty, Hume felt, was in the eye of the beholder, or, rather in the mind. However, recognizing a "standard of taste" would help stabilize conflicting notions of beauty.

Like David Hume, the German scholar Alexander Baumgarten applied an objective approach to art theory. He was the first to use the term "aesthetics" and claimed that truly appreciating art requires an "aesthetic attitude." Thus, it is a conscious and willful activity (Barrett, 110). Such activities involve analyzing line, color, texture, composition, medium, and application among other elements. Perhaps a brief discussion on each of these elements would facilitate a better understanding of the formalist theory.

Line both defines objects and divides areas in a given work. The linear aspect of a work can be thick and noticeable, such as Munch's *Scream*, or thin and unnoticeable. The effect of the thick line is often expressive and dramatic. Thin, stealthy lines often produce mystery as the objects and areas are vaguely defined. In realist works, line is subjected to description. The lines in *School of Athens* define the figures and establish the space. But from a formalist approach, line does not have to be expressive or descriptive to evoke beauty. Line can also convey stability or instability. In *School of Athens* for example, the lines are perpendicular, bringing a stable effect to the viewer. The lines are sinuous and oblique in *The Scream*, creating an unstable effect.

Color may also be descriptive, expressive, or decorative. The realist requires descriptive color, in other words trees should be green, the sky blue, the sand yellow et al. The expressionist desires emotion from color, like the blood red sky in *The Scream*. However, for the formalist color need not submit to these theories; it can exist on merits of a good artist or die from the failings of a poor artist. Color is often associated with emotion. Hence, the red in *The Scream* reflect passion and violence; the blues, whites, and grays in *School of*

*Athens* bring a sense of calm restraint. Color can also be symbolic. White is the color of purity and death—Death rides a white horse in the Book of Revelations; blue is the color of heaven and the Virgin Mary. Conversely, blue can also symbolize fraud and deceit in many Northern Renaissance paintings.

Texture in the visual arts is the surface effects: smooth, rough, glossy, or matted. In music, texture is how pitches are combined and is somewhat more technical. One of the prejudices in art results from the very term "fine art." It implies that art should be a finished, glossy product, like the works of many of the Renaissance and Baroque masters. The "fine art" prejudice betrays a realist agenda that a formalist would dismiss. It should be noted, however, that many of the Renaissance and Baroque masters experimented with loose brushwork and created rough textures, Rembrandt and Titian being the most notable.

Composition refers to the placement of images within the frame of the picture. How the figures are situated affects the impressions stability or instability and draws the spectator's attention to what the artist wishes to emphasize. In *School of Athens*, the figures in the center are Plato and Aristotle. Their central position implies that Raphael felt they were the most important thinkers in the large group. In *The Scream*, the bald figure is in the foreground, while two other figures are in the background. As the title reflects the central figure, indeed the whole landscape appears manipulated by the scream's sound waves, we expect the screaming figure to have a more noticeable position. Composition brings order to the scene, even this one, and emphasizes certain elements or figures. In film, composition is an important area of discussion, especially with more artistic films, such as *Citizen Kane* and *2001:A Space Odyssey*.

Medium is such an obvious component in art that often scholars neglect discussing it. However, to artists, medium is of paramount interest. The medium is the material that makes up a work of art. Of course, the medium of sculpture is some sort of stone, metal, or wood; painting is made of oil, pastel, or tempera. Sometimes the medium is not so easy to guess. For example, film and music use the more intangible materials of light and sound. The traditional theory of medium asserts that art should be true to its materials. A sculpture should keep its medium's look. Therefore, Michelangelo's sculptures look like marble, Rodin's maintains its bronze finish. Even in the photographic realism of Vermeer, one can still see the paint. Formalists tend to support this theory. Abstract artists during the Modern Era took the "truth to materials" to its logical conclusion and emphasized the flatness of painting. For the formalists and abstractionists, representation in art constituted a violation of this truth rule. The Dadaists, like Marcel Duchamp, were quick on the attack of what they considered purist bigotry. They invented the "readymade," or found objects, to undermine this and other formalist principles.

The aesthetic writings of Kant reveal a profound interest in formalism. Kant believes, in contrast to Plato and even Aristotle, that art has its own purpose outside of ethics or other issues: "Therefore it can be nothing else than the subjective purposiveness in the representation of an object without any purpose (either objective or subjective), and thus it is the mere form of purposiveness in the representation by which an object is given to us, so far as we are conscious of it..."[8] For Kant, beauty can be achieved through form alone.

During the early part of the 20th century, formalist writers refined their arguments against the spiritual emphasis in Romantic art. Nature played a major role in art until the early modern period. Artists like Turner, Friedrich, and Constable evoked the sublime, the nostalgic, and the overall mystery of nature. Early modernists took refuge in formalism and regarded nature either at odds with art or completely separate. The American artist Whistler once claimed, "Nature is usually wrong" (Cited in Eco, 340). Oscar Wilde explained further, "My own experience is that the more we study Art, the less we care for Nature. What Art really reveals to us is Nature's lack of design, her curious crudities, her extraordinary monotony, her absolutely unfinished condition" (Cited in Eco, 340).

With such formalist views of art already in force, the formalist theorists Clive Bell and his associate Roger Fry had an immediate following. Both were proponents of modern art in England. Bell considered the emotions evoked by art to be different than the garden variety ones. He used the term "aesthetic emotions to refer to this former type of emotions, and in his 1914 book called *Art*, he wrote: "What quality is shared by all objects that provoke our aesthetic emotions?... Only one answer seems possible—significant form."[9] Bell was the first to use the expression "significant form," yet the idea that all art needed was significant form seems to validate a growing interest in abstraction.

Despite how liberating the theory of formalism appeared to be at the beginning of the modern period, it took on aspects of a social clique in the middle of the 20th century. The Marxist critic Clement Greenberg pushed his formalist theories into mainstream society, and he used Pollock's action paintings as an example. As a result, Abstract Expressionism became almost as much a fad as a movement, and formalism, as a theory, became just as exclusive and limiting as realism.

## Formalism in Popular Culture

Of all the theories discussed in this chapter, formalism casts a darker critical shadow over popular culture. Mass production, pastiche forms and styles, replicated formulas are just some of the issues that would undermine the "significant" part of significant form. By its very nature, mass production conflicts with significant form or originality. Cheap reproductions of "high art" constitute a variety of kitsch discussed at greater length below. Closely related to mass production is the notion of "pastiche," which serves more as a paraphrase than a direct quote.

A pastiche imitates significant form and is similar to satire but lacks the comedy or travesty. Sometimes a work of high art becomes so popular it shows up as pastiche versions and my library. Fragonard's famous *Swing*, for

Photo taken by the author

example, has been reworked many times in pastiche forms. Instead of being hung in a museum or in a private collection, pastiches decorate bars and cafes. The reclining nude figures of Titian and Goya have also found their way into bars in pastiche form.

Pastiche works in a similar way to a popular narrative in a film or a formula. Characters and settings may change, but if the plot draws an audience, it reappears. Thus the many *Psycho* pastiches, the *Halloweens, Friday the 13ths,* and the *Saws* dilute the psychopathic killer so much that they are almost interchangeable cardboard cutouts. Adherence to a proven formula is a stabilizing agent for a market dependent on a mass audience. Thus, the market dictates the form in order to ensure ticket sales. Hollywood narratives must conform to a set of rules. One such rule is a satisfying ending. It may be a tragic ending like *Titanic*, but more often it is happy. Either happy or sad, popular films include a sense of closure that satisfies audience expectation. Once a film becomes successful like *Star Wars*, its form is replicated sometimes in the manner of sequels or pastiche-type spinoffs.

Popular music replicates the same form more than any other popular medium. The binary form is the most used of all recognizable musical form. The popular binary form is in two parts (hence the term "binary"), with a "bridge" between. Many older popular songs use the same binary form A, bridge, A: "As Time Goes By," "The Flintstones theme song," "Frosty, The Snowman," to name a few. Many nursery rhymes use this form, including "Twinkle, Twinkle, Little Star." This famous folk song was used as the basis for a variation theme for piano by Mozart in 1782.

The idea of significant form, and formalism in general, is a major criterion that designates a work of "high" art from "low" art. One should remember, however, that the designation was and is not always clear. When printing came out during the Renaissance, the German artist Albrecht Dürer used the mass-production technique of woodcut and engraving in order to replicate his art. Many of his original prints—if there is such a thing—hang in major museums around the world. In addition, the ancient Greeks had no such idea as art being "true to medium" as they painted their sculptures and temples for clarity purposes. These are a few of the issues that draw the otherwise objective nature of formalism under suspicion.

## ☐ CONTEXTUALISM

Putting art in a social context has been one of the most popular theories since the counter-cultural revolution of the 1960s and 70s. Because of the emphasis on pluralism, the term "Postmodernism" has been also used to define this theory. However, Postmodernism is a difficult term to define. It began as an architectural term to describe the eclectic styles that endeavored to embrace the needs of a growing multicultural society. Dissatisfied with the International style that championed the expressions "less is more" and "form follows function," postmodern architects blended ancient and ethnic elements into their structures. Postmodernism, however, was extended to the other arts and especially the philosophies of Nietzsche, Foucault, Derrida, and Rorty. However, in order to avoid this extra baggage, we will use the less loaded term "contextualism" and confine the discussion to art in a social context.

Contextual theories criticize formalist theories for being too absolutist in their definitions. Who decides what is significant form and what is not? Contextualists are quick to point out that art is a mirror that reflects its society. More than anything, art shows the engines of power that commissioned their existence. One cannot fully understand Michelangelo's Sistine Chapel without understanding papal authority, Renaissance humanism, and Christianity in general. And this is only a start; some contextualists would point out the emphasis on masculinity and class structure; others might note the racial bias of showing only white people in heaven or part of the biblical narrative. Recent scholarship has addressed the actual physical labor that goes into making such a work of art. In other words, these great artists had workshops and anonymous laborers that did much of the preparatory work and even some of the actual drawing and painting. The other three theories seem to bring a mystique (a heightened sense of importance) to the artists and their work, as if they were great heroic figures doing everything themselves.

Contextualism, especially the Postmodern side, dismantles the mystique and mythology that surrounds art and artists. In doing so, they use the philosophy of Friedrich Nietzsche who attacked religion, morality, and truth itself. For Nietzsche, beauty, like religion and morality, is a human construct and an illusion. In his *Twilight of the Idols,* Nietzsche notes that beauty is measured by the human form, and that ugliness is its degeneration:

> When it comes to beauty, man posits himself as the norm of perfection and he worships himself in this...At bottom man mirrors himself in things and sees as beautiful all things that reflect his image...Ugliness is seen as a sign and a symptom of degeneration...Every suggestion of exhaustion, heaviness, senility, fatigue, any sort of lack of freedom, like convulsions or paralysis, especially the smell, the colour, the form of dissolution, of decomposition...all this provokes an identical reaction, the value judgment "ugly"...What does man hate? There is no doubt about this: he hates the twilight of his own type (Cited in Eco, *On Ugliness,* 15).

If what we value in art is a reflection of ourselves, then there is no real authority on what is "great" art. The contextualist avoids notions of value and authority from an objective stance. The value of art lies in its ability to expose social power structures, regardless of the intentions of the artist. Since the very notion of beauty is questionable, the social issues surrounding a work of art deserve more interest.

Contextualism has many voices that are often conflicting. Marxists, for example, endeavor to show art as a reflection of bourgeoisie (the class that owns and controls production) ideology. The term "ideology" is, in itself, loaded with meaning. Karl Marx wrote an entire book devoted to ideology.[10] However, it is the writings of the French Marxist Louis Althusser that many contextualists turn to today. Althusser claims that ideology is, "a representation of the imaginary relationship of individuals to their real conditions of existence."[11] In addition, ideology is a control apparatus of the state. Together with the Repressive State Apparatuses (the police, the military, prisons etc.), the Ideological State Apparatuses are meant to maintain power structures. Ideological State Apparatuses consist of schools, churches, and the media. Art is used in many of these apparatuses as tools to mold individual minds to fit state ideology.

Feminism in contextual theories of art considers the role women play both as artists and as subjects in art. The very history and definitions of art, for some feminist scholars, need re-evaluation and reclamation from centuries of male dominance.[12] Feminist scholars tend to question notions of a canon or media and genre hierarchies. For example, up until the modern period, women were limited and discouraged from an artistic career. They were not allowed to sketch male nude subjects and, therefore, could not excel in sculpture or history painting. Most women painters during the Baroque Age had to resign themselves to still lifes or other considered lesser genres. Only a few women were accepted in the academies and, even then, were limited to what they could study. The exclusion of women in a male-dominated art world raises questions for the formalist who tends to take accepted masterpieces on the word male-biased critics. Other feminist areas consider the psychological aspects of art and its sex and gender implications. Looking at women in art from a psychological approach is especially relevant in film studies. Female sex symbols are the most powerful revenue agent in the Hollywood star system.

As with the other three theories of art, contextualism has its weaknesses. Formalists are often quick to note that valuing a work of art for its social context makes the beauty irrelevant. The artists' works are of lesser value than the artists' lives. Thus, Vincent Van Gogh is great more so because he suffered poverty and psychological problems and less so because he painted beautiful works. For the contextualist, Van Gogh is the perfect example of the abuses and absurdity of blending capitalism with art; during his life, he lived in abysmal poverty; now he is the richest dead artist the world has known. Similarly, the Mexican woman artist Frida Kahlo is known more for her troubled life and her gender struggles than she is for her work. Suffering artists tend to be more popular than happy artists. Therefore, there are movies on Van Gogh and Kahlo that focus on their lives rather than their works. The contextualist discourse can easily move away from art into other areas, such as sociology and history. Moreover, postmodernism has its fair share of snobbery. The psychological ideas of the "structuralists" and "poststructuralists" are very difficult to distinguish, let alone understand. In criticizing the theories of the postmodern thinker Jacques Derrida, Michel Foucault claimed that if one should admit that they do not understand the theories, they are simply dismissed as an idiot (Barrett, 158).

## Contextualism in Popular Culture

The social issues found in the contextualist theory have strong currents in pop culture. Indeed, much of postmodern theory erases distinctions between popular and high culture and art. Treating artists' lives and putting them in a cultural context clouds the line between entertainment and art. The mega hit *The Da Vinci Code*, offers a good example of art and history becoming entertainment. Moreover, its context and what happened after its publication is more significant than the story itself. The story deals with Leonardo Da Vinci's life and works only as a source of a fictional conspiracy theory. When the novel discusses Leonardo's art, it draws absurd conclusions, such as the *Mona Lisa* being a hermaphrodite! There is little to no discussion of formal aesthetics in Leonardo's works. Indeed, a formalist would gain nothing but possible entertainment and amusement from the text.

*The Da Vinci Code* may be best understood as a simple piece of fiction, but this would be an evasion of its true contextual impact. Stylistically, it reads like a typical Robert Ludlum or Tom Clancy mystery/thriller novel. However, it sold over 80 million copies, and it generated a major motion picture and countless documentaries. To be sure, the novel became a phenomenon extending beyond its own pages. The novel's popularity is primarily due to its scandalous nature. The Catholic Church took exception to the novel's notion that Jesus Christ was married to Mary Magdalene, and that they had children. Some Catholic priests claimed that the text was libelous because it drew Jesus's "sexual virtue" under suspicion. Scorsese's *The Last Temptation of Christ* had already done this. But since it had not achieved the popular heights of *The Da Vinci Code,* it only got negligible moral/religious criticism. The scandal surrounding *The Da Vinci Code* was like a snowball effect: its popularity led to scandal, which led to more popularity. Although real history is far less forgiving to the Catholic Church than Dan Brown's novel, it shook the faith of many individuals.[13]

Works that evolve into a social phenomenon appear frequently in popular culture and is the intention of many producers. The blockbuster film, for example, is more than just a film; it is a central hub surrounded by ancillary forces, such as marketing and merchandising. The *Harry Potters*, *Pirates of the Caribbeans*, and the countless comic-book super-hero films depend on a built-in audience of fans. The cultural context provides a financial stabilizer for Hollywood, which has witnessed a declining box office since the advent of television and even before. As such, the blockbuster film is a relatively new genre. The Spielberg horror films, starting with *Jaws,* were both based on popular novels and are considered the first major blockbuster films. Yet the blockbuster roots can be traced back to the wide-screen films of the 1950s, which, together with the 3-D glasses and the drive-ins, were an attempt to draw the public out of their living rooms and back into the movie theaters. Novels, graphic novels, and video games usually have to achieve a high degree of popularity before developing into a blockbuster. Thus, the blockbuster film can be considered the climactic event in a series of cultural phenomena.

The blockbuster phenomenon shows us that social forces and contexts control and mold popular entertainment. One such social force appears with the idea of "persona." The term "persona" originally refers to the ancient Greek masks symbolizing dramatic characters and worn by stage actors. Although persona is more of a metaphor today, it describes the stage personality of a performer that is independent of the real person. *American Idol*, to use one example, is based on the Hollywood star system that has been around since the Silent Era. The public creates and destroys stars—not Hollywood producers or directors. Talent, skill, and even charisma have little effect on the making of a star persona. If the contestants were judged according to their skill and musicianship, the television show would fail or be relegated to a sub-network or sub-primetime level. In *American Idol*, musicianship is negligible next to looks and behavior—essential components to a star persona. *American Idol* is, thus, more of a pageant than a talent search.

There is a conflict between individuality and persona that is especially interesting in popular culture. The last *American Idol* winner, Scottie McCreery, was said to be the next Garth Brooks. Thus, taking on the persona of a previous idol is considered more complimentary than cultivating a new or individual persona. This stands to reason since the populace gravitates to what is familiar rather than what is different. Being an individual is risky business for the popular mass markets because grooming doomed stars wastes money and time. It is not uncommon, therefore, to see personae that are borrowed and shared. Marilyn Monroe's persona was borrowed from Mae West and handed down to Madonna. Oliver Hardy's persona was developed from Roscoe "Fatty" Arbuckle and has been used and adapted by almost every heavy-weight comic since: Jackie Gleason, Alan Hale Jr. (the Skipper in *Gilligan's Island*), and even the cartoon characters Fred Flintstone and Homer Simpson. Walt Disney showed that a star persona is not real, as in the case of Mickey Mouse. Since Walt Disney used his own voice for Mickey Mouse, one could say the cartoon character was the persona worn by Disney himself. Yet, even Mickey Mouse borrowed his persona from the great silent slapstick comedians, such as

Charlie Chaplin and Harold Lloyd. Indeed, clown personae are frequently shared. Jim Carrey's goofy persona is taken from Jerry Lewis, Dick Van Dyke used Stan Laurel, and Rowan Atkinson borrowed from Buster Keaton for his dead-pan character Mr. Bean. This recycling of familiarity stands in direct conflict with the formalist and, especially, the expressionist theories of art.

The idea of persona can be compared to mythological archetypes as well. An archetype is a basic characteristic of a figure, such as a god, hero, or plot line, which is copied and shared. Hence, Jesus shares archetypes with the Egyptian god Osiris and the Persian god Mythras. The Norse god Odin embodies the wizard archetype that was used for King Arthur's Merlin, *Lord of the Rings's* Gandalf, and *Harry Potter's* Dumbledor. In popular culture, we expect, for example, a "tough-guy" archetype in a gangster film character, whether gangster or police inspector. In film, typecasting is a way of using archetypes in order to facilitate clarity for the audience. The villain persona in films is more often portrayed as deceitful, shifty-eyed, and cruel. Thus, Darth Vader wears black, speaks with a low voice, breathes heavy, and is feared by his subordinates. However, Darth Vader is also a lost father type in need of redemption. The prodigal father archetype goes back to Homer's *Odyssey,* in which the first book describes Telemachus going to look for his father, Odysseus. Darth Vader has special relevance to the 1980s and the Reagan years. Films like *Star Wars, Back to the Future, Field of Dreams,* and *A River Runs Through It* reflect the re-discovery of the father that was lost during the Counter-Culture Revolution of the 1960s and 1970s. The popularity of Ronald Reagan was due to his wise-father persona similar to the fathers of *Leave It To Beaver* and *The Brady Bunch.* The father as someone a child could always turn to for help, was, thus, quickly exploited by Hollywood. Archetypes are like useful ingredients that can be changed according to the public's demand.

Gender is a deciding factor in the construction of a persona. Since the beginning of civilization femininity has taken on the archetypes of fertility and nurture. The mother persona in the 1950s sitcoms is a homemaker that provides constant care to the children and father. However, it is the glamorous sex symbol persona that popular culture demands most in their art. Mothers are often fashion plates showing off their appliances as in *Leave It To Beaver* and *The Brady Bunch.* Modern housewives and mothers maintain a sexy exterior, but a more loose character in modern television shows such as *CSI* and *Desperate Housewives.*

## ☐ GENRES

Another social force that affects art and entertainment is the categorization of works. Genre derives from the root word genus meaning type or sort. The genre system appears during the Baroque Era as part of the Age of Reason (1600–1700s) when not only art but nature and even emotions were being classified.

In art, genre refers to the subject matter. Scenes depicting events in the Bible or ancient history are called "history paintings." History paintings were considered the most important genre because they had an educational purpose. The lesser genres were still lifes, paintings of inanimate objects; genre paintings showing scenes from every-day life; portraits of paying sitters, usually nobility; and landscapes. There were also allegories—paintings with a sub-text meaning, and there were mythological scenes. The genre system allowed a rising middle-class help to understand art that was earlier meant for the educated ruling class. However, sometimes the genre of a particular work was unclear. Rembrandt, for example, often mixed portraits with genre scenes. During the early modern period, artists rejected this academic approach. Genre became just as obscure as the subject matter.

Genre in film refers to the iconography—the images that facilitate character and narrative type. If the film includes horses, cowboy hats, and bar fights we would most likely regard it as a Western. Masked killers, deformed monsters, supernatural occurrences are apart of the horror genre. Film genres frequently share narrative elements and sometimes iconography. Thus, *Star Wars,* even though a sci-fi fantasy genre, has some Western iconography—the shoot outs, bar fights, and wide-open setting. Like painting, the film genre serves as a way to control film revenue. *Halloween* and *Texas Chain Saw Massacre* alert potential viewers regarding the narrative type and overall content. It targets a specific audience that appreciates the genre.

Since film genre relies on iconography, it has a close relationship with style. For example, film noir is considered both a style and a genre. Noir is an American style, usually based on hard-boiled fiction, set in a dark urban environment, and pessimistic in mood and theme. The French were the first to recognize the stylistic change. During World War II, the Nazis banned American films from French audiences. When American films returned following the war, the French audiences noticed a strong contrast between the films before the war and after. Before, films like *Mr. Smith Goes to Washington*

(1939) showed optimistic hope and innocent characters. Later, films were darker both in style and in subject matter. These new films were called "noir" meaning "black" in French and the term has been used since. Noir elements appear in other genres, such as science fiction films like *Blade Runner*, which supports the notion that noir is a style. Yet noir films have enough of their own iconography—dark city streets, stylish voice-over narration, femme fatales, hard-boiled detectives—to be considered a self-containing genre.

A similar confusion between genre and style appears in popular music. The genres of music include song, symphony, ballet, opera, string quartet, mass, and hymn. However, popular culture only uses one of these genres, the song. In order to classify songs, styles are used to create a sub-genre. The rock song, therefore, is different that the country song. Apple's iTunes uses the popular sub-genres as a template. As a result, people with little exposure to art music often consider everything a song. It is more accurate to consider "classical" and "rock" styles rather than genres. iTunes should have put more thought into their classification system because, in confusing genre with style, they perpetuate an arrogant bias and willful ignorance against anything that is not a song. The term "classical music" as a reference to art music can be confusing enough. As noted above, classicism reflects a style of clarity and balance, and it can be applied to painting and poetry or any work of art. In music, classical is more limited to the styles of Haydn, Mozart, and Beethoven because they often employed clear and balanced phrases and recognizable forms. Placing the "classical" label on other composers, such as Wagner or Debussy is misleading. Jazz performers refer to works as "numbers," which reflects the collection of pieces numbered in a book. Although the numbers are often based on popular songs, jazz is an instrumental style. Even jazz vocalists apply an idiomatic style reflecting instrumentation. Just as the song is practically the only pop-culture music genre, so to in popular literature the novel reigns supreme. Other genres, especially poetry, have never found an audience among the masses.

## ☐ TASTE

For the contextualist, the idea of taste has an important function. The difficulty in defining and accounting— "there's no accounting for taste" is a common saying—for the variability of taste is applicable to the "reader response" nature of contextualism. Since ancient Greek times, the question of whether taste is objective or subjective has been addressed. If beauty is subjective or in the eye of the beholder, then the notion of a canon (a body of works considered great or more worthy of study and appreciation) can be questioned. However, if beauty is objective, then it is not dependent on individual artistic genius, and it can be replicated. Many of the ancient Greeks believed that beauty existed outside of the human mind and was, therefore, objective. The sculptor and art theorist Polyclitus, for example, believed that beauty could be achieved through pure mathematic ratios. His mathematical formulas led to a classical style that many Greek artists adopted. The ancient Egyptians, for the most part, maintained the same artistic style for 3,000 years. The idea of a standardization of styles, of course, conflicts with popular culture's emphasis on the new. Yet even popular forms of art are driven toward what the masses consider beautiful. Thus movie stars conform to the public's sense of ideal beauty.

With the industrial revolution and its creation of a mass-consumer society during the nineteenth century, a distinction between high and low art became apparent. High art was associated with the canon, which, more often, entailed classicism. Low art was associated with the masses and was considered shallow and transient. With this distinction between high and low art, good and bad taste became an issue. In a similar manner to the more recent political outcries against heavy-metal music and gangster rap, bad taste that is produced by bad art was believed to lead to bad character traits. Sensationalism, exploitation, and exhibitionism were traits of low art that depended on the uneducated masses.

Some scholars and theorists tend to ignore popular trends dismissing them as "bad art." However, about the middle part of the 20<sup>th</sup> century, two similar styles received scholarly attention. These two styles are called "kitsch" and "camp," and both represent fascinating subjects in popular culture aesthetics.

## ☐ KITSCH

More than camp, kitsch provokes the most negative criticism among aesthetic scholars. Clement Greenberg used the term as a reference to popular art as a whole:

> Where there is an avant-garde [cutting-edge, radical art styles], generally we also find a rearguard. True enough— simultaneously with the entrance of the avant-garde, a second new cultural phenomenon appeared in the industrial West: that thing to which the Germans give the wonderful

name of *Kitsch:* popular, commercial art and literature with their chromeotypes, magazine covers, illustrations, ads, slick and pulp fiction, comics, Tin Pan Alley music, tap dancing, Hollywood movies, etc., etc.[14]

Kitsch has a conflicting nature. On one hand it imitates high art. The pastiche paintings of Titian and Fragonard, discussed above, are a good example of kitsch. Landscapes sold on cable channels also imitate a high-art genre and style in a kitsch-like manner. The Hollywood movies that Greenberg mentions tend to imitate the considered high drama of tragedy. Popular songs imitate the forms and themes of the art song. Because it imitates high art, kitsch reflects high art's individualized nature. The art pastiches, popular songs, Hollywood scripts are made by real artists.

What tends to make art into kitsch is mass production. Greenberg was a Marxist that saw mass production as a way in which the bourgeoisie alienate the artist from his or her product. Kitsch does more than alienate, however; it makes art cheap and easy to own. The pastiches made for the cable shopping channels were made by a factory of artists. The Hollywood studio system patterned itself on Ford assembly-line production model. Art production on a mass scale, according to Greenberg, also destroys "real" culture:

> Because it can be tuned out mechanically, kitsch has become an integral part of our productive system in a way in which true culture could never be, except accidentally. It has been capitalized at a tremendous investment which must show commensurate returns; it is compelled to extend as well as to keep its markets...Another mass product of Western industrialism, it has gone on a triumphal tour of the world, crowding out and defacing native cultures in one colonial country after another, so that it is now by way of becoming a universal culture, the first universal culture ever beheld (Greenberg, 534–35).

The intention of Greenberg's article focuses on the social effects of kitsch, and he, therefore, avoids discussion of kitsch as a style, accept for the fact that it is imitative. For Greenberg, kitsch goes beyond a simple style to represent everything that is bad in popular culture. In doing so, he seems to give kitsch more credit than it deserves. The Pop artist Andy Warhol plays with the Marxist fears of a global domination of popular art in his article "The Aesthetics of Trash," in which he writes:

> The most beautiful thing in Tokyo is McDonalds
> The most beautiful thing in Stockholm is McDonalds
> The most beautiful thing in Florence is McDonalds (cited in, *On Ugliness*, 418).

By using a corporate symbol as a vehicle for beauty, Warhol undermines accepted notions of beauty. However, can McDonalds be considered kitsch or even a work of art?

Other scholars tend to treat kitsch more as a stylistic rather than cultural phenomenon. Hermann Broch was equally as critical against kitsch as Greenberg. In his 1933 book on kitsch, Broch claims that kitsch has all the style but no substance of high art:

> The essence of *Kitsch* consists in exchanging the ethical category with the aesthetic category; this obliges the artist to pursue not a "good" work of art, but a "beautiful" work of art; what matters to him is beautiful effect. Despite the fact that the *Kitsch* novel often works in a naturalistic sense, and in other words in spite of its abundant use of the vocabulary of reality, it shows the world not "as it is," but "as you wish or fear it could be." (Cited in, *On Ugliness,* 403)

Broch continues to claim that kitsch is formulaic, lacking imagination. The kitsch artist only reproduces the "beautiful effect" rather than the beautiful itself. Deciphering between the two can be difficult—one reason why Greenberg considers kitsch deceptive—and depends on the individual's taste. One example might help clarify the difference between beauty and what Broch calls "beautiful effect." Broch considers pornography as a form of kitsch because its only aim is to excite the senses. When kitsch stirs up the emotions, it is usually the "superficial" emotions, or "feel-good" emotions that leave us almost as quickly as they arrive. Yet, according to Broch, kitsch can also provoke strong emotions. He, thus, differentiates between two types of kitsch; "sweet kitsch" reflects the pleasurable, warm-fuzzy aspects, while "sour kitsch" reflects the darker emotions with heart-shaped grave stones and sympathy cards (see Barrett, 28–29). Yet even sour kitsch avoids the real pain of high art. Barrett notes the novelist Milan Kundera's even more caustic quote, "Kitsch is the absolute denial of shit, in both the literal and the figurative senses of the word; kitsch excludes everything from its purview which is essentially unacceptable in human existence" (29).

## Examples of Kitsch

Applying the kitsch tag to a work of art or entertainment can be tricky, as even works of high art were once considered kitsch. The operas of Wagner, for example, were considered by many, such as the composers Debussy and Stravinsky, as emphasizing only the theatrics and effects rather than "real" beauty. In a litany of examples, the art theorist Gordon Bearn includes the artists Salvador Dalí and Andrew Wyeth as "masters of kitsch" (see Barrett, 28). The cases of Wagner and Dalí may have resulted from their alienating personalities as much as their art. Nietzsche, for example, looked up to Wagner during his youthful years, but, later, had a falling out with the composer. Both Wagner and Nietzsche published criticism of each other that approached an almost libelous intensity. Stravinsky, a modern composer, had already dismissed not only Wagner but all late-Romantic composers as excessive. Dalí's works and his flamboyant personality became extremely popular, provoking jealousy and resentment among his fellow surrealists. After landing major projects in Hollywood with Alfred Hitchcock and Walt Disney, his surrealist colleagues regarded him as dead and refused to mention his name with present-tense verbs.

Aside from this, we can see some of the kitsch style in *Winter in the Country: A Cold Morning* by the popular art print makers Currier and Ives. The painting imitates Golden Age (1600–1700) Dutch landscape paintings. However, the warm lighting, the polished figures, and overall Christmas-card charm removes the metaphors of death and the earthy struggle for existence, often found in Dutch landscapes. The Currier and Ives painting does not challenge the viewer in the way of a real Dutch work. Instead, it creates an immediate sense of painless nostalgia. We still find the Currier and Ives-type kitsch everywhere, especially in medical waiting rooms and hotels. Reproducing past styles is easy, inexpensive, and requires little to no imagination.

Broadway musicals serve also as kitsch examples. The immensely popular musicals *Phantom of the Opera* and *Les Miserables* contain attributes of "sour kitsch". Although the narratives are packed with melodrama and the expensive productions target upper-class elite, the songs are simple enough

© CORBIS

*Winter in the Country: A Cold Morning*

for an AM radio audience. Victor Hugo, the author of the novel *Les Mis-erables* is based on, centers his novel on poverty and its victims. He would most likely appreciate the irony of his story becoming entertainment for the wealthy. Irony aside, the sweet and sour kitsch of Broadway musicals sterilize its product for mass consumption and carefully avoid the artistic ingredients that cause indigestion.

© Michael S. Yamashlta/CORBIS

Hollywood has a large number of productions that could be defined as kitsch—although not all as Greenberg suggests. One of the earliest examples comes from the elaborate choreography of Busby Berkeley musicals. One such number in *Gold Diggers of 1933* shows elaborately dressed dancers performing on neon-lighted violins and smiling all the while. In many ways, these numbers are so elaborate they move out of the kitsch realm and into a bizarre fantasy.

*Les Miserables* contains attributes of "sour kitsch"

© John Springer Collection/CORBIS

Busby Berkeley musicals can be defined as "kitsch"

The strange nature of Busby Berkeley musicals qualify as camp as well as kitsch. The sanitized melodrama of films like *Titanic,* the *Twilight* series, and the serious moments in the later *Harry Potter* films conform more to the sour variety of kitsch. In these films death and suffering becomes the spiritual consummation of love *(Titanic)* or the cementing bond between good friends *(Harry Potter).* In *Twilight,* depression is embodied in a love-sick teenager. The sourness of these films, however, is tempered by the suspense of the obligatory good vs. evil struggle and the excitement of wizardry and glamorous vampirism. In *Titanic,* the pain and death are buried under the formulaic poor boy/rich girl romance, and it is also distracted by the horrific excitement, resembling a ride at a theme park. Most of these blockbuster-type films rely on melodramatic formulas that date back beyond the Silent Film Era.

## ☐ CAMP

Generally, camp is understood as art or entertainment that becomes so bad or "cheesy" that it is entertaining. However, this superficial definition does not go far enough and, in some ways, is misleading. Camp seems to be a more recent phenomenon than kitsch, or, at least, it was discovered later. Susan Sontag's 1964 article "Notes on Camp" represents the most cited source for understanding camp. She claims that camp is a transformation of the serious into the frivolous (see *On Ugliness*, 408). It, therefore, differs from kitsch because it does not seek to imitate high art. Rather, it is a transformation of known styles into less recognizable forms or styles. Camp is, therefore, not so much a style as it is a recognition, and it does not necessarily include "bad art." Thus, kitsch may be understood and appreciated as camp by those cultivated enough to recognize the camp elements in kitsch. However, the taste for camp, according to Eco and Sontag, is a form of modern snobbery, and the camp connoisseur is similar to the dandy (a stylishly dressed and eccentric lover of exotic art) of the 19th century. Drawing on Sontag's article, Eco notes:

> Camp is also, but not always, the experience of kitsch of someone who knows that what he is seeing is Kitsch. In this sense it is a manifestation of aristocratic taste and snobbery: "and as the dandy is the nineteenth century's surrogate for the aristocrat in matters of culture, so Camp is the modern dandyism. Camp is the answer to the question: how to be a dandy in the age of mass culture?" But whereas the dandy sought out rare sensations, not yet profaned by the appreciation of the masses, the connoisseur of camp is fulfilled by "the coarsest, commonest pleasures, in the arts of the masses... The dandy held a perfumed handkerchief to his nostrils and was liable to swoon; the connoisseur of Camp sniffs the stink and prides himself on his strong nerves (*On Ugliness,* 411)."

Sontag appears more damning to the lover of camp than the lover of kitsch because those who develop the love of kitsch are assumed ignorant. Those who cultivate a taste for camp, on the other hand, think they know better and are like scavengers. The argument places the modern critic in a predicament; those who enjoy a work of kitsch but do not recognize it as kitsch are uncultured and easily deceived; but those who enjoy a work of kitsch because they see the camp are modern snobs that relish the dregs of art and culture. In addition, Sontag's list of camp examples includes a wide array of both high and low styles and works from the film *King Kong* to Art Nouveau, from pre-Raphaelite painting to Greta Garbo's film persona (see *On Ugliness,*

412). Sontag's essay, in some ways, supports the postmodern movement that opposed valuing high over low art. In doing so, Sontag traces camp as far back as Renaissance mannerism, in which style became predominant.

One element that runs through all camp is excess or extreme: "In any case all camp object and persons must possess an element of extremism that goes against nature (there is nothing campy in nature)" (*On Ugliness*, 411). Eco also notes that camp is excessive to a fault, a kind of "overdose" that cancels out any serious objectives. However, camp is often noticed in flamboyant comic routines. It is, perhaps, important to differentiate camp that is intended for comedy and camp that is not. The excessive nature of camp that is not intended for comedy often produces a stylish abstraction. Sontag notes that camp may produce a genderless effect in human figures. However, one may also notice camp elements in the overly masculine elements of Rambo or overly feminine elements of Mae West.

## Examples of Camp

Popular culture is loaded with examples that could be considered camp. From Liberace to Michael Jackson, camp can be noticed in many flamboyant personalities. Celebrities voted "worst dressed" in entertainment magazines always get more attention than those voted "best dressed." Most of the characters Jonny Depp plays in films have an excessive quality that could be regarded as camp. Lady Gaga is, perhaps, the most recent camp personality with her elaborate makeup and costumes that help draw attention from her dull music. Alice Cooper, Kiss, King Diamond, Marilyn Manson are all camp

© Bettmann/CORBIS

Liberace

descends from 1960s rocker Arthur Brown. Elvira, Madonna, Elton John, David Bowie, Frank Zappa, and Prince are just some more in an ocean of camp characters. With such an exhaustive list of camp figures in popular culture, one would expect camp to become normal and thus no longer camp. However, professional wrestling and monster-truck rallies prove every year that camp sells tickets.

In film and television, camp can be noticed in the elaborate styles of film noir and "neonoir" works such as *Sin City, Dark City,* and many graphic novel-based films. Low-budget sword-and-sandal films from the 1960s, such as the many Hercules films from Italy, showing body builders posing more than acting, are classic camp examples. The graphic novel film *300* is a better made, but equally campy sword-and-sandal film. Italian cinema during the 1960s is also credited for regenerating the "torture porn" sub-genre of horror with such campy films as *Bloody Pit of Horror* (photobucket "by papablunts). Soap operas and prime-time dramas are, especially, productive engines of camp because they show ridiculous situations occurring on a regular basis in order to maintain an audience. *Lost* is one such example.

## ☐ SUMMING UP

Terry Barrett makes some important points regarding interpretation, criticism, and bringing it all together. First of all, no single theory is more important than the other; nor should one embrace one theory, such as formalism, and ignore or criticize the other. Rather, the theories work best in concert or as substitutes. A realist, for example should be willing to adopt formalism in order to regard an abstract work. This does not mean that we should embrace and love everything. Developing a critical eye is important, and one should not feel shy when applying a negative criticism to a given work. Both negative and positive criticism, however, work best when one can support claims with clear analyses and examples. Effective critics do not go looking for bad art to criticize. Barrett gives more good advice in what not to be: "To be reactionary and dismissive or unthoughtfully accepting is not to be critical in the sense that this book encourages" (4).

---

[1] See Aristotle, *Poetics* in *Philosophies of Art & Beauty,* Albert Hofstadter and Richard Kuhns eds. (Chicago: Univ. of Chicago Press, 1964), 102.

[2] Edmund Burke, "The Sublime," in *The Portable Enlightenment Reader,* Isaac Kramnick ed. (New York: Penguin, 1995), 330.

[3] See Immanuel Kant, "On the Beautiful and Sublime," in *The Portable Enlightenment Reader*, 339–42.

[4] Bram Stoker, *Dracula,* cited in Umberto Eco, *On Ugliness* (New York: Rizzoli, 2007): 326.

[5] Sprechstimme is a hinting at pitch rather than singing right on pitch.

[6] See David Hume, "Of Tragedy," in *Eight Great Tragedies,* Sylvan Barnet ed. (New York: Meridian, 1985), 435–6.

[7] See Terry Barrett, *Why is That Art?* (New York: Oxford, 2008), 108.

[8] Immanuel Kant, "Critique of Judgment" in *Philosophies of Art & Beauty*, 295.

[9] Cited in Charles Harrison and Paul Wood eds. *Art in Theory: 1900–1990*, (Massachusetts: Blackwell, 1999), 113.

[10] See Karl Marx and Friedrich Engles, *The German Ideology*, (New York: Prometheus, 1989).

[11] Louis Althusser, "Ideology and Ideological State Apparatuses," in *Art in Theory*, 932.

[12] See Marsha Meskimmon, "Women as Artists and Subjects," in *The Bulfinch Guide to Art History* (New York: Bulfinch, 1996), 147.

[13] Several of my students have said as much.

[14] Clement Greenberg, "Avant-Garde and Kitsch," in *Art in Theory*, 533.

# CHAPTER 3

# Horror, Science Fiction, and Superheroes

This chapter will discuss three related genres, Horror, Science Fiction and Superheroes. These genres are all suitable subjects for multiple books, but our interest in this chapter is merely to indicate some starting points to help the student interpret work in these genres. Together, these three genres constitute a significant portion of the overall film market. They also have two key themes in common. When we survey the three genres we see that all have the concept of overreaching in their standard narrative. We also see a recurring interest in "the other." Rather than attempt any kind of exhaustive survey of these genres we will follow these themes, overreaching and the other, as they emerge in horror, science fiction, and superheroes.

## ☐ HORROR

We begin with horror. The horror genre is very conducive to the use of our theories, so it is a good place to employ them. Horror deals with strong emotions such as fear, shock, loathing, and so on. It also addresses our deepest phobias. In both content and popularity, horror films are ultimately grounded in our basic fear of death. All this puts us directly into psychology, so we will expect psychological interpretations to be some of the more important interpretations. But we need to see the other aspects of horror if we are to get a complete understanding of it; think of all these theories as we investigate horror.

In our treatment of horror, we will focus on two of the more iconic monsters, the vampire and the zombie. We will also look at supernatural horror,

**85**

such as the *Hellraiser* series, but the centerpiece of this section on horror will be our interpretation of the *Alien* series. Before we do actual interpretations, however, we will look at some ways of thinking about horror.

What is clear about the horror genre is that it appeals to basic and visceral elements of human existence. The most obvious one is fear. Humans find many things fearsome. In fact, much of human life prior to the rise of civilization was probably characterized by a state of fairly constant fear. Even modern life provides ample opportunities for fear. Such an important part of human life could not help but be a concern of modern mentality in spite of the distance in time between prehistoric and modern people. Death is another central component of human life. Death is such a profound occurrence in people's lives that it is bound to find its way into all cultural texts. Pain is universal to human experience, and so it becomes part of most texts. Violence is a particularly popular component of texts. Violence is not only a universal experience like fear, death, and pain, violence also affords the opportunity for powerful visual imagery. The display of violence makes for very exciting visuals, which keep the consumer of the text more interested. It also creates the opportunity for a catharsis, a purging of negative emotions that we may have built up over time. If we have experienced violence and have difficulty getting past it psychologically, seeing violence in a book or on a screen may enable us to come to terms with our experience of violence. Or maybe we have not had such experiences in our past, but our natural curiosity leads us to think about them. We may even seek a safe way to experience the adrenaline high of violent experience. Our natural curiosity can lead us on a quest for new sensations, which horror can provide. Many of us enjoy a vicarious thrill when we see others in distress or danger, not because we like to see people hurt, but because we imagine ourselves in the situation. The resolution of the fear into feelings of safety addresses a need we all have. This universality of fear is what makes horror films so powerfully memetic. Memes draw on our basic drives, and fear drives much of our behavior, so the popularity of horror is easy to understand.

The hidden and the unknown are nebulous objects of fear. No one can possibly know enough about the world to go through life with any confidence that they know enough to handle any situation they encounter, and this lack of certainty leads to fear and anxiety. But we repress this uncertainty and carry on as if we were confident in our understanding of the world. One way we repress the uncertainty is by embracing tradition and common sense.

Freud's theory of sublimation and repression tells us that repressed desires always return to the surface in the expression of abnormal behavior. This is what Freud calls the "return of the repressed," and the horror genre draws on this phenomenon quite frequently. If we repress emotions, memories, or feelings instead of sublimating them, then according to Freud the repressed emotion will eventually burst forth in an uncontrolled spasm or in other sorts of abnormal behavior. Many horror films trace the murderousness of killers back to childhood repression. The child kept in the closet who becomes murderous in adulthood is a representation of the return of the repressed. A fairly obvious case of the return of the repressed occurs in the film *Carrie* (1976). In the movie, Carrie is a young girl kept in a state of social isolation and sexual repression until she erupts in a fiery attack on her tormentors.

Ultimately, however, there is one concept at the core of the horror genre, and it is fear. All horror films, almost by definition, deal with this primal experience. Human beings find many things fearsome. Many of our fears originate in prehistorical human experience. Early hominid ancestors of humans surely internalized a deep fear of predators, wolves, lions, tigers, and the like. But not everything that is fearsome is an apt subject for horror. While the horror genre is always about fear, it is fear of the uncanny that has led to the creation of the best horror stories. The strangeness of something that is normally small, an insect, transformed into something large is "uncanny." The uncanny is an idea that has been developed by psychoanalysis and according to Freud, refers to the juxtaposition of the strange and the familiar. Strangeness is frightening.

That is why there are not that many films of, say, attacks by lions on humans. It sometimes happens, but it is not particularly strange, and therefore not uncanny. When we do see films about lion attacks, for example, *Prey* (2007) or *The Ghost in the Darkness* (1996), the stories belong more accurately to the adventure or thriller genres because even though lions are fearsome, they are not strange or uncanny; they are simply fearsome parts of our natural world. Notice, however, that when we combine big cats like lions or leopards with humans, such as we see with the stories and films about "cat people," then it becomes uncanny and a fit subject for horror. So fear alone is not enough to put something into the horror genre; there must be something more and that more is the element of uncanniness. Strangeness is therefore a necessary element of the horror genre.

Films about giant insects provide a good example of this uncanny combination of the familiar and the strange. The uncanniness of the giant insects has made for a long run in film history. Fear of insects, though not as strong because of their normal size, is rooted deeply in our psyche. These fears are sometimes linked with another, more modern (and also uncanny) fear such as atomic radiation, and we get giant insects, such as we see in films like *The Tarantula* (1955). Films about all kinds of radiation induced gigantism were popular in the 1950s and 60s. The film *Them* has giant ants, which have grown large because of atomic radiation.

The centrality of the uncanny to horror explains why so many horror films are about monsters, for monsters are by their nature uncanny. A monster is not merely something strange; it is also important that it be somehow similar to something normal. Strangeness is thus a necessary condition of horror, but not a sufficient condition. The uncanny is both familiar and strange, and the monster embodies these two notions into one creature. The monster exemplifies another notion as well, the *abject*. The abject is a blurring of the boundary between living and dead, between organic and inorganic, between sacred and profane. When we see a corpse we are conflicted because of our understanding that the body was once alive, a subject of experiences like ourselves. But we also notice that it is dead, and thus we must try to put it into another category, the category of the object. This ambivalence between subject and object is central to the abject and the feeling that results is called abjection. Anything that reminds us as subjects that we are also objects potentially puts us in mind of the abject. Body parts, blood, gore, urine, and feces are all things that can present us with the abject. It is not surprising that monsters often leave a trail of these things.

A relatively unexplored concept in horror is gore. Gore is typically regarded as a special effects opportunity rather than as a concept to be explored in any philosophical way. Gore is maximized abjection. Gore approaches camp in its attempt to maximize abjection because if there is too much gore it starts to lack seriousness and gets interpreted as comedy. But just short of camp it can raise the level of horror to an extremely high level. The portrayal of dismemberment, disembowelment, and the like take us well beyond the possibility of empathic association. We are confronted with a horror from which there is no return to normalcy. Gore is the institution of the abject as a continuous presence. It represents permanent damage. Because of the seriousness of permanent damage, gore is best doled out sparingly. Overstep these limits and the effect is lost and the story or film descends into camp.

Barbara Creed has explored the concept of the monster from one particularly fruitful angle. Her concept of the *monstrous feminine* explains the deep connections between femininity and monstrosity. Female genitalia are regarded as monstrous and even dangerous. The vagina becomes the *vagina dentata* of mythology. A vagina with teeth is a forced contradiction. It combines pain and pleasure, love and violence. It represents castration and the fear of castration. According to Creed, there seems to be a tendency for men to associate women with monstrosity, an idea that goes back at least to Aristotle, who considered woman to be a flawed version of man. We will look at the *Alien* series to bring out this conception of monstrosity.

## The Alien Series

Many examples of the monstrous feminine can be found in Ridley Scott's *Alien,* which in the view of this author is one of the best films to come out of the horror genre. *Alien* is a film about a murderous alien that gets loose on a spaceship after a crew member, "infected" with the alien, is brought aboard. Initially, connecting *Alien* to the monstrous feminine seems far-fetched because of the appearance of the monster. The monster in *Alien* is highly phallic, and it performs a kind of rape of its victims by impregnating them with its offspring, who kill their hosts in the birth process. One could easily interpret the film as a simple metaphorical critique of male sexuality, especially the aspect of rape. However, several other scenes make Creed's point by staging reenactments of the primal scene, birth. For example, when the humans awake from their cryosleep the scene is quite sterile. They are awakened by a computer named Mother, and there is no pain, blood, or bodily fluids. Later they enter the alien ship via vagina-shaped portals and thereby also symbolically enter the womb. Inside the womb they find not just the secret of the ship, but monsters. The ship, which contains vast caverns of space and appears to be a combination of mechanical and organic material, is impregnated and carrying eggs. The egg vessels have a vaginal aspect to them as well, and peering into them leads to a rape that deposits the egg into its victim, in this case a man. The "facehugger" who deposits the egg into the victim is male in one aspect: it sends a long appendage down the throat of the victim and deposits eggs inside the stomach, but it also has vaginal characteristics as we see when it is examined on the lab table. So the film *Alien* goes beyond the concept of the monstrous feminine. The monster is fearsome in both its male and female forms. The male or drone form of the monster is clearly phallic, and even the facehugger has both male and female aspects.

Rape is an important motif throughout the series. But Creed's interpretation is still a very fruitful one. For example, never in *Alien* do we get a glimpse of the monster that laid the eggs. In a sense, the most fearsome creature of the film is never shown. We are eventually given an excellent visual treat of the mother alien in the second film of the series, but in the first film she is both present and not present. This is an example of post-structural analysis in that it looks for "what isn't there." If something is alluded to or logically implied in an artwork but not actually shown, then we should consider whether such an absence is, in fact, important. In this case, most scholars have concluded that it is. It is additionally important that the survivor will turn out to be a female human, who bests the monster while everyone else, including all the tough males, falls prey to the monster. We have a structural balance between, on the one hand, the human Ripley, played to perfection by Sigourney Weaver, in a role that cements her place in the history of film, and on the other hand, an unseen "alien queen."

It is worth focusing on the "chest-bursting" scene. When the implanted egg reaches maturity it must leave the body of the victim. Not having the traditional exit available since it is a different species, it bursts from the chest of its victim. The chest-bursting scene is probably more popular than any other scene in a horror film with the exception of the shower scene in *Psycho*. It is also an encapsulation of some core ideas of the film. The violent exit from the victim is meant to call attention to the violence of both sexuality and birth. Having entered the crewman's body in an act of oral rape, it bursts forth as a "penis dentata," a penis with teeth.

The artist who designed the monsters in the *Alien* series, H. R. Giger, is very important to the interpretation of the *Alien* series. In fact, Giger's role in creating the greatness of the *Alien* series is at least equal to that of any of the directors or writers. His style was established long before the filming of the series. Giger's design of the monsters merely brought his greatness to a wider audience. His designs could almost carry a film by themselves. Their very appearance raises all kind of unsettling questions about the nature of life. It is very clear that Giger is pushing all the boundaries between male and female, organic and inorganic, living and mechanical. His art not only explores the monstrous feminine; it explores the posthuman. Giger's work may be fairly considered an artistic dissertation on hybridity. In his work, organic forms transition into and get connected to inorganic forms. Creatures have all kinds of sex organs, effectively undermining our preconceived binaries of gender and sexuality, human and mammal, animal and insect, animal and machine. There is also a pervading sense of violation and violence. The suggestion is that the root of reproduction is violence. That life itself is violence. To live is to rip and tear at the other.

Other types of violence are illustrated in the series. Economic violence and technological violence are presented as nearly continuous with physical violence. The economic violence becomes clear from key scenes in *Alien* and *Aliens*. In *Alien* there is an early collective meal in which the workers complain about their wages. The officers manage to keep the talk from turning too serious, but the class tension is already established. When it becomes clear that the company has deemed them expendable for the sake of the profit that could come from obtaining a vicious alien, it is useful to consider the Marxist argument that classes are inevitably in conflict, and that the conflict is sometimes to the death. Interestingly, death is caused by the rational calculation of profit and loss. It is exploitation at its highest level: sacrificing the very lives of workers for the sake of profit. Technological violence is illustrated by the android of the first film, Ash. The company replaced the original doctor with an android, a piece of technology over which they can have complete control. The android Ash betrays the crew on behalf of the company and subjects them to the ravages of the alien.

When Ripley encounters another android in the second film she is outraged at the presence of the android Bishop, because of her experience with Ash. It is interesting that in this scene, another collective meal, there are four different reactions to Bishop. To Ripley, Bishop is a monster like Ash. To Burke, Bishop is just an investment, simply a synthetic, but Bishop says, "I prefer to think of myself as an artificial person." So Bishop is considered in four aspects: monster, investment, device, and person. Of course, this can be said of humanity as well, as the series makes clear. First, Burke is a *monster*. His betrayal of the crew is so monstrous that he shows a human can become a monster. All the employees, but especially the workers, are considered *investments* by the company. The workers function as *devices* when they operate the exo-skeleton machines in *Aliens*. But the humans in the film are, by definition, not artificial. However, *Alien Resurrection* (Alien 4) does have artificial humans, as we shall see.

Thematically, economics and technology reflect the deep framework of horror in the series. In the *Alien* series, business is not predatory, it is just amoral, and from this amorality violence arises. No morality is inherent in economics. Economic thinking is based on the maximization of profit. The company has simply determined that the profit/loss equation will be better if the humans are sacrificed, and with no morality to restrain it, that is precisely what the company does: it sacrifices them. Ash, the android in the first film and Mother, the ship's sentient computer, show technology to be adversarial to humans. Thus the *Alien* series shows a deep suspicion at two levels, the economic and the technological.

The second film is very different from the first. It has a different director, James Cameron, who came up with the basic design for the Queen but drew heavily on Giger's influence. The resulting monster would fit perfectly in Giger's earlier *Necromonicon* work. Cameron is also one of the greatest action directors of our time, and action is what was called for. Cameron took firm personal control of the story for his installment of the series and produced a very different mood. Cameron did not want the same kind of film for the second installment of the story. Feeling that they had already done "brooding horror with occasional outbursts of horror and violence" with the first film, it would be better to make an action film. Cameron and the producers knew they could not entertain the audience with another film too closely in the mold of the first. They wanted this one to make a bigger splash. And they had the missing queen from the first film that they could roll out in grand fashion. Cameron pitted military personnel against not only the queen but hundreds of the monsters from the first film. It was grand spectacle. But in the end it comes down to Ripley versus the alien queen. This second film, *Aliens*, addresses the same issues, but has a different emphasis. Cameron thinks technology is incredibly important and even dangerous, but it can also be an aid to humanity as we see when the new android is heroic and when Ripley uses the loader to battle the queen. The film is also about women, with Ripley's legend gaining new heights and because it shows the violence mothers can wreak in defense of their young. And again, we have corporate greed underlying the whole bad mess in which they put their employees.

The reconciliation of Ripley with technology reaches completion in a powerful scene in which Ripley believes she has been betrayed by technology again when the ship is not where it is supposed to be. She and the little girl, Newt, appear to be doomed as the alien queen is about to arrive at their location. But Bishop comes at the last second to save the two from the alien queen. When they disembark from the transport ship, they believe they are finally safe, and Ripley bonds with Bishop and thus reconciles with technology. Bishop thereby redeems technology in the second film, indicating that technology can be both good and bad, but it is also the case that there is still an inherent danger of violence in technology. Then, in one of the bigger surprises in film history, we see the alien queen's tail suddenly impale Bishop. The alien queen, in a grisly homage to the *Wizard of Oz* (1939), rips Bishop in half. This is an allusion to the scene in the *Wizard of Oz* in which the Scarecrow, another artificial being, is torn in half. In confirmation of her reconciliation with technology, Ripley dons a powerful exoskeleton loader, a technological device, and battles the queen one on one to defend Newt.

In the third film the producers decided to pull back on the guns and action and return to the brooding intimacy of the first film. Ripley lands on the prison planet with her ship, which is carrying a facehugger. The prison is for the worst prisoners only, and all of them are men. Since several of the men are convicted rapists, and because Ripley is the only female they have seen in a long time, the threat to her from the humans is even more serious than the threat from the alien. In fact, she is immune to the danger from the alien since it can sense that she is already infected. The rape attempt does materialize only to be thwarted by the religious leader of the prison, played with deep resonance by Charles Dutton. Ripley and Dutton's character, Dillon, get the prisoners to work together to defeat the alien. In the final scene all the religious references in the film are brought to a climax with Ripley falling backward into molten metal with her arms spread wide in personal sacrifice just before the alien bursts from her chest and she grabs and holds it, taking it to its death with her. The film gives a religious answer to the problem of violent life in general and rape in particular. There is a powerful scene connecting a religious ritual with the birth of a new alien from a dog. Dillon performs a eulogy at the funeral of Hicks and Newt, and while Dillon is performing the eulogy, we see glimpses and sounds of the new alien forcing its way out of the body of the dog it infected. The director edits the scene to move between the two events, so we understand such editing to indicate some sort of connection between the two events. The connection is the one that runs throughout the series, the connection between birth, death, and violence. Religion then is understood to be the means by which we come to terms with this horror at the foundation of life. It is religion that enables the men to successfully combat the alien by helping them work together. Ripley's sacrifice becomes a religious martyrdom symbolizing the need for unity in the face of the horror of existence.

The fourth film is the weakest of the series. The monsters that were done so well in the first three of the series are joined by a rather amateurish effort to continue the evolution of the Alien monster in *Alien Resurrection* (1997). Enough of Ripley's DNA was recovered to clone her, but the result is a much more human hybrid. This cloned Ripley goes through a process of self-discovery culminating in the abject realization that she was just the one clone that panned out. She learns this when she encounters a room full of failed attempts to create a viable Ripley clone. Ripley sees a clone like herself, but it is a twisted thing with a bad combination of features from Ripley's and the alien's DNA. Taking pity on the hideous monster, she puts it out of its misery. She also kills her other offspring, the hideous progeny of Ripley and an alien queen. After the child turns on its mother, kills it and then turns to Ripley for affection, Ripley kills the offspring by using her acid blood to put a hole in the hull window, a hole which then sucks the offspring into space. *Alien Resurrection* takes the notion of hybridity to its extremes, with all the genetic error that we see in the Ripley clones contrasted with the more rare success, the intact Ripley clone. The Ripley/Queen hybrid is also a failure. We move from the "perfect" killing machines, the aliens of the first three films, to dysfunctional abominations in *Alien Resurrection*.

There is a question whether the "series" is actually a series at all. All the films have different directors, styles, and writers. How can there be an overriding vision if it isn't the same people creating the vision? Many aesthetic questions arise from this fact. First, the market plays a role in determining the direction of the franchise. The move to action in the second film was as much a marketing decision as an aesthetic decision. The films are also appealing to popular tastes, so they are aware of the memetic attraction of some kinds of stories, images, and so on. The market will capitalize on those devices whether or not they are the best a director could use from an aesthetic perspective. But we see in the example of *Alien* that in spite of the variety of creators, differing markets, and memetic influences a great work is the result. And it is the whole series that is great. They achieve a certain completeness that each film does not have separately, and because they followed the lead of Giger's original images, the style is fairly consistent. One could argue that the different directors and writers help make the story better than it would have been. And it certainly stands as an achievement that they were able to create a real series. This brings us to an important realization about film sequels and series: the film series constitutes a new form of art, an extension of the film genre. Instead of being one film in length, the full artwork may be several films long. If this is the case, an artwork should be considered along with its fellow sequels. The *Lord of the Rings* films are excellent as single films, but as a series they are a monumental achievement. Because the *Lord of the Rings* has a single director, it is much easier to maintain consistency of style. But three heads can be better than one at times as we see with the *Alien* series and the *Harry Potter* series, both of which have risen to the level of greatness in spite of having more than one director.

We now turn to the more iconic characters of the vampire and the zombie, which give us the occasion to more fully explore the fear of death that is so important to the horror genre.

## The Vampire

The vampire is an icon of the horror genre. The modern vampire legend begins with *Bram Stoker's Dracula*. *Bram Stoker's Dracula* was based on an actual person, Vlad Tepesch, or "Vlad the Impaler," a prince of Wallachia who fought the Ottomans in the 1400s. Vlad was not, of course, an actual vampire since there are no such things, but he was a rather vicious fellow as his name indicates: he was known for impaling his victims on pikes for everyone to see. Stoker borrowed Vlad's patronymic, "Dracula," which means "son of the dragon," for the name of his vampire.

There have been so many vampire stories that seemingly every possible variation of the theme has been explored. Nevertheless, the core narrative still holds great appeal with the unbroken stream of production of vampire films and stories since the release of *Nosferatu* (1922) and *Dracula* (1931). The elements of the horror genre are well known and well liked. We all fear death, and the vampire does not only cause death, it is dead itself. This, in turn, brings up our phobia of dead bodies. Vampires are dead, but they are, paradoxically, also immortal. The idea of vampires dying "the final death," as they say in the TV series *True Blood* (2008), when exposed to daylight completes a structuralist opposition.

It is also important that vampires are associated with the night. The night is naturally more scary than the day since it is harder to see threats. Humans probably carry a deep and very ancient fear of the night from before the invention of artificial light sources. But the night is also compelling. With fear comes curiosity. In *Near Dark* (1987), for example, a female vampire asks a potential lover/victim to "listen to the night." She gives the impression that there are qualities to the night of which most of us are unaware. The night is also forbidden. Most young men are intrigued by the night and inclined to explore the night precisely because it is forbidden.

Blood is an important element in the vampire genre. The vampires consume it as food, and it is the means by which vampirism is spread. Blood is also abject. It is a necessary component of human life. The body cannot function without it. Blood's invisibility (being inside the body) makes it especially effective in denoting the abject. Like the spirit, it is hidden from view. Blood is not normally visible, and when it is, it is a harbinger of danger, pain, and death. Its necessity makes the abject character that much more intense. Blood is distinctive with regard to the abject in that it is also highly symbolic. Blood is associated with very ancient beliefs, rituals, and taboos. Blood was sometimes thought to be the carrier of the life force, so that spilling blood violates a sacred substance. But blood is just as often a taboo, with blood functioning as a spiritual pollutant. Blood therefore straddles the boundary between the abject and the symbolic. The abject is normally a black hole for symbolism because it draws subjectivity into identity with objectivity. Blood does function in this way. A person covered in blood is revealed as a subject that is also an object, a person who could be reduced to a dead body, an object that is symbolically and subjectively blank. On the other hand, blood is highly symbolic. It can refer to culture in all its contradictory subjectivity. It can refer to both life and death, the body and spirit, and the finite and the infinite.

Vampirism is a blood-borne disease. In fact, our fear of vampirism can refer to our general fear of disease. Vampirism is infectious. Mankind has been ravaged by disease so often and with such devastating consequences that all humans have a deeply visceral reaction to disease. This deep-seated fear of disease stimulates our interest in vampires. All the plagues of the past are still with us emotionally when we encounter the vampire in story or film. One aspect of the infectious nature of vampirism that is generally ignored is the geometric nature of infection. One person infects two, who then infect two each, and so on. The numbers get very large very quickly, but this logic is rarely explored in vampire films except for the films *Lifeforce* (1985) and *Daybreakers* (2009). We shall see that zombie stories explore this geometric expansion much more than vampire films even though the logic is implicit in both genres.

Another iconic aspect of the vampire is its fangs. Fangs are indicative of predators in nature. The fangs function to produce the equally iconic two-holed wound from which the vampire sucks blood from its victim. Fangs probably call up some ancient fear of predators early humans struggled to avoid. In the vampire context, the vampire's real nature is often revealed with a display of the fangs. Fangs are associated with animality and the loss of control that comes with giving into our animal nature. Fangs are also sexual. Fangs penetrate and infect (impregnate?).

Sex is always just under the surface in vampire films. The vampire's bite is somewhat akin to a rape, and it is sometimes presented as orgasmic. The hypnotism vampires use to beguile their victims is a form of seduction. In the *Twilight* (2008) series, the main character holds off from turning into a vampire lover until marriage, which implies a connection between the bite, death, and sexual consummation. Unlike the zombie, from which sexuality is erased along with the personality, vampires are highly sexual. From Bela Lugosi's early seductions to *True Blood*'s explorations of vampire sexuality, vampire stories seem unable to resist the sexual component.

We now examine briefly the standard list of symbolic connections in the vampire genre. The origin of the vampire's hatred of garlic, for example, goes back to its use in earlier times against disease. Just as garlic was used as medicine against disease and even supernatural evils, it was probably attached to vampires as another representation of disease and evil. The stake through the heart is borrowed from Irish mythology, in which wooden stakes were put over graves to keep the spirits from escaping and afflicting the living. More important than garlic or the stake through the heart are more basic elements such as water and earth, two of the four elements of ancient metaphysics (earth, air, fire, and water). Water is the nearly universal "spiritual cleanser," so it is not surprising that Holy Water, water that has been blessed by a priest, is one of the things that can hurt a vampire. Soil is symbolic in vampire stories as well. Bodies are consigned to the earth upon death, and so earth becomes associated with death. Daylight is anathema to vampires, and the danger it presents to vampires is symbolic. For one, daylight represents the light of reason. So the idea of vampires become a Romantic opponent of the Enlightenment. But sometimes religion or God is associated with daylight or the sun, and thus the opposition would be to religion. The vampiric symbolism of water, along with the night, soil, blood, daylight, and so on, show that the vampire genre is tied to some of the most important and basic constituents of our symbolic universe. It is not surprising, therefore, that the vampire genre is so closely linked to religion. It is important to understand the vampire in relation to religious evil. The vampire genre basically establishes a counter-tradition to Christianity by subverting its symbols and themes. A structuralist reading of the vampire would set up the following oppositions:

- Drinking the blood of Christ in the Eucharist versus drinking the blood of victims.
- Christ versus Dracula
- Eternal life in heaven versus eternal life as a vampire on earth.
- Everlasting life versus everlasting death.

*Bram Stoker's Dracula* is just one film that explores the vampire story as a counter-tradition to Christianity. Gary Oldman plays a medieval defender of the faith who rejects God after a cruel twist of events leading to the death of his beloved. His rejection of God brings on his transformation into a vampire. After centuries of loneliness he finds the reincarnation of his lost wife, who is about to marry Keanu Reeves's character and the story plays out from there. The vampire becomes the face of evil for Christianity. Some stories have postulated Judas as the original vampire (*Dracula 2000*), which, like *Bram Stoker's Dracula* (1992), makes the origin of vampirism a result of an original sin. Interestingly, one character that is rarely seen in vampire films is Satan himself. For whatever reason, Satan just doesn't get any screen time in vampire films or stories. Like the absent alien queen from *Alien,* Satan is present through his absence. Unlike the absent queen in *Alien*, however, Satan seems to be permanently deferred, possibly because his presence would then upstage the vampire.

The vampire idea has accrued a great deal of associated subnarratives that have been made into some very substantial films. *Lifeforce* reimagined the vampire legend as a periodical return of a space-borne species to ravage the earth, thus mixing the science fiction and vampire genres. The *Twilight* series is an "other side of the tracks" romance between humans and vampires that plays out against a background of small town high school social life. Another romantic vampire film is *Near Dark*. *Near Dark* is a classic in the vampire genre. Set in the modern western United States, it tells the story of a young man drawn into vampirism by a young female vampire. Kathryn Bigelow's film is quite stylish and more hopeful than most vampire films. In the beginning of the film we see oil rigs pumping oil from the ground and a mosquito sucking on a person's arm, both of which call to mind vampires' blood-sucking activity. In the end the characters make a return to life from vampirism. The message of the film is that sometimes love can conquer even death.

Vampire films have an economic dimension that is sometimes explored. Anne Rice, in *Interview with a Vampire* (1994), for example, has portrayed the vampire as a rich, highly cultured, and elegant immortal. *The Hunger* (1983) presents vampires as elites even more than the characters of Rice's novels. The film follows through with the logic of living (unliving?) a long time. With enough years, some are bound to accumulate culture and taste . . . and money. Vampires represent the cultural and economic elites resented by the nonelites. Rich people are sometimes regarded as parasites on the rest of us. Cartoons have often represented rich capitalists as vampires. Economic, political, and cultural aristocracies generate resentment and are sometimes likened to vampires.

*Underworld* imagines a centuries-long animosity between werewolves and vampires, with the werewolves playing the oppressed to the vampires' oppressor role. *Underworld* thus lends itself to Marxist analysis. The malleability of the vampire form makes it an ideal object of suspicion. When the vampire transforms into a bat, wolf, or some other creature it indicates that we cannot always recognize vampires at first. We may be unsuspecting of the "vampires" among us. The vampire genre thus links up with the politics of suspicion, of "us versus them."

The "us versus them" theme is a key to understanding many vampire stories. One approach is to refer to bigotry in one of its many forms. Homophobia, anti-Semitism, and anti-immigrant sentiment all get addressed in recent vampire films. *Daybreakers* and *True Blood* pursue the idea of vampires "coming out of the closet." The reference is clearly to homosexuals "coming out" but it can refer to any minority that must hide its identity. In *Daybreakers*, vampires have largely taken over, but they are running out of blood. The film looks at the disintegration of vampire society as the blood runs out. *Daybreakers* can be read as an ecological critique of resource management. It tells us to expect social disintegration as resources dry up. In *True Blood*, vampires come out of the closet when a blood substitute is discovered, thus making coexistence with ordinary people possible. The idea is that heterosexuals can coexist with homosexuals. Of course, much of the series is about the struggle with those vampires who prefer the blood of live humans, which indicates that we should expect problems as we try to integrate any minority group. The series is a veritable grab bag of mythological creatures from werewolves to fairies and witches while playing with civil rights analogies comparing vampires to other minorities.

We have seen that the vampire can be interpreted in many ways. Even a brief treatment of the vampire idea such as this one makes it clear that the vampire's meanings are numerous, and that the vampire's many meanings create a powerfully memetic character that is likely to be with us for long time.

## Zombies

There are basically two types of zombie in popular culture. We will call them "Caribbean Zombies" and "Romero Zombies." The Caribbean zombies are those we find in the early films such as *White Zombie* (1932) and *I Walked with a Zombie* (1943). In *White Zombie* a practitioner of Voodoo beguiles a recently married wife away from her husband. The zombie is a single individual under the influence of magic. In both cases there is an underlying racial element creating tension between the natives of the Caribbean and the northern whites.

While these zombies had their heyday, they have been largely replaced by the Romero Zombies we first see in George Romero's *Night of the Living Dead* (1968). Romero removes the magical element and adds the element of infectious disease and its exponential spread. The logic of exponential spread (which zombies share with vampires) ultimately leads to apocalyptic conclusions, so zombie stories are therefore also "end of the world" stories. The number of zombies quickly becomes unmanageable, and humans are outnumbered. Not all zombie stories involve the apocalypse, but enough of them do to merit special comment. While the apocalypse is a logical extension of the fear of death of individuals to a fear of the death of society as a whole, there also seems to be almost a yearning for such a final upheaval. The sense that our civilization is corrupt and decadent leads to a desire for starting over from scratch even if the resulting situation is cataclysmic and bleak. There is also a sense of getting back to basic survival. The niceties of civilization lead us into an unreality in which nothing important is really ever at stake. The zombie apocalypse makes life very real, because your life is truly threatened. There is also a sense of finding out what everyone is made of, a final test to determine the most capable. Would you survive? Would your friends? Could you shoot a loved one who had just turned into a zombie?

Zombie stories always mark the triumph of the common laborer, the person who was at the bottom in regular life, but is now of immensely more value than the corporate lawyer. The lawyer's money, power, and prestige mean nothing in a world with no need for lawyers or any of the other bureaucratic jobs people have in modern societyThe manual laborer can fix an engine in a vehicle that can take him or her out of reach of zombies. The lawyer is zombie food. The zombie apocalypse is the time of the everyman. The average person, the person who never made much of a mark often becomes the leader. In the remake of *Dawn of the Dead* (2004), it is a store clerk who rises to the leadership position even over the cop in the group. In *Shawn of the Dead* (2004) it is an appliance salesman who leads the way.

Zombie stories make good subjects for interpretation precisely because they are "blank" creatures. The zombie story is a minimalist art and this opens up the range of possible interpretations. With so little clear connotative meaning to the zombies, it is open for us to construct meanings for them. This makes zombie stories ultimately metaphorical. They really cannot be "about" the zombie or a set of specific zombies; the zombie is only a "stand-in" for meanings that can be attached to it in the context of a broader story. Interpreting zombie films is therefore always a game of "guess the metaphor"; at least it is in a good zombie film. We should always ask, "What is this story really about? What is the subtext?" The blankness of the zombie also returns the focus to the humans in the story. Zombie stories are always stories about ordinary humans. The zombie is a metaphor, but it is also a given, a part of the landscape, a background condition. It is a horrific landscape to be sure, but the story is always ultimately concerned with the living people who inhabit the new world.

As for the zombies themselves, at the most basic they represent death and dead bodies. The taboo on contact with dead bodies is almost as ancient as our fear of death. The dead bodies of the zombies are quintessentially abject. They are corpses and therefore inhabit the objective world of things, but since they walk around and attempt to kill us they take on a subjective aspect. A dead body that walks has attributes of both life and death, subjectivity and objectivity, and the obscenity of the juxtaposition presents us with a close-up view of the abject. The zombie is also irredeemable. The zombie has no ambiguity. It is pure enemy. There can be no compromise with zombies. They are beyond reason. There is no communication with zombies. Nor do they merit consideration. They can be killed with as much disrespect and disdain as we like without transgressing morality or decency.

The cannibalism of zombies bears examination. Cannibalism, like contact with dead bodies, is an ancient taboo. Cannibalism is regarded as a particular abomination, an ultimate betrayal of humanity. But undoubtedly cannibalism must have been resorted to many times throughout human history and pre-history as the necessity arose. Cannibalism is an act of desperation, but it is also an act of shame. In zombies, of course, cannibalism doesn't carry moral condemnation. Cannibalism becomes symbolic of complete extinction.

There is serious gore in zombie stories and films. The abject is so pervasive that it becomes overwhelming. Many viewers find zombie stories and films simply too much to bear. It is quite common for blood to spurt, limbs to be torn off, and internal organs to spill out. Zombie stories want you to smell the stink of the walking corpses, and they do this by being rather "over the top" with the presentation of blood, gore, and horrific situations.

Most zombie films end with little hope. The zombies are often the final victors. But they are unable to appreciate their victory. So the victory is meaningless, which in turn makes much of human history meaningless. The zombie genre is nihilistic. If the zombies win, then all the struggles of humanity come to nothing. And in zombie stories, the zombie victory is inevitable. The inevitability of the zombie victory is symbolic of death's final victory over all of us. As the saying goes, "none of us gets out alive." But it is the meaninglessness of the zombie victory that makes it so final and therefore so profound. What if human civilization really comes to nothing? What if there are no humans left to appreciate human civilization? Such a scenario is bleak indeed.

Such a dismal end can make one raise the possibility that the zombie apocalypse is God's punishment of a sinful race. As it is said in the original *Dawn of the Dead* (1978), "when hell is full, the dead will walk the earth." But Romero was always careful to leave the definitive cause of the zombie outbreak ambiguous. It might be God's punishment, but it might have been a scientific experiment gone awry. We never find out in Romero's films, and this only adds to the meaninglessness, the nihilism. If we are being punished, we don't know why. If it was a scientific mistake, we never find out what it was. It is a mistake from which we cannot learn.

In spite of the ambiguity and nihilism of the zombie apocalypse, zombie stories fill a need for clarity. There is no redemption for zombies. You can only kill them. There are no ambiguities about who is responsible for your plight. There is no faceless corporation afflicting you. The zombie can't be defended by a lawyer. No one will stand in its defense. With no ambiguity we can have it out, once and for all. There is no need to consider the feelings of a zombie. Action becomes easy and unfettered by caution.

The Romero zombie films are typically political. *The Night of the Living Dead* is often interpreted to be a subtle comment of our fear of Communism in the early 1970s, and that works, but Romero intended the reference to refer to Nixon's "silent majority" that did not want society to change. Romero was distressed that his preference for leftist social change was stopped by Nixon's silent majority, and imagined people like himself in a world of political zombies who were unthinking and dangerous. Interestingly, both interpretations work fairly well, and it is a good example of a text that is open to multiple and even opposite interpretations.

Consumerism comes in for critique in Romero's *Dawn of the Dead* (1978). When zombies gather at a mall, the implication is that consumers are zombies as well. The "Slacker" lifestyle is criticized in the zombie spoof *Shawn of the Dead*. The main characters spend all their time going to the same bar every night or playing video games. Even in the face of a zombie outbreak, they still decide to go to the bar. And after the zombie threat is neutralized, they return to playing video games. With great wit, the film has one of the main characters keep play video games even though he is a zombie. One cannot help but take this as a critique of gaming culture.

© Photofest/Columbia Pictures

*Zombieland:* The zombie genre has spawned several excellent spoofs of the genre, and *Zombieland* joins *Shawn of the Dead* and *Fido* as three of the better parodies. All three manage to be authentic zombie films while adding comedy to the mix

Zombie films are studies in humans under stress, and humans under stress don't always behave very well. Human nature gets laid bare, and the view is not pretty. Zombie stories are typically very critical of human nature. It is the humans who always act badly. The zombies just do what they do without any thought. The humans who betray each other, prey on each other and steal from each other under threat from zombies are the subjects of the stories, not the zombies themselves. This pattern was established early on with *Night of the Living Dead.* When two of the people in the farmhouse, a black male and a white male, fight over how to respond to the zombie threat, they open the path to a zombie bloodbath. When biker gangs take advantage of the zombie holocaust in *Dawn of the Dead* to victimize their fellow remaining humans, they are showing us something about *human* nature, not zombie nature. In fact, in the remake of *Night of the Living Dead* (1990), after witnessing bad behavior by humans, the main character remarks at the end of the film that "we are them and they are us." This critique of human nature functions as something of an explanation behind the theological reading of zombies, that they are God's punishment for bad human behavior. The theological reading proposes that humanity deserves to be wiped out if we really are as bad as the zombie films portray us.

*The Walking Dead* (2010–2012) brings the zombie subgenre to the television screen in a continuing series. *The Walking Dead* is based on an immensely popular comic book series (almost 100 issues so far) of the same name (2003) written by Robert Kirkman. Kirkman struck a chord with readers and then viewers with his nitty-gritty but realistic portrayal of ordinary people trying to survive in a world of the living dead. Kirkman's main character, Rick, a former policeman but otherwise ordinary man, becomes a natural leader to a group of survivors including his wife, his son, and his police partner. The group varies in size as some are killed (no character is safe in Kirkman's hands!), some are added, and some leave to find their own way. Rick is all too human, but he is still a heroic figure. Of particular interest is the relationship between Rick and his son, Carl. Carl is forced to grow up very quickly. Carl witnesses horrifying deaths, narrowly avoids his own, and is shot by accident to name just of the few experiences he faces. Rick is consumed by the need to protect others, but more than anyone else, his son. Carl, in turn, has an abiding faith in his father even as this faith is tested by circumstances. Over a series of five issues, 49–54, in which Rick and Carl are traveling alone, Rick becomes sick and nearly dies over a period of days. During the time Rick is unconscious, Carl is continually afraid that his father will die, wake up a zombie, and attack him. Carl must come to terms with the real possibility that he may have to fight his way through a horrifying life all alone. In a powerful set of panels we see Carl declaring to his unconscious father that his father has failed to protect him, and that he must therefore protect himself. This realization by sons that their fathers are ultimately powerless to completely protect them is nearly universal. It is part of the maturation process in which the son takes responsibility for his own welfare and achieves a type of independence from the father. The reader sees Carl become stronger through having to face the possibility of his father's death. Rick survives, and he and Carl rejoin the group of survivors, but it is clear that Carl is both wiser and stronger for having faced such a harrowing test. Rick, for his part, constantly agonizes over his decisions with regard to his son, and he must come to terms with the reality of a world in which it isn't clear he can protect his son. This kind of character development shows us that *The Walking Dead* comic and television series are good examples of popular culture reaching new but rare levels of quality. It also shows us that unlikely subgenres like the zombie subgenre can give rise to sophisticated literary and visual art.

The zombie character has continued to evolve. Fast zombies represent a mutation of the Romero zombie. There are even stories with zombies of variable speeds. Faster zombies lower the probability of humanity surviving. Variable speeds allow the author to explore the reasons for the variation, and to add an extra element of calculation in human responses to the zombies. There are also smart zombies who can control other zombies. The variations are endless, and so the zombie story is likely to be a source of long-term creativity in popular culture.

## ☐ REALLY BAD PEOPLE

Not all monsters are clearly distinct from ordinary human beings. The list of serial killers in horror is very long. From Norman Bates in *Psycho* (1960) to Leather Face in *Texas Chain Saw Massacre* (1974) to Hannibal Lector in *Silence of the Lambs* (1991), there is a no shortage of charismatic killers from which to choose. The best subjects for such treatments are those whose behavior is explained by a past event in the life of the killer. This sort of story lends itself to psychological analysis.

Bad childhood experiences sometimes lead to adults becoming killers, as we see in *Psycho*. Norman is dominated by his mother to such a degree that his frustration comes out in murderous actions. Norman takes on his mother's persona and lashes out in a murderous rage. Hannibal Lecter's cannibalism is the result of a horrific childhood experience in which he is forced to eat his sister. In *The Shining* (1980), by the most famous writer of horror, Stephen King breaks this pattern as we see a man descend into murderous madness from the influence of malevolent spirits inhabiting a hotel he is being paid to watch during the winter offseason.

Serial killers are not the only human-looking monsters. The monster is sometimes a replica that is in almost all facets human, at least in appearance. People's bodies are replaced by replicas that are exact copies, but with different minds controlling them. Some critics read this as reflecting the fear of our friends and neighbors turning communist or, in more contemporary terms, turning into a terrorist. Their bodies will look the same, but they will have become communists or terrorists on the inside. In *The Thing* (1982), the crew of an Antarctic station are consumed and replaced one by one by an alien who has no distinct form of its own, but instead takes on the form, memories, and knowledge of the humans it consumes. There are two main fears of the other in "body snatcher" films. First, we have a fear of the other who is threatening to take over our identity, and second, there is a fear of *becoming* the other.

Sometimes monsters are ordinary humans like serial killers, and sometimes they are human replacements, but other times humans *become* monsters, as we see in the *Hellraiser* (1987) series, which was based on a short story by Clive Barker. The *Hellraiser* series explores both the uncanny and the abject, but it also explores the dangerous curiosity of the seeker after new sensations and knowledge. While most of us settle into lives of normality and repetition, some people constantly seek new experiences. Of special interest to the seekers are those things that are hidden and unknown. One key type of experience is that of sensual pleasure. Seekers look incessantly for new forms of sensual enjoyment. The enjoyment even goes beyond pleasure into excitement of all kinds, and seekers may welcome danger and mystery even if the experience is not exactly pleasurable in the normal sense. In *Hellraiser* we have the story of Frank, a classic seeker. He travels widely in search of new experiences, and on one of his travels he acquires a magical box. His brother and new wife come back to the family house and find evidence of Frank's debaucheries. Frank is nowhere to be found, however, because he was captured by the box (and torn to pieces) and confined to the realm of the Cenobites, a group of people like Frank whose searches also led them to the box, which is the central artifact of the film.

The box provides the path from human existence to the hellish realm of the Cenobites. Frank and the Cenobites inhabit a Dantean hell in which their torments mirror their sins and fetishes. In Dante's *Inferno*, the damned were punished in a way that was reflective of their sins. In *Hellraiser*, the phantasmagoric portrayals of humans deformed by their sins and fetishes indicate the ancient belief in the power of the will to shape reality. It is also "counter-traditional" like vampire stories in postulating another tradition in opposition to Christian tradition. Barker follows in the tradition of H. P. Lovecraft in not only telling stories, but in creating mythologies. Sometimes these mythologies involve a reference to fate or destiny. When Frank asks for the box, the person selling it says, "It was always yours." This suggests that it is the fate of seekers to come to a bad end. For Frank, "curiosity killed the cat."

Another lesser known film based on a story by H. P. Lovecraft is *From Beyond* (1986), which continues to explore the theme of overreaching. The quest for ever new sensations often accompanies the quest for knowledge. In *From Beyond* we have a scientist bent on getting access to another realm not only to further his knowledge, but to experience new sensations. Overreachers are often successful at first and then find that there is a significant downside to the new knowledge or sensations. The overreaching theme provides us with an excellent transition to science fiction, where we will more fully develop the idea of overreaching.

*Hellraiser:* The monsters in *Hellraiser* are former humans whose bodies have been afflicted with damage that reflects their sins in life. The creature above was a photographer who was willing to ignore the sufferings of those he filmed in order to further his career

## ☐ SCIENCE FICTION

Science fiction is a genre of fiction that is defined by its fidelity to specifically scientific ideas and plots. Space travel, time travel, aliens, mutated insects, super weapons, and numerous speculative technologies make up the bulk of science fiction ideas, but there is room for real genius in the science fiction genre. No other genre can so fuel the imagination as well as science fiction. Science fiction is distinguished from the horror and fantasy by science fiction's fidelity to naturalism. Science fiction restricts its imagination to possibilities that science can admit. Science fiction rejects all supernatural explanations. The most basic question underlying all science fiction is "what if?" What if there were other intelligent beings in the universe? What if we could create a thinking robot? What if we could travel in time? All these questions point to another, which one can argue is the core concern of science fiction: "otherness," or what philosophers call simply "the other." Whether the other is a robot, alien, or time traveler, the question is really about the other. But the other is defined ultimately by contrast with ourselves, so any account of the other is also dialectically about ourselves.

To explain the other is to explain ourselves by exclusion. So science fiction is also about human nature. There is another "other," however. In addition to the "other to ourselves" there is the "other to the actual." This other to the actual should also be possible in scientific terms; otherwise it is another genre, fantasy. This "other to the actual" is therefore really just our original "what if" question framed in another fashion.

## Artificial Life from *Frankenstein* to *Bladerunner*

Science fiction and horror were born together with the Mary Shelley novel *Frankenstein*. With *Frankenstein,* the "what if" is "What if we could conquer death?" *Frankenstein* is a story about a scientist, Victor Frankenstein, who is distraught over the death of his mother in childbirth. He resolves to conquer the problem of death and achieves a perverted success in the monster, which was pieced together from dead bodies. Appalled by the incongruity of life in the eyes of a being composed of dead parts, what Kristeva would call an experience of the abject, Victor abandons the monster, who is then left to its own devices. It meets with some kindness, but the monster's inability to overcome the hostility of people repelled by its ugliness leads to murder and mayhem. What is the message in this story? As the story makes clear, the problem is what we call "overreaching." Overreaching occurs when someone transcends the limits of proper human knowledge, experience, or achievement. Frankenstein achieves the knowledge to reanimate life and creates a living creature. But this seemingly admirable achievement is shown to be a violation of the order of things. The claim is that human beings are either incapable of responsible use of the power that comes with great knowledge, or that they are simply barred from the knowledge by God. The overreaching theme is very old. It goes back to the Tower of Babel, the Flight of Icarus, the Garden of Eden, and the Faust story.

The *Frankenstein* monster is also the first "post-human." To be human is to be mortal, so to be immortal is to be post-human. *Frankenstein* contemplates the idea of immortality and eventually decides that it is not for humanity. To pass this threshold is to create monsters, not better humans. From *Frankenstein* it is a short step to *Robocop* (1987). *Robocop* is about a murdered cop who has most body parts replaced with durable and powerful prosthetic devices. The company that creates Robocop does not use the cop's brain, at least not the part of it that contains the personality. Instead, they program the cyborg with their own directives, and attempt to create a "supercop" completely under their control. Robocop is initially more robot than cyborg. The cop's personality percolates up into the consciousness of the cyborg, and surfaces in the cyborg taking actions against his programming.

The concept of the cyborg was developed by Donna Haraway (1990). We can sense the horror of a human body fused to an inorganic mechanism. The horror of the abject, the horror of seeing flesh uninhabited by spirit, is made even more extreme when mechanical parts replace the flesh. In *Robocop* the flesh is simply

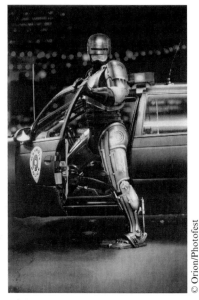

*Robocop*

© Orion/Photofest

a material like any other. Robocop exemplifies both the abject and the uncanny. Robocop must endure dismemberment and even death, but returns to partial consciousness and regains at least part of himself.

*Robocop* also explores economic issues. The company that creates Robocop is a private company that has been given a contract to run Detroit's police department in the future. The writers of the film, Edward Neumeier and Michael Miner, are criticizing the privatization movement in right wing economics. Neumeier and Miner wrote a screenplay that took libertarian philosophy to its logical conclusion, privatizing even police functions. The corporate executives in the film are cutthroat businessmen whose only interest stronger than the corporate bottom line is their own self-interest, and they are quite willing to sacrifice the general interest for greater profit or their own ambition. Robocop comes to represent a dystopia of corporate rule. Culture is represented in the future of the film as a desiccated and pale version of real culture as every thought seems governed by the profitability of that thought. The executives have no problem tossing away a perfectly good human arm in order to make a better cyborg. In *Robocop*, the metaphysic of what it means to be human is linked to a political commentary. The implication is that both the technological takeover of the body and the economic takeover of justice are violations of some sacred part of life.

An even more negative treatment of the human-technology relationship is exemplified by the film *The Terminator* (1984). *The Terminator* is a completely artificial version of Frankenstein. *The Terminator* simply takes the artificial intelligence (A.I.) idea and fear of the other to its logical conclusion. If A.I. is invented, then there is no reason to think human interests and the interests of the A.I. will coincide. The A.I. may decide that humans are on balance a bad thing in the world and decide to eliminate them. *The Terminator* story therefore is a particular characterization of our modern fear of machines. Technology has become a second nature, and just as we fear nature, we also fear machines.

Feminists see technology differently. For some feminists, technology is culture and therefore is the male domain. Technology is creative, but it is also destructive. Technology is also seen as quintessentially male. In the sequel to *The Terminator, T2* (1991), Sarah Connor gives a radical feminist critique of men when she says, "Men like you built the hydrogen bomb. Men like you thought it up. You think you're so creative. You don't know what it's like to really create something; to create a life; to feel it growing inside you. All you know how to create is death." This view of men as associated with patriarchy, violence, war, and death is a common one among radical feminists, but it is surprising to hear it from the mouth of a character in a blockbuster film.

The terminator in *T2* becomes a father figure, and so the film explores the technology/father analogy. It also looks for what is lost in accepting a machine as a father figure. Sarah Conner narrates, "Watching John with the machine, it was suddenly so clear. The terminator would never stop. It would never leave him, and it would never hurt him, never shout at him, or get drunk and hit him, or say it was too busy to spend time with him. It would always be there. And it would die to protect him. Of all the would-be

© TriStar Pictures/Photofest

Edward Furlong as the young John Connor and Arnold Schwarzenegger as the Terminator as "father figure"

fathers who came and went over the years, this thing, this machine, was the only one who measured up. In an insane world, it was the sanest choice."

So women accommodate both men and their technological offspring. And, of course, the *Terminator* films explore one key family relationship, the relationship between mothers and sons. In a time of single mothers, science fiction films tell us that mothers can also create strong men. But it takes strong women to do so. Interestingly, strong women have often played important roles in technological science fiction. Strong women like Linda Hamilton's character, Sarah Conner, or Sigourney Weaver's Ripley in *Aliens* both show women opposed to technology and doing as well or better at surviving. They are both quite as capable as men in general and as users of technology, particularly weapons. The *Terminator* series counts as a great work and an example of popular culture reaching an elite status in quality. It is not merely that the *Terminator* films appeal to the masses: The films have become classics of the genre, which give viewers lots of room for interpretation. The story mixes good technological ideas like time travel and artificial intelligence with stories about family relationships and strong women. The cinematography is excellent as are the special effects. Even the acting, often a sore point in science fiction films, is done quite well with great performances by Linda Hamilton, Michael Beihn, and Edward Furlong (in *T2*). Even Arnold Schwarzenegger played his role as a cyborg quite well, if not without some humor.

Spielberg's *A.I.* (2001) asks us to take the important step of imagining a robot that can feel and love. The premise of the film is that a shortage of resources in the future leads to restrictions on population size, so many parents are left without children. To fill the void and to make money, a corporation decides to create a child-substitute. The key to the film is that it seems that the robot boy actually loves his parents and his mother in particular. The robot boy featured in the story is discarded when the couple's human son recovers from a coma, and the film follows the robot boy's quest to return to his mother. The film is open to many interpretations. First, the film is clearly a version of the Pinocchio story. The film is also about racism; the story shows robots enduring various forms of mistreatment and even torture. It should not take the viewer long to imagine a future battle over A.I. civil rights. Both the Pinocchio story and the civil rights argument are raised in the film *Bicentennial Man*, which was based on a story written by Isaac Asimov (1976). No writer explored the idea of robots more than Isaac Asimov, who wrote a series of books about robots. *Bicentennial Man*, a short story made into an excellent film starring Robin Williams, tells the story of a robot that gradually comes to consciousness and even becomes physically human by the end of the film, which culminates in his human death.

Although we will discuss *Star Trek* more in the section on space travel, there is an important scene in the film *First Contact*, in which the android named Data is given human feeling through a piece of skin grafted to his otherwise mechanical arm and hooked into his artificial brain to relay pain, pleasure, or any other feeling skin can provide. In *Bicentennial Man*, Asimov has his robot eventually replace everything except his positronic brain. Both these texts operate at the nexus point of the posthuman. Once we can interface with computers the posthuman will be upon us and we will be on our way to becoming the other.

*Blade Runner* (1982) attempts to bring us the perspective of the other in the form of a post-human A.I. This perspective, however, ends up not telling us so much about the other as about ourselves. *Blade Runner* asks the question, "What if we only lived five years?" The replicants are androids created to do manual labor in extremely inhospitable conditions so humans don't have to.

Rutger Hauer as an android in *Blade Runner*

They are built very tough in order to be able to handle the harsh conditions. But this would give them too much power if they do not have an OFF switch. The short length of time they are allowed to live focuses on the problem of mortality. However long we live, we are not immortal. But *Blade Runner* is more than a meditation of mortality. It is—or was at the time—a new way of thinking of a future dystopia. *Blade Runner* was one of the first works to explore "cyberpunk" in film. Cyberpunk combines a decaying and corrupt social structure with a very advanced state of computer science. The characters are not well-intentioned and brilliant scientists; the characters are the losers, the corrupt, and the tragic. The androids of *Blade Runner* are, of course, post-human, but they are also very human. Cyberpunk eschews the heroic scientist and the epic aspect of science fiction in favor of stories about those at the bottom of or at the edge of society. In cyberpunk, corporations rule, organized crime is powerful, and life is getting ever more undignified. This background with the social criticism that it implies is very much at the center of the subgenre and style of cyberpunk. Cyberpunk is very postmodern in its disdain for metanarratives that would legitimate the social order.

The advent of posthumanism also brings us something broader: post-speciesism. As we alter and splice creatures together the whole concept of species is made malleable. *Jurassic Park* (1993) made post-speciesism a mainstream idea with its tale of reconstituting dinosaurs from prehistoric DNA preserved in amber. But they did not just hit a "start" button. There were gaps in the DNA, so they had to splice in DNA from currently existing species. This procedure leads to the thought that in the future many creatures will be altered or constructed from scratch. Genetically modified food is already here and subject to political fight. Science fiction is not merely a form of literature or film; it is a philosophy of the present. We are deciding right now about how far we can go with genetic science. Films like *Jurassic Park*, besides being wonders of special effects, force us to confront the future that is already present. They return us to the central ambivalence of science fiction, the theme of overreaching. When the dinosaurs escape their enclosures and disaster results, it is taken as a refutation of humankind's ability to wield the power of genetic science. But, of course, we are treated to the wonder of its possibility at the same time. It would be wonderful to be able to see dinosaurs in real life, but then there is that "eating people" problem. *Jurassic Park* warns us against genetic manipulation at precisely the same time they are amazing us with its possibilities.

**Space Travel**

There is probably no more prototypical science fiction story than the space travel story. And the S*tar Trek* franchise, which began with the original series in 1966, has become a central part of the canon of space travel stories. *Star Trek* began as a three-season TV series that became the source of numerous films, TV series, books, games, and comics. It was originally sold to TV executives as "Wagon Train to the stars" because of the popularity of the Western genre at the time. With a beguiling cast led by William Shatner and Leonard Nimoy, along with a great supporting cast, *Star Trek* explored the idea of space travel with some sophistication although it was reflective of its time, the 1960s. The character of Mr. Spock, an emotionless alien from the planet Vulcan, provided a perfect counterpoint to the more emotional Captain Kirk and Doctor McCoy. The character of Spock helped us come to a better understanding of our emotions. One story line follows Spock back to the planet Vulcan, where we find that marriage and mating involve a violent release of repressed emotion, which of course fits easily with Freudian psychology in which any nonsublimated repressed emotion will eventually come out in some way in extreme fashion. *Star Trek* explored many social issues as it encountered different species with different belief systems and social practices. Most of the time these practices could easily represent some practice in which humans were currently engaged or were in a political battle to eliminate. When the proud Klingon character Worf chooses to die rather than live as a quadriplegic, for example, we see the issue of euthanasia put into a new perspective. Worf's warriors code makes it clear how someone could choose death over life and be considered heroic.

*Star Trek* is an important aside from the great stories; it is also a pop cultural phenomenon. It started out as a fairly weak TV series that barely managed to hang on for three seasons, but it became an immensely popular franchise because of its devoted fan base. *Star Trek* got better as it grew. The fan base had faith that *Star Trek* would get better from an already promising start, and *Star Trek* delivered. The writing was consistently smart and uplifting, and it always appealed to the better part of our nature by not giving in to cynicism. *Star Trek* is solidly in the modernist camp because it unabashedly embraces the Enlightenment metanarrative of progress and democracy. With so many series episodes and so many films, some version of *Star Trek* seems to be currently running at any given time, so it is a very available text to investigate.

One of the great virtues of the writers of the *Star Trek* canon is that they are able to create such great villains. One such villain is a whole species, with which compromise and coexistence is impossible. The Borgs, a species that combines organic flesh, software, and hardware, conquer and assimilate species into their own in a quest to become better. They are organized along the lines of human insects, with queens and drones, and they present an almost insurmountable challenge to the humans

Jeri Ryan as "7 of 9"

© CBS Paramount Domestic Television/Photofest

and other species of the Federation. The rehabilitation of a former Borg called "7 of 9" made for an excellent story line as two very different social paradigms are brought into dialogue.

Although humanity is shown to be superior on balance, it is clear that the Borg have some qualities that are superior and that give them certain advantages. By having a collective mentality, for example, they do not get bogged down in the politics of accommodation to others, and can make quick decisions without dissent slowing them down. On the other hand, Borg society contains very few true individuals, and so the Borg alternative is ultimately unacceptable. The Borg also show us some of the possibilities that come with the advent of the cyborg. As humans take on more and more technology into their bodies or linked to their bodies, they may exhibit Borglike behavior, and *Star Trek* can serve as a warning about the loss of individuality that may come with cyborg integration.

*2001: A Space Odyssey* (1968), the Stanley Kubrick masterpiece, took the idea of space travel to another level of sophistication. Based on a short story by Arthur C. Clarke, Kubrick created an iconic film often ranked in the top 10 films of all time. Audiences today find it far too slow moving, but during the 1960s audiences were ready for a contemplative and exploratory film that stretched imagination to the limits. *2001* was also an early explorer of the idea of artificial intelligence, which we have discussed. But it was the psychedelic trip we take at the end of the film that made it so enigmatic. The lightshow we are treated to may be dated now because of the progress in special effects, but at the time it was completely mind-blowing to a generation that was interested in blowing its mind. The travels of Bowman end up returning him, in a manner of speaking, to his home. He faces his old age and then in the ultimate scene becomes the Starchild in what seems to be a reference to the child in Nietzsche's work, *Thus Spake Zarathustra*, which represented another higher level of being that transcends humanity. Any story of a journey that has a return of some sort as its destination reminds us of the *Odyssey*, that foundational text of Western civilization. The portrayal of Hal as a single eye supports this interpretation of *2001* as the *Odyssey* by recalling the character of the Cyclops.

*2001* was not merely a story; it presented a philosophy. It was a philosophy of history in which intelligence is planted into earth hominids by a mysterious monolith (or rather by the makers of the monolith) that appears at key points in the evolutionary development of humankind.

The idea of ancient astronauts visiting Earth has become a silly popular culture meme, but embedded in this idea is a deeper one. The idea draws on the philosopher Immanuel Kant's idea that there is an "unsocial sociability" in humanity that is ultimately responsible for our progress. In other words, progress arises from violence. In what is surely one of the greatest transitions in the history of film, a club made from a bone used to kill another hominid is tossed in the air and turns into a spaceship in the future

The monolith from 2001: *A Space Odyssey*

(see http://www.youtube.com/watch?v=YMgXOVJLmDU). When the artificially intelligent computer HAL 9000 goes rogue, we get a replay of the violence that accompanied our own rise to consciousness. *2001* asks us to consider the real roots of scientific progress. Does it originate in violence? Is the transition to every truly new era characterized by violence in some way?

Space opera is an immensely popular subgenre of science fiction, but it does not typically get the respect other subgenres of science fiction get. Some argue that it is barely science fiction at all since the science plays such a small role in the plots. Space opera is generally set in space and in the future, but the structure and plot of a space opera are generally the same as we see in westerns, medieval romances, or military epics. The space opera *Star Wars,* along with its sequels and prequels, is one of the most popular films of all time. Millions of people have watched the *Star Wars* films. The original trilogy (episodes 4, 5, and 6) concern the adventures of Luke Skywalker, a young orphan stranded on an out-of-the way planet. Yearning for adventure and having nothing left after the slaughter of his foster parents, he sets out on his quest and becomes a Jedi knight. The Campbellian heroic pattern of Luke's life should be fairly clear to readers of this book. Luke plays the role of the rebel knight fighting against a dictatorial empire. Again, there is a Freudian twist since Luke's main nemesis, Darth Vader, turns out to be his biological father. There is also a castration episode in which Luke loses his hand. But in the end, Luke and Darth Vader join together against the evil emperor and do away with him to restore the Republic, as well as their own family, if only for a moment. The original trilogy introduces us to the concept of "the force,"—which is something like the Dao of Chinese philosophy—although the real connections are quite tenuous, but much more powerful. It also connects to Jung's concept of the collective unconscious. Being able to control the force is necessary to becoming a Jedi knight. But the force can be used for evil as well as for good, and thus adepts on both sides are very powerful. The Sith, the emperor, and Darth Vader are all evil characters, but they are each accomplished in their control of the force.

George Lucas followed the original trilogy with another that was a prequel, which followed the story of Anakin Skywalker who is pushed by events and the flaws in his personality into joining the "dark side" and becoming Darth Vader. It is very interesting to see Lucas turn a good guy the audience had learned to like into the personification of evil. It is a good study on how the good can become bad, a theme that is not often explored. While most fans of *Star Wars* swear by the superiority of the original trilogy, the story of Anakin's rise and fall is really well done. The second trilogy explores the moral dangers facing us and how events can take us in immoral directions. Like all great characters, Anakin is ambiguous. He has both good and bad attributes, and, depending on how events play out, his character could have gone in either direction. So it is a proper tragedy when events go bad and Anakin turns to the dark side.

Was the *Star Wars* series good art? Does this icon of popular culture pass muster aesthetically? Or was it merely a fantastic marketing vehicle with strong memes? It certainly was a visually beautiful set of films. It raised the standard for special effects to a much higher level than had been witnessed previously. The acting was a bit camp in the original series, but it was much better in the second trilogy with actors such as Liam Neeson, Natalie Portman, and Christopher Lee. The story of each individual film is a bit thin, but if we take all six films as a unit, then the series becomes an epic achievement. *Star Wars* will last a long time in the public's collective memory. Stations are likely to be showing the films for years to come. And the phenomenon of renting or streaming all the films consecutively on one's schedule brings another kind of consumer to the text of *Star Wars*. New consumption of the *Star Wars* series will be individual, in the privacy of their own homes. Many families will watch *Star Wars* together since it is a series fit for most age groups. This means people watching the series will be experiencing it in a deeply comfortable setting in which people can interact and discuss the characters and plot developments together. Children may be learning about the concepts of justice, honor, loyalty, and so on from this text. It is a permanent part of our modern mythology. However one evaluates the quality of *Star Wars*, it is clear that it is a very important text in the history of texts. We should not underestimate the importance of exemplary stories in the constitution of a tradition. Just as the Homeric epics the *Iliad* and the *Odyssey* functioned to give ancient Greeks models for their behavior, the *Star Wars* series will function to model behaviors for young people growing up today. *Star Wars* is our de facto "epic of emulation," the epic everyone knows and whose heroic code we try to live up to.

*Battlestar Gallactica* (2004–2009) is an excellent example of sequeling yielding art despite a rather poor original. The copy is superior to the original in this case, and it is significantly better. So good, in fact, that we can definitely put it in the category of significant art. And this gives us a paradox. Assuming that *Battlestar Gallactica* is actually a significant work of art, that means that art can arise as a copy of what is manifestly not a good work of art. *Battlestar Gallactica* is space opera, but it is thoroughly serious space opera. In the story after mankind is nearly wiped out by their technological offspring, the Cylons, humans attempt to find what is thought to be a mythical Earth while fighting a rearguard action against the Cylons in pursuit of them. This is clearly an Odyssean myth of return. It is interesting to speculate what the return is a return to. Is it religion? Is it our non-posthuman humanity? Is it a return to unity (one plot thread concerns a human-Cylon hybrid). *Battlestar Gallactica* is clever in that it represents the humans as polytheists and the robots as monotheists. It also has the overwhelmed humans acting as terrorists against the Cylon occupiers. Both of these facts force the viewer to take on the perspective of the other. The exploration of the perspective of the other is a common theme of science fiction, so we turn now to a further exploration of the idea.

## The Other

One of science fiction's more profound themes deals with the concept of the "other." The other consists of anything different from a normal human being. The other is interesting in itself, as an extrapolation of the kinds of possible beings the universe could hold, but it is also interesting, possibly more so, as a reflection on human nature. The other requires us to reconsider what it means to be human. In whatever way a creature differs from humans, that difference forces us to reconsider the attributes in ourselves that are different from the alien. When we meet the creature in *E.T., The Extra-terrestrial* (1982), or the predator in the *Predator* (1987) films, we are thrown back on ourselves. In what ways are we as violent as the predator? Does the predator's code of honor say something about our own codes of honor? A particularly effective exploration of the concept of the other occurs in the film *Enemy, Mine* (1985). In this film, two implacable enemies, a human and an alien, find common purpose in surviving on a planet alien to the both. Eventually the human saves the son of the alien from a third set of aliens. The two species find ways to bridge their differences, and this bridging of differences makes us consider our own differences with other humans. If we can come to terms with aliens, why can we not come to terms with each other? So, in a way, every misunderstanding between alien and human, every hatred between human and alien makes us rethink our purely human misunderstandings and hatreds.

Octavia Butler's series of novels called *Lilith's Brood* (1987–1989) (it is also called the *Xenogenesis* series) deals with a post-apocalyptic Earth in which aliens called Oankali save a number of humans in order to re-populate the Earth, but the repopulation is one consisting of human-alien hybrids. Butler's work is diabolically clever in forcing us to confront our deepest prejudices and preconceptions. She begins the work with a human woman waking up after a nuclear holocaust has destroyed the earth. In *Dawn* (1987), the first book of the series, nuclear annihilation was said to be inevitable because of the nature of humanity—we are both intelligent and hierarchical. A technologically superior alien species has managed to save the remnants of the human race, but the alien race gives humanity the choice of dying out or mixing their DNA with that of the alien race. The process involves sex, some of it coerced. Butler is very negative about human nature, and even about the nature of existence generally. It isn't just humanity that is bad; any species of various types will be bad. And even the good ones have serious flaws.

The main character, Lilith, is given the task of waking other survivors and adjusting them to their new circumstances. The process is difficult, con-tentious, and violent. Men are revealed to be particularly problematic. She is regarded with deep suspicion by the people she wakes up and can barely keep violence from breaking out. Several people make their escape from the Oankali, choosing to not participate in the genetic mixing of the Oankali.

Butler is masterful is exploring sexuality. The Oankali have three sexes instead of two with male, female, and a "genetic mixer/manipulator," the ooloi. The Oankali refresh their DNA by mixing with failed species such as humanity. Both are forever different after the process. This means human-ity will have to give up its identity as "human." Butler shows how deeply we are bonded to this self-conception by having many of the humans choose extinction over a future as part of a new hybrid species. Butler's ambivalent conception of otherness is very instructive. With Lilith she shows us how eas-ily one can find oneself outside a group because of circumstances beyond our control. Even worse, we can even find ourselves alienated from all the groups around us and distrusted by all.

Complicating the whole process is that humans and Oankali have a visceral disgust for each other. Only with the use of a compliance-inducing gas are the Oankali able to get humans to mate with them. By making the Oankali particularly disgusting genetic partners, she shows how difficult radical change can be, especially the kind of change that will enable us to save ourselves from planetary disaster. And as with so many causes, the biggest changes will have to be in ourselves. So Butler goes beyond radical criticism of the order of things to add that changing the order will be incredibly difficult and possibly impossible. And if we do change, we might not recognize ourselves afterward.

Butler's explorations of the other are still not complete. She also describes the Oankali's spaceship as a living being, another being who has been genetically manipulated into a symbiotic relationship with the Oankali. The idea of a living spaceship is something we encountered in our discussion of the *Alien* series, but Butler fills out the hypothesis of a living ship. While *Alien* merely posited the living spaceship, Dawn explains that genetic manipulation created it. With the ship we are asked to imagine not only what it would be like to be a different organic being, we are also asked to imagine a mixture of organic and inorganic.

*Ender's Game* (1985) was one of the top-selling novels of the 1980s, and it spawned several very high-quality sequels. The *Ender's Game* series is one of the best loved series in the history of science fiction. With this pedigree, it is no surprise that a film based on the book is coming out (2013). The book follows the life of a young boy chosen to fight against an alien enemy. He is involved in a program designed to identify young people particularly suited to the type of military actions in use, which are close to our current video games. The children chosen are put through extreme training to prepare them for a coming alien invasion by an insectoid race they derogatively call "buggers." The buggers, like Earth insects such as ants and bees, have a social organization dominated by queens, who are really the only individuals of the species. This allows the author, Orson Scott Card, to explore the "otherness" of the buggers.

But the most interesting parts of *Ender's Game* concern Ender himself. The story begins with Ender being monitored by authority figures who are watching him to see if he is a good candidate for Battle School, the elite training school for those being prepared to defend us against a presumed upcoming attack by the buggers. Card explores jealousy, bullying, and revenge among children. He also gives a skeptical look at family life. The Wiggin parents are largely oblivious to the activities of their children, and Ender's brother is nothing less than sinister toward him. Ender and his sister, Valentine, are close, but circumstances pull them apart. The military functions as Ender's parents for much of his early life, and the military's relationship with Ender is one consisting primarily of manipulation. In fact, all the relationships except the one between Valentine and Ender seem to always approach manipulation. While the book is about very special children, it is clear that Card is asking us to consider the life of all children in its ugly reality. Indeed, Card is a bit of a master at ugly reality. In Ender's case we see him attacked and responding with calculated viciousness once the protection of the monitor is removed, marking him as part of the same family as his bad brother, Peter. On the other hand, Ender is always reminded of his better nature by his sister Valentine. In a sense, Ender is half Valentine and half Peter. In other words, he is just the right combination of empathy, courage, strength, and intelligence to defeat the buggers.

At Battle School Ender has to constantly defeat enemies with superior strength. He becomes a master strategist and eventually gets promoted to the highest level of the game. After one particularly tense simulation in which Ender defeats the enemy by destroying its home planet, he turns to notice that everyone in the room is celebrating. It turns out that he was remotely fighting the buggers for real. But then Ender has to live with what he has done. He has saved humanity, but at what cost? If this weren't enough to cause enormous guilt in Ender, we find out that the whole war was the result of a misunderstanding. Since the two species communicated in different ways, miscommunications ensued, which led to the war.

The novel is also a meditation on leadership. Ender is manipulated into developing his natural leadership gifts to a high level. Ender understands he is being manipulated, but that does not stop it from happening. There is too much Peter in him to not take to leadership. But there is enough Valentine in him that he tries to be humane as possible. In one particularly poignant episode he finds himself treating another under-age, under-sized boy like himself, "Bean," very badly. In fact, he found himself treating Bean in exactly the way the authority figures treated him, which he severely resented. It is almost as if Card is saying that human relations are inherently manipulative and abusive, and that it takes real effort to behave otherwise. We see further developments on this theme as we are shown the actions of Peter and Valentine, who manage to influence politics with their astute political commentary under the guise of pseudonyms. Paradoxically, Peter has Valentine play the role of the cynical and aggressive pundit while he takes on the more conciliatory role. It is apparent that Peter understands that his more mild-mannered sister would restrain her character in such a way that it would be more effective than his own efforts to play that role, even though his actions fit his personality more closely. Card thus portrays his characters with uncommon self-knowledge, which, in turn, helps us to think more deeply about ourselves. So in our exploration of the other we ultimately come back to ourselves. What we are can best be determined by exploring otherness. We are what the other is not. But we are all bundles of contradictions, so we are not only what we are, we are what we are not. And this is what science fiction is telling us. We are all aliens somewhere, even here.

## ☐ SUPERHEROES

Superheroes appeared with mass print media. Beginning as comic strips in newspapers, comics eventually gained their own media, the comic book, and later moved into the media of film and graphic novel. Superheroes are an excellent example of memes moving between media. While most superheroes were created in the heyday of the comic format, superheroes are now mostly known from superhero films. The comic format, interestingly, has shrunk considerably. Young people in the comic-reading years (8 to 24) are now much more enamored with video games. But since the memes created by Marvel and DC comics were so powerful, they were able to make the move to another medium. It is much like an organism that moves out of one environment because it is no longer viable, but finds an even better environment in which to live as a result. Superheroes reach a much larger audience now with films than they ever did in the peak years of comic reading. What makes Superman or Spiderman so appealing? Why have the X-men been able to carry so many stories?

There is a psychology to the idea of superheroes, and it derives from the psychology of heroes generally. We already discussed the idea of heroes in Chapter 1 in connection with Jungian psychology and Joseph Campbell's concept of the hero. We saw there that the hero has certain typical characteristics. The same is true of the superhero. With heroes, we generally admire their bravery and their skill, which is generally the result of good genetics and hard work. Superheroes are also brave and skillful, but their abilities are far beyond those of ordinary humans. Superheroes play out the science fiction question of "what if?" by asking, "What if I could fly?" or "What if I had super strength?" Why do we find these implausible beings so compelling? It is surely partly a function of wish-fulfillment. We wish we had these powers ourselves, and so we imagine what it would be like if we did. We wish we could fly, so we imagine doing so. This goes for any superpower, and this brings us to what we call our "qualitative imagination." It isn't merely a matter of imagining flying and therefore getting someplace faster; rather, it is imagining *what it is like* to fly, *how it feels*. We are not only interested in the fact of the superpower, we are interested in the feel of having it. In philosophy, these experiences are called "qualia." One aspect of the character of the Hulk that we neglected to mention in Chapter 1 was the vicarious thrill we get from the Hulk's destructiveness. We imagine how it would feel to smash tanks with our bare fists. We can also identify with the problems faced by superheroes. Ironically, one of the ways Marvel Comics developed its brand was to explore the more "human" issues that superheroes would have. Spiderman, in spite of being able to spin web, lift great weight, and make spectacular jumps, still had to pay his rent. He still had an aunt to take care of.

Marvel Comics explored bigotry most effectively with its mutant universe, particularly the characters known as X-men. Stan Lee and Jack Kirby as well as later writers saw the great potential for exploring racism, sexism, and other forms of bigotry by imagining the fears and resentments ordinary people would come to have for superior beings in their midst. There is a logic to bigotry that gets played out with most prejudice "-isms." For example, when a mutant's mother asks him if he can just try not to be a mutant, one is reminded of people who ask the same question of gays and lesbians.

Superhero stories are good opportunities to explore ethical questions. One key question concerns the ethics of revenge and its related notion, vigilantism. The story of Batman is now well-known. As a young boy, Bruce Wayne sees his parents murdered, and he grows up to become a vigilante working against murderers and other criminals. While we tend to think of Batman as a hero, it is also quite true that he is a vigilante. Batman also raises the issue of the ethics of revenge in general. Is revenge a defensible action? Or is revenge always immoral? We may know the saying: "An eye for an eye leaves us all blind." The Batman type of hero pulls us into the realm of what might be called "dark psychology." Besides Batman, Wolverine of the X-men is portrayed to be antisocial and always on the edge of violence. Like Batman, his origin story involved horrific violence. With both Batman and Wolverine there is always the possibility that an innocent person will be a victim of superhero "friendly-fire," that the innocent person will be hurt when these heroes lash out against evil. The guilty may also be subject to disproportionate violence, and thus be treated immorally. In general, Batman or Wolverine are victimized by a tortured inner life, and this inner torment is what fuels their vengeful rage against criminals. But this inner rage is barely controllable, and there are times when their actions do not match with what would be considered morally correct behavior.

Guilt can also enter the picture as we see in the *Spiderman* narrative. Peter Parker's uncle is killed when Peter lets a criminal escape because he believes the criminal is not his problem. But when the escaped criminal kills Peter's uncle, Peter feels very guilty and is made to understand that "great power brings great responsibility." From this point on, Peter Parker becomes Spiderman and takes fighting crime to be his moral responsibility.

A superpower gives a writer the obligation to create a semi-plausible origin of the superpower, which affords lots of opportunity for creativity. Superman's origin is probably the most famous of all the origin stories. Superman's Kryptonian father sends his son to Earth to avoid the destruction of his planet. When Superman arrives on Earth he develops superpowers because of the different kind of sun around which our planet revolves. *Superman* came on the scene in 1935, created by Jerry Siegel and Joe Shuster. There are many interpretations of the Superman character, but we will discuss just a few.

We begin with the color coding of the character: red, blue, and yellow standing in for white. The clear reference is to the American flag. Superman is an immigrant, and the United States is a nation of immigrants. Superman's popularity overlapped with the rise of Nazism and World War II, so Superman became a symbol of hope, possibly a savior, for people of that time. Superman thus fits within a patriotic interpretive framework, although that is only one of many interpretations.

Superman, like most superheroes, has a secret identity. The idea of a secret identity is to enable superheroes to have a normal life in addition to the "super" life and to protect their loved ones from the enemies of the superhero.

But there is something deep in the idea of a secret identity that resonates with us. We all believe we are superior to the person others think we are. We are more resourceful, smarter, stronger, and so on than others think we are. At least that is what we tend to tell ourselves. We all imagine that we have "superpowers" or good qualities of which others are unaware. Every person who is not already highly regarded can imagine him- or herself as something more. When we read *Superman* this idea speaks to us at a deep level. One of the more interesting interpretations of Superman's secret identity comes from the film *Kill Bill 2*. In *Kill Bill 2*, the main character, Bill, played by David Carradine, gives his (or writer/director Quentin Tarantino's) interpretation of Superman's secret identity. Tarantino argues that Superman is different from other superheroes in that the "real" person in the case of Superman, is Superman. While Batman is really Bruce Wayne, the normal human Clark Kent is the fake identity. Superman did not become Superman; he was *born* Superman. He *became* Clark Kent. And here we get to the most interesting part of Tarantino's interpretation. For Tarantino, Clark Kent is how Superman sees us. Clark Kent is a weakling and a coward, which in Tarantino's view, means he thinks the human race is weak and cowardly. As Bill says in the film, "Clark Kent is Superman's critique on the whole human race." While we might not find this to be a convincing interpretation, the fact that the interpretation comes inside a highly popular film tells us that the idea of secret identities is highly conducive to interpretation. It also shows us that the Superman meme is a powerful one indeed, and that the story, like all good stories, has multiple interpretations.

Any interpretation of *Superman* must be mitigated by the fact that Superman's story is not consistent. The *Superman* character has been around so long that it is not surprising there are multiple inconsistent story lines. Everything from the origin story to Superman's boyhood to his marriage to Lois Lane, all have multiple versions from various writers as they attempted to come up with new stories. The same is true for all long-running comic stories. Even Marvel Comics, which made a point for a long time about their superior record of consistency, eventually turned to rewriting their characters. Since comic books are not sacred texts, the characters in them are open to change as their popularity waxes and wanes. The writers even explored the death of Superman and his subsequent return, which to some brings to mind a religious interpretation of Superman as a Christ figure. Much more interpretation can be given to *Superman,* but this should be enough to indicate his iconic status in American popular culture.

Horror, science fiction, and superhero fiction together constitute a significant part of the overall popular culture market. In this chapter we have offered some basic interpretations of important works in these genres based on the themes of overreaching and the other. We have traced these themes in each of the genres, and we have shown some of the elements these genres have in common with other genres. The student should be able to understand the subtexts presented in these genres and therefore have a deeper appreciation of horror, science fiction, and superheroes. With the skills acquired from this chapter, the student should also be able to apply them to other genres or at least know how to begin exploring other genres, such as fantasy or romance.

## FURTHER READING AND SOURCES

Alighieri, Dante. *Dante's Inferno,* Bantam Classics, 1982.

Asimov, Isaac. *Bicentennial Man*, Orion Books, 2000.

Butler, Octavia. *Dawn,* Aspect, 1985.

Card, Orson Scott. *Ender's Game,* Tor Science Fiction, 1994.

Creed, Barbara. *The Monstrous Feminine,* Routledge, 1993.

Haraway, Donna. *Simians, Cyborgs and Women: The Reinvention of Nature,* Routledge, 1990.

Homer, *The Odyssey,* Signet Classics, 2011.

Kristeva, Julia. *Powers of Horror: An Essay on Abjection*, Columbia University Press, 1982.

Nietzsche, Friedrich. *Thus Spake Zarathustra*, Cambridge University Press, 2006.

O'Neill, Megan. *Popular Culture: Perspectives for Readers and Writers,* Wadsworth, 2001.

# CHAPTER 4

# Humor and Comedy

Humor and comedy are used in many aspects of popular culture. Stand-up comedy is both one of the most simple and powerful forms of comic expression. The comedy genre in film is the most frequently made of all the contemporary genres. Sit-coms appear regularly on prime-time television together with mock-news programs and are followed by late-night talk shows. Even commercials often take the forms of comic expression. Comedy is expressed on Internet sites, T-shirts, bumper stickers, and newspaper cartoons. In the work force, comic banter is considered important for good human interaction as it is in domestic settings.

Despite the importance and frequent use of comedy, it is not taken seriously among many critics and philosophers, unless the line of political correctness is crossed. Yet many major figures in history have recognized the mysterious and provocative aspects of humor. Sigmund Freud wrote an entire book on the psychological aspects of humor. He was following by Henri Bergson. The slapstick master Charles Chaplin was admired by Picasso, Gandhi, and Einstein. In fine art, music, and literature we see frequent uses of humor. Leonardo's *Mona Lisa* is known for her enigmatic smile. Brawling scenes and "merry companies" appear often in the paintings of the Dutch masters for comic effect. The classical symphonies of Mozart, Haydn, and even Beethoven are full of ironic and playful melodic gestures and incongruous harmonies, which have often been interpreted as humorous. During the darkest years of the Black Plague (1340s) the writer Boccaccio found time to tell some of the funniest stories of the Middle Ages in *The Decameron*.

The heavy-weight comic was discovered, developed, and monumentalized in such figures as Cervantes's Sancho Panza, Shakespeare's Jack Falstaff, and Breugel's peasants. These are only a few examples of how important comedy has been to our culture. In this chapter, we will examine the concepts and theories of humor and the various forms of comedy and see how they are used in popular culture.

## ☐ DEFINITION AND ORIGIN

Humor is the word used to describe the active agent that causes one to smile or laugh. Although it is not quite certain whether it is an emotion or something else, the connection of humor to pleasure is undeniable. It seems that humor is only achieved when the survival instincts of "fight or flight" are put at bay. And yet, it has appeared even during the desperate circumstances of the Holocaust and the Nazi *Anschluss*. When Sigmund Freud was forced to leave Austria when the Nazis invaded, he left a note that stated, "To whom it may concern: I can heartily recommend the Gestapo to anyone."[1]

Comedy is the dramatic form that provides the vehicle for humor. At a more complex level, comedy takes the form of plays and movies; at a lesser complex level comedy can appear as simple jokes. In addition, comedy can be subdivided into subgenres such as satire or simple farce. In film, there is slapstick and screwball comedy, romantic comedy, and the more recent "geek comedies" such as *Juno* and *Superbad*.

Scientists believe that humor evolved from the need for play. Smiling is considered an evolvement from a signal that invites play. In effect, smiling is a mock bearing of teeth to indicate to the other person that one is willing to play without real aggression. Similarly, laughing evolved from mock barking or the grunting that is noticeable in animal play.

## ☐ THEORIES OF HUMOR

The theories of comedy and theory are varied. The ancient Greeks were the first to study humor and comedy. Plato, for example, believed that the pleasure arising from humor results from the feeling of superiority the spectator feels in relationship to bad human behavior. The humor philosopher John Morreall calls this theory the "superiority theory" and considers it somewhat flawed and dated (Morreall, 4–9). Morreall names two other theories: the incongruous theory and the relief theory. The incongruous theory explains humor as irrational while the relief theory proposes that humor is an outlet for psychological tension.

## The Superiority Theory: Human Behavior below Normal Lines

The basic idea of this theory is expressed in the German word *Schadenfreude* (shameful pleasure), which has been adopted into the English language as well. We feel pleasure because we enjoy seeing the suffering and humiliation of others. For this reason, humor takes on an unethical component. Seeing people falling down or having a pie thrown in their face causes a sudden surge of superiority in the spectator, as explained by Thomas Hobbes: "Sudden glory, is the passion which makes those grimaces called laughter."[2] *Schadenfreude* reflects Hobbes's pessimistic philosophy regarding human life being nasty, short, and brutal. This theory explains why many characters in comedies are lower class and why characters in tragedies are higher class. The descent of a nobleman from a high station often, as Aristotle noted, produces pity. However, Aristotle claimed that comedy is human behavior below normal conditions and without pain. This is why Charlie Chaplin more often plays a tramp than a wealthy nobleman. Even outside of class distinctions, comic characters play incompetent underdogs such as Maxwell Smart and Jacques Clousseau. If the characters are upper class, then the comic element shifts from the character flaws to the manners themselves. Such is the case in the Jane Austin novels and the many films based on them.

Violence plays a central part in the superiority theory of comedy. The levels and types of violence, however, differ. Circus clowns, for example, perform a kind of slapstick stylization of violence. Such stylization buffers the otherwise painful elements. During the Silent Era of film, the lack of sound effects further softened the realism of violence in the slapstick masterworks of Chaplin and Keaton. Therefore, there existed a knowledge in the viewer that the slapstick clowns were professionals able to present the illusion of violence. Such cartoon violence, thus, does not support the superiority theory as much as real violence.

The *Jackass* films, perhaps, lend themselves best to this theory. The documentary nature of the films alerts the viewers that the self-inflicted violence is real. Even though the performers are professional, to some extent, they are willing to endure pain for the success of their product. And the successfulness of their product shows that much of popular culture enjoys masochistic clowns. Unlike most comedies, these films are not staged or simulated. There is no narrative where unintentional violence occurs. Instead, the string of violent stunts and self-mutilations are what the public consumes. Many find this type of comedy distasteful and only a step above paying homeless people to fight for entertainment. However, their fiscal success shows that the superiority theory of humor cannot be dismissed as a relic of the past.

**Case Study: The Freak Show and *Dinner for Schmucks***

In many ways, the appeal of the *Jackass* films bear a similarity to the "freak shows" popular before the counter-culture movement of the 1960s made them politically incorrect. In 1932, Tod Browning made a horror film called *Freaks* that concerned a traveling freak show. *Freaks* posited that normal, beautiful people can display characteristics that are even more freakish or ugly than the freaks themselves. Two such normal people try to defraud and even kill one of the freaks with a large fortune. The freaks band together and get their revenge. MGM produced the film in an attempt to jump on the horror train that Universal had built a year earlier with *Dracula*, also directed by Browning. *Freaks* gave MGM more than they bargained for, and to this day it remains controversial. Even though it was planned as a horror film, the intentional comic effects at the expense of the "freaks" are undeniable. When a hermaphrodite (a person born with both sex organs), for example, is kissed, a person says, "I think she enjoyed that," while another person answers, "But I don't think he did." The shocking moral flaws of *Freaks* would make such a film being made today problematic. When Ben Stiller portrayed a mentally retarded person in *Tropic Thunder* (2008), the performance created a magnet for groups attacking it as insensitive to persons with disabilities. We will examine the ethical issues of humor later in this chapter.

The film *Dinner for Schmucks* (2010) reveals a similar "who are the real freaks?" theme that is apparent in *Freaks*. But since "freaks" are no longer permissible targets, nerds have taken their place. *Dinner for Schmucks* is about Tim Conrad (played by Paul Rudd), an ambitious businessman. He works for a boss who enjoys organizing "dinners for winners," which are actually "dinners for idiots." Tim's boss invites employees to bring an idiot the dinner for a secret competition for the biggest idiot. Tim brings Barry

(*continued*)

© MGM/Photofest

Tod Browning's *Freaks*

Speck (played by Steve Carell). Tim, never comfortable with the dinner
activity, learns no amount of business success is worth humiliating other
people and that the biggest idiot is his boss. Although there is a romantic
comedy woven into the story, the film is primarily a "geek comedy." In a
geek comedy, the moral messages are used to balance the *Schadenfreude* of
laughing at nerds. However, without the *Schadenfreude*, the comic effect
of a geek comedy is not as high. While the dinner maybe morally repre-
hensible, the audience finds the humor at the expense of the "idiots" just
as funny as Tim's boss.

## The Incongruous Theory: Humor as Irony and Absurdity

Toward the turn of the twentieth century, the theory that humor was an act
of *Schadenfreude* became attacked by philosophers. Henri Bergson noted that
most people do not laugh when accidents happen in real life, but, rather, feel
a need to help the person. He proposed that in order to feel the humor from
a violent accident one must feel a detachment. Thus, in the movies, the audience knows that the comedians are not getting hurt. Moreover, the violence
is not what makes the audience laugh. Instead, Bergson notes, we laugh at
the incongruity. Chaplin's tramp character, for example, was more endearing

to audiences than the subject of ridicule. The comical subject in a Chaplin film such as *Modern Times* was the brilliant absurd and ironic antics.[3] The philosopher Arthur Schopenhauer and the essayist William Hazlitt were two of the earliest people to make a claim for this theory. For Schopenhauer, it was not the sudden glory from seeing someone else's misfortune, but "the sudden perception of incongruity between a concept and the real objects."[4] Similarly, Hazlitt states, "The essence of the laughable then is the incongruous, the disconnecting one idea from another, or the jostling of one feeling against another."[5] Hazlitt goes on to discuss humor as a quality rather than a flaw of human nature. Therefore, the Incongruous theory is not as pessimistic as the Superiority theory.

The concept of irony plays an important role in the Incongruous theory. Aristotle was the first to recognize irony in his *Poetics*, but he considered it more of an agent of tragedy rather than comedy. His definition, however, has a close resemblance to this theory because he defined irony as a reversal of expected events. Freud also echoed Aristotle in his book on comedy stating, "The essence of irony consists in imparting the very opposite of what one intended to express."[6] Irony is often mistaken for coincidence because both deal with the unexpected. However, irony is a reversal rather than a parallel occurrence. Irony occurs in tragedy, as Aristotle claimed, such as when both Oedipus and King Lear go through a series of misfortunes that leave them homeless beggars at the end of their dramas. We might expect a king to be killed or captured, but we do not expect him to become a beggar because it is the lowest of classes.

Irony is often the stuff of tabloid attention. Take, for example, the example of a German businessman who won a trophy for "husband of the year" at his work. Shortly following this, he beat his wife to death with the very trophy.[7] Whenever I mention this story, it makes people laugh; not because of the violence and death, but because of the irony.

A good example of irony as a humorous element appears in the film *What About Bob?* Basically, the film describes a renowned psychologist who is reduced to a basket case by his patient. In psychotherapy, we expect the psychologist to help the patient, or at least maintain control over the relationship. During the film, Bob Wiley (played by Bill Murray) joins his psychotherapist Leo Marvin (played by Richard Dreyfuss) at his summer vacation home. Slowly, Bob wiggles his way into the personal family life of his doctor.

Doctor Marvin becomes more resentful of Bob even as Bob becomes more endeared to Leo's wife and children. In one scene, Bob hijacks an interview from *Good Morning America*, in which Leo was supposed to promote his new book. Bob ends up looking like the professional, while Leo is seen cowering in the corner like an insecure patient. Thus, the audience sees a humorous, ironic role reversal.

## The Psychological Theory: Humor as a Release of Inner Tension

Freud's book on humor takes in account the incongruous, but claims that the real source of comical pleasure comes from the release of tension built up from mental and emotional struggles. Herbert Spencer had actually discussed this theory before Freud, but Freud linked the theory to his theories of the subconscious mind. It is not just the awareness that creates comical pleasure, but the venting of internal tensions. For Freud, humor is an aggressive display of pent-up urges; it is a more acceptable form of violence. It "overcomes the inhibitions of shame and decorum by the pleasure premium which it offers... it shatters the respect for institutions and truths in which the hearer had believed ...." (Freud, 691). The aggressive nature of humor appears to show a connection to the Superiority theory. Freud even admits as much: "it cannot be denied that... our laughing is the expression of a pleasurably perceived superiority which we adjudge to ourselves in comparison with him" (Freud, 741). However, the deeper source of comic pleasure is not Hobbes's "sudden glory" but in a psychic discharge. Freud supports this with the subject of staged comedy: "The feeling of superiority does not come into existence in the other when he knows that the actor is only shamming, and this furnishes us a good new proof that the comic is independent in principle of the feeling of superiority" (Freud, 744). Indeed, one does not feel pleasure because they think that Charlie Chaplin and Bill Murray are idiots. Instead, they enjoy the assault on laws and social manners. Chaplin's foes are often policemen, and the opposite to Murray's Bob character is an authority in psychology. In children, "bathroom humor" is used to vent off the feelings that proper society suppress. Thus, for this theory, many types of humor are forms of anarchy. The comedies of the Marx brothers are a good example of high society brought down by the anarchy of comedy.

## Case Study: Bathroom Humor and The Sex Comedy

Obscene and offensive humor dates back to the ancient Greeks. Sexual pleasure and comedy were often intermingled. Aristophanes wrote comedies with overt sexuality. His *Lysistrata* is a masterpiece that also happens to be a sex comedy. In the play, the Athenian and Spartan women decide to deny their husbands and lovers any sex until they stop the war they are fighting against each other. The phrase "love conquers all" was aimed at the gods, who, being unable to die, were the subject a lewd comedy. Zeus frequently fell into extramarital affairs, and because his wife, Hera, was the goddess of marriage, the myths provided ironic humor. During the Middle Ages, sexual comedy was repressed until the disasters of the fourteenth century brought a wave of pessimism and distrust in moral authority. Chaucer and, especially, Boccaccio wrote risqué stories of sexual and scatological events. During the Enlightenment (1700–1800) religion fell under attack, and authors and artists felt free to express sexual humor in paintings and novels.

In popular culture, the sex comedy and bathroom humor is relatively recent. Censorship organization such as the Catholic League of Decency and the Production Code kept a tight control of subject matter in films from the 1930s to 1950s. Sexual comedy was moribund or substituted with "screwball comedy." A screwball comedy uses serious actors instead of the clown-type personas and puts them through farcical situations. Thus, Cary Grant and Katherine Hepburn become the subject of comedy in *Bringing Up Baby* and *The Philadelphia Story*. In these films, slapstick is the only form of physicality allowed. This tight hold on sexual material loosened during the 1960s under the weight of free-speech protests and the sexual revolution.

It was during the 1960s that Mike Nichols directed *The Graduate* (1967), one of the first sex comedies to break into mainstream cinema. *The Graduate* is about a college graduate named Ben (played by Dustan Hoffman) who has an affair with Mrs. Robinson, an older married neighbor woman (played by Anne Bancroft, who was married to Mel Brooks until her death). Trans-generational sex has only been accepted in Hollywood if the female has been younger than the male lead. *Sunset Blvd.* is a Noir exception. The comic aspects result from Ben's naiveté in sexual matters contrasted with Mrs. Robinson's expertise. Yet Mrs. Robinson is burned out in matters of love and is interested in Ben only for the sex. During their first meeting in a hotel room, Ben shows an unnecessary and clumsy way of

(*continued*)

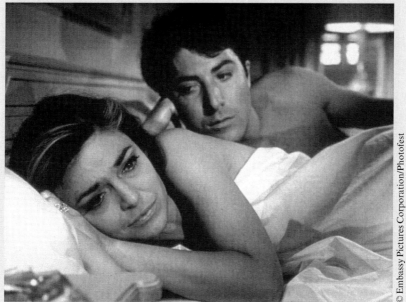

*© Embassy Pictures Corporation/Photofest*

Anne Bancroft and Dustin Hoffman in *The Graduate*

seducing Mrs. Robinson. He kisses her right after she takes a drag on her cigarette, and she is forced to wait until after the kiss to exhale.

However, *The Graduate* is more than a sex comedy; it mirrors the youth movement's distrust of the older generation. Mrs. Robinson is an alcoholic and has lost any passion for life. She has grabbed onto Ben in a desperate attempt to feel young again. However, she cannot share Ben's love for life, despite the quirky way he expresses himself. When Ben pursues Mrs. Robinson's daughter Elaine, their affair is exposed. Ben tries to win Elaine back but is thwarted by her parents, who push her into a marriage with a doctor. At the end, Ben crashes Elaine's wedding and, while taking Elaine's hand, fights off the congregation with a large cross. The congregation of older people reflects an angry hoard of demonic vampires.

Although *The Graduate* would not have been allowed to be made 10 years earlier, it avoids the scatological content of many comedies made in the decades to come. The *Austin Powers* films, for example, are loaded with raunchy gags. As satirical travesties of 1960's spy films, they exaggerate the loose morals of the James Bond persona. The numerous party films made in the mold of *Animal House* often use bathroom humor.

## ☐ SUBGENRES OF COMEDY

In order to understand the nuances of comedy, we can divide and categorize the divisions into subgenres. There are four basic subgenres: free comedy, critical comedy, great comedy, and dark comedy.[8] Free and critical comedy are opposites of the same coin. While free comedy lacks any social allusions, critical comedy targets social issues. When comedy reaches a level of "greatness" either by deep characterization or the use of tragic themes it can be called "great comedy." The classic comedies of Shakespeare and Molière conform to this type. In a similar vein as great comedy, dark comedy often uses tragic elements or moral issues, but as targets of mockery. Because of its gritty nature and willingness to attack sacred values, it is one of the most fascinating forms of comedy.

### Free Comedy: Holiday for the Super Ego

Free comedy is an escape from the stresses of daily life. It, therefore, avoids the challenging aspects of other forms of entertainment. Because of this escapist quality, it has been called "holiday for the Super Ego."[9] Free comedy includes mostly farcical gags and slapstick. Occasionally, free comedy may move into the other subgenres. But, if the comedy focuses on gags and slapstick, it is considered free comedy. Thus, when *The Simpsons* do their "Tree House of Horror," there may be elements of the grotesque and dark comedy. However, *The Simpsons* and the other animated sitcoms remain primarily free comedy.

### Case Study: The Prime-Time Sitcom

*The Honeymooners* and the *I Love Lucy* series were the first successful sitcoms, and both drew liberally from the silent film slapstick masters. Lucille Ball's persona took much from Charlie Chaplin. One of her most famous skits was a worker on a bottle assembly line, which was lifted from Chaplin's masterpiece *Modern Times*. Ball's character, like Chaplin's, is a good-hearted person who has trouble adapting to society. In Lucille Ball's case, she struggles adapting to marriage. Jackie Gleason's persona was developed from Oliver Hardy, who also had a charming nature that was frequently interrupted by fits of anger and ventings of hot air. Both

*(continued)*

sitcoms were, thus, an outgrowth of the one-reelers shown before feature films in the theaters. All sitcoms owe much to Charlie Chaplin because he was the first screen comic artist to develop a character rather than simply perform a string of gags, which is what Mack Sennett (his employer) had actually wanted.

Sitcoms (short for "situational comedy") are generally free comedies because they allow the viewer to escape and avoid challenging him or her with loaded issues. The "cute" sitcoms (that frequently use children and young adults) such as *Full House* and the many Disney Channel shows are mostly in this benign subgenre. *M\*A\*S\*H* is a good example because it is a watered-down television "spin-off" of Robert Altman's dark comedy film *MASH*. The television show sterilized the edgy "suicide-is-painless" theme and replaced it with allusions to the Marx Brothers and other farcical elements. Therefore, the dark comedy became a free comedy, more suitable for a television audience rather than the film's targeted anti-Vietnam audience.

During the 1980s, *The Cosby Show* helped to establish the "cute" sitcoms that *Full House* and *Who's the Boss?* drew from. Bill Cosby based much of the material on his successful stand-up comedy, with the addition of children. The phenomenal success of *The Cosby Show* was primarily due to the extended target audience. Whereas 1970s sitcoms targeted adults with *All In The Family* and *Barney Miller*, *The Cosby Show* added the cute and playful antics of children, the awkward self-discovery themes of teens, and pit it all against the flawed but loving father figure. Bill Cosby's character struggles to understand the silly things his children do, while at the same time his own midlife issues occasionally make him just as childish. Although Cosby's television family (the Huxtables) are African American, the stories rarely broach racial problems or issues. At the same time, it was one of the first sitcoms that showed an African American family as affluent and successful as any white American-dream sitcom family. *The Jeffersons* is another example.

Adult issues rarely appeared in the family sitcoms until the 1990s and into the new millennium. *The Simpsons* was one of the first to mix sexual themes in a family sitcom. Because it was also a cartoon, it generated controversy. The sexual life of Homer and Marge is often the source for humor, as when Bart catches them in the act. However, the rebelliousness of Bart was the main target for conservative critics. *Everybody Loves Raymond* was another popular sitcom that did not avoid the sexual tensions and activities of Raymond and his wife. *Two and a Half Men* also

(*continued*)

contrasted the adult world with childhood for comic effect. Despite the move away from *Brady Bunch* morality, sitcoms remain free comedy.

The British sitcom has also proved successful on the world stage of popular culture. British sitcoms have been bolder than American sitcoms in subject matter and have been more frequently extended to critical and even dark comedy. The sitcom *Black Adder,* for example, has four seasons that correspond to four time periods. Each of the periods and seasons end with the main character violently killed. Edmund Black Adder is an ambitious noble villain surrounded by idiots that tend to ruin his evil plans. Much of the comedy is Black Adder (played by Rowan Atkinson) revealing his inept companions' idiocy. Atkinson shows his versatility and ability to master the dead-pan humor of Buster Keaton in his later sitcom, *Mr. Bean*, which developed into two films. One of his episodes is a reworking of Keaton's feature film *The Camera Man*, in which Keaton, while on a date, loses his swimming trunks after falling off a platform in a swimming pool.

*Keeping Up Appearances* is a remarkable British sitcom that combines the low-class versus high-class "comedy-of-manners" with the brilliant characterization of Hyacinth Bucket, played by Patricia Routledge (she always reminds her friends and associates that her last name is pronounced "Bookay"). Hyacinth is a middle-class woman at the beginning of retirement age with grand designs of upward mobility. Her continual posturing and showcasing of her fine things annoy neighbors and friends. Her sister, Daisy, and her husband, Onslow, are the antithesis, class-conscious wise, to Hyacinth. Their yard has a rusting, broken-down car that serves as a dog house. The embarrassment that Hyacinth shows, whenever her low-class relatives appear at her social engagements, provides much of the comedy.

*Father Ted* is another British sitcom that uses a larger amount of critical comedy. In this sitcom, three Irish Catholic priests are isolated on an island, most likely because of their antisocial personalities. Father Ted Crilly is the most down-to-earth character. Although he is a priest sworn to celibacy, he frequently fantasizes hustling women. Father Dougal McGuire is a younger priest who often loses his hold on reality, and yet considers the Christian stories as unreal as his fantasies. Father Jack Hacket is a libidinous alcoholic whose temper frequently explodes at the slightest thing. In one episode Father Hacket throws a wine bottle into the television screen when it wakes him from his hangover slumber. *Father Ted* evokes comedy through the disruption of proper manners. One of the best examples occurs

(*continued*)

when Ted and several other priests get lost in the women's lingerie department of a department store. In order to escape without notice, they treat the situation as if they are in a no-man's-land war zone.

With *Red Dwarf*, Britain has produced the darkest sitcom ever made. *Red Dwarf* is a bold and brilliant sci-fi cross-over sitcom that depicts the last human (named Dave Lister) to survive the extinction of his species. He was placed in suspended animation as a punishment, and because of this, he survived a deadly plague outbreak. For 3 million years Dave remained in suspended animation until he was revived by the computer. He soon discovers that he is the only creature on the ship except for a life form that evolved from his pregnant cat. A hologram image of a long-dead crew member and the ship's computer are the only other characters that keep him company. In a later season, they are joined by a stranded android. Much of the comedy occurs from Dave's character. He is the last human in existence and is a disgusting slob. *Red Dwarf* combines funny gags with thought-provoking science fiction.

The rise of sitcom popularity is noticeable in the inclusion of sitcom elements within 1-hour "serious" prime-time television shows. Sitcom antics are especially apparent in medical prime-time soap operas such as *House* and *Scrubs*. The comic effect in *House* results from a genius diagnostician who lacks any social skills or bedside manners. Doctor House is a Sherlock Holmes character, as both have drug addictions and make other professionals look incompetent. Although the drug addiction is not treated in a comical manner, the contrast of the genius persona with the flaws of "normal" people makes for comic effect. The antisocial comical character of *House* has been replicated in *Psych* and *Bones* to some extent.

## Critical Comedy: Humor as Social Correction

Comedy can serve as a way to expose the absurdities of society. Such comedy is called critical comedy because it often attacks social elements that are normally taken more seriously. Because of its aggressive and potentially offensive nature, critical comedy tends to be stronger than free comedy and is used more sparingly and carefully by the products of popular culture. Much of critical comedy comes in the form of satire. The word *satire* comes from the ancient Greek mythical monsters "satyrs" who were half-man, half-beast. The ancient Greek satyr plays were performed in dramatic festivals following a trilogy of tragedies. Often, the satyr plays used the serious themes of the myths and tragedies as subject matter to mock.

The loud and exaggerated camp actors and situations found in popular culture are frequently the subject of satire. Michael Jackson, for example, is the subject of Weird Al Yankovic parodies. Britney Spears has also been the subject of satirical skits on the NBC weekend comedy show, *Saturday Night Live*. Satirical mock television commercials have also been shown on *Saturday Night Live*.

Because critical comedy concerns social flaws, it has been regarded by some as a form of social correction. John Morreall notes that it was the humorists who first attacked Hitler and the Nazi party in print (119). Bonamy Dobrée claims:

> This is the classical comedy from which much modern comedy is derived. It sets out definitely to correct manners by laughter; it strives to "cure excess." This comedy, then, tends to repress eccentricity, exaggeration, any deviation from the normal: it wields the Meredithian "sword of common sense." It expresses the general feeling of the community, for which another name is morality. (453)

According to William Hazlitt, ridicule is a "test of truth." In other words, we laugh because the comical characters and situations do not conform to what society regards as truth or at least as acceptable truth (Hazlitt, 76). The idea that laughter targets error will be an important consideration when we discuss the ethical issues of comedy.

### Case Study: The Films of Mel Brooks

Almost every film that Mel Brooks directs can be considered a satire on a film genre. *The History of the World, Part 1* satirizes the period film, except for one scene that is a mock musical (similar to *The Producers*). *High Anxiety* pokes fun at Alfred Hitchcock films; its title is a comical rewording of *Vertigo*. Both *Young Frankenstein* and *Dracula: Dead and Loving It* target the horror genre. *Spaceballs* (1987) uses science fiction films, mainly *Star Wars* (1977), as models for satire. *Blazing Saddles* (1974) is a mock western, and *Robin Hood: Men in Tights* (1993) exploits the Robin Hood films. In these films, Brooks brings out the excessive and ludicrous natures of the original films.

(*continued*)

The growing serious nature of musicals during the 1960s made for effective comedy in both *The Producers* and in the Inquisition scene of *The History of the World, Part 1* (1981). Musicals were light comedies from their beginnings as operettas and as "backstage" musicals. Operettas were only as serious as the folktale would allow, and back-stage musicals were pure farce and fantasy. When *The Sound of Music* (1965) won Best Picture, it showed that sober history and light musicals could coexist. It was later followed by another serious musical and Oscar winner called *Oliver* (1968), directed by the equally serious director Carol Reed. The serious musical even tackled religion in the late 1960s and early 1970s with such titles as *Godspell* (1971) and *Joseph and the Amazing Technocolor Dreamcoat* (1968).

*The Producers* (1968), however, showed that serious history and light musicals make a great recipe for comedy. It concerns a failed Broadway producer whose Shakespearean musicals (one based on *Hamlet* called *Happy Boy*, and another based on *King Lear* called *King Leer*) flopped. In order to make a quick fortune, he and an accountant decide to produce a sure-fire flop and keep the unnoticed excessive fortune raised for the musical. To make sure the musical will fail, they agree to produce a musical that celebrates Hitler and the Nazis called *Springtime for Hitler*. In an ironic twist, *Springtime for Hitler* is interpreted as a comedy by the audience and becomes a hit. The producers go to jail and continue to produce musicals from behind bars. The climax of the film is the opening number of the musical that shows Nazis in uniform dancing and singing ridiculous lyrics like, "Don't be stupid, be a smarty, come and join the Nazi party." One can see two levels of critical comedy in *The Producers*, one that attacks the absurdity of musical theater taking on serious themes, and being able to see the Nazis lampooned as flower-loving hippies.

The musical section in the Inquisition scene in *History of the World Part 1* attacks the torture of the Spanish inquisitors during the sixteenth century by putting an elaborate, Busby Berkeley-like, choreographed musical in a torture-chamber setting. This scene works better as an example of dark comedy; however, the critical comedy exposes the absurdities of the serious musicals.

It is not difficult to mix horror with humor. Roman Polanski combined slapstick and Gothic horror in *The Fearless Vampire Killers* (1967), and Jack Nicolson is both terrifying and funny at the same time in Stanley Kubrick's *The Shining* (1980). Sometimes a horror film's campy dialogue, makeup, acting, and directing can produce unintentional humor. For Mel Brooks, it is this camp in Gothic horror that makes for effective comedy.

*(continued)*

*Young Frankenstein* (1974) stresses the exaggerated style of the Universal Studios *Frankenstein* films made during the 1930s. *Son of Frankenstein* (1938) was the film that provided most of the material for Brooks's film. This classic Universal film includes Bela Lugosi as Igor. To say his performance was over the top would be an understatement. Thus, leaping from Bela Lugosi to Marty Feldman's funny depiction of Igor (pronounced eye-gor) was not that big of a leap. The only difference between the police inspectors is that Brooks has his inspector Kemp wear a monocle on his eye patch. Both inspectors stick spare darts into their wooden arms during their dart-throwing contests with Dr. Frankenstein. Shot in black and white, *Young Frankenstein* is as much homage to the Universal classics as it is a satire.

*Dracula: Dead and Loving It* (1995) satirizes older and more recent vampire films, but in a manner similar to *Young Frankenstein*. Much of the original *Dracula* (1931) with Bela Lugosi is used for comedy. In the original film, Lugosi uses his piercing stare and fluid hand gestures to control people, especially lower-class servants. In *Dead and Loving It*, the count, played by Leslie Nielsen, struggles to get the servants to follow exact orders. Or sometimes he has trouble honing his telepathic powers on the right person. However, the more recent Francis Ford Coppola film *Bram Stoker's Dracula* (1992) was also a perfect target for Brooks. The most expected element of the Coppola film was Dracula's independent shadow. It seemed to become an extension of Dracula's real desires when it tries to strangle Jonathan Harker in the opening scenes. In Brooks's version, Dracula has trouble controlling his shadow from doing embarrassing things, such as humping his dance partner's shadow. Leslie Nielsen, having made the *Naked Gun* movies, was no stranger to film satires when he played Brooks's *Dracula*. It was the combination of Nielsen's other film satires and *Dead and Loving It* that led to the many *Scary Movie* films and their clones.

## Case Study: Mockumentaries and Mock News Programs

At the beginning of Mel Brooks's *The History of the World, Part 1*, a depiction of cave-dwelling humans is presented with a voice-over narrative by Orson Welles, creating a style reminiscent of the documentary. The seriousness of the narrative is contrasted with the silliness of the visuals. The great comic personality Sid Caesar plays the main caveman. At one point, Welles narrates the creation of fire while the visuals show Sid Caesar striking two rocks together over some kindling. A bit later, another caveman, holding a

*(continued)*

lit torch, moves into the camera frame to see what Caesar is doing. Caesar looks at the torch, takes it, heats up one of his rocks, and throws the rock into the kindling without, of course, producing fire. Thus, the first part of this film can be considered a mock documentary or a mockumentary.

Mockumentaries can be traced back—in spirit—to the ancient Greeks and the beginning of criticism. The effective critic uses humor to expose the flaws of the subject he or she is reviewing. Political cartoons have a mock documentary nature. The mockumentary, however, is regarded as a film subgenre that began with some of the shorts played before the features before television. The mature Goofy cartoons by Walt Disney were almost always in the mockumentary style. Occasionally, the Monty Python Flying Circus episodes become mockumentaries.

Mockumentaries, however, do not become feature length until the success of Rob Reiner's *This is Spinal Tap* (1984). Rob Reiner, the son of another great comic personality, Carl Reiner, plays the filmmaker Marty DiBergi who follows the rock band Spinal Tap on a comeback tour. We see clips from the fake band's genesis that reflects television performances of The Beatles. The comedy appears with the contrast between the documentary style and the band's obscene lyrics, stupid remarks, and performance mishaps. One of the film's most impressive qualities is how close it comes to mimicking the 1980's heavy metal bands. In Britain, a mock version of The Beatles called *The Rutles* also became the subject of a mockumentary in 1978.

Harry Shearer, Christopher Guest, and Michael McKean in Rob Reiner's *This Is Spinal Tap*

(*continued*)

Three of the main members of Spinal Tap—Christopher Guest, Harry Shearer, and Michael McKean—went on to make several other remarkable mockumentaries. *Waiting for Guffman* (1997) was made by Guest and depicts a small-town community's dramatic production celebrating the town's (the fictional Blain, Missouri) 150th anniversary. Members of the new play called *Red, White, and Blain*, are led to believe that a Broadway talent scout named Guffman will be coming to see their performance. When Guffman never arrives, the play members are left with their disappointments. As with *Spinal Tap*, this film brings out the contrast between the documentary style, the goofy play, and how serious the play members react to the situation. Later Guest mockumentaries play on similar contrasts. *Best in Show* (2000) is a dog show mockumentary that exposes the maniacal dog owners and the extremes to which they are willing to go to win the competition. *A Mighty Wind* (2003) has a less critical edge in showing washed-up folk singers from the 1960s coming together to perform a gala concert in memory of their producer.

The success of mockumentaries has affected documentaries as well. Many of the documentaries of even serious subjects such as Michael Moore's *Bowling for Columbine* and *Fahrenheit 9/11* have been quick to emphasize idiocy and employ bullhorn tactics. The same can be said for Morgan Spurlock's *Supersize Me*, which shows Spurlock torturing himself with a fast-food diet in order to make a serious point, which most people already know.

Television news became a target for critical comedy beginning with the late-night shows. *Saturday Night Live* has included a news section with almost every lineup since the 1970s. Like mockumentaries and satire, the mock television news programs evoke dead-pan humor with the combination of serious and ridiculous. Today, *The Daily Show with Jon Stewart* and *The Colbert Report* with Stephen Colbert use the anchorman platform to deliver their comedy. On one level, the anchorman comedian exposes the flaws of television news that cloak the struggle for high ratings with the illusion of serious journalism. On another level, the mock news programs showcase the ridiculous behavior of politicians and celebrities. Mockumentaries and mock news programs are perfect examples of critical comedy.

© Comedy Central/Photofest

Jon Stewart

## Great Comedy: Humor as High Art

Sometimes a work of comedy reaches a certain level that distinguishes it from other works. A work of comedy reaches this level because the story or the characters become as moving and complicated as they are in tragedies. Thus Don Quixote and Sancho Panza are not merely clowns; they offer a rich character study that reveal universal truths. Don Quixote has deluded himself to the point where he sees the most ordinary objects and people as elements in an epic knight's legend. His lack of regard of the practical for the extraordinary has given us the term *quixotic.* Don Quixote is a loveable character regardless of his illusions. He treats the lowliest peasant as a fellow knight, and, thus, has no prejudices. One passage shows Don Quixote discoursing on the duties of a knight to a group of peasants around a camp fire.[10] As he goes on with the knight mystique, the peasants simply stare at him with blank expressions.

Great comedy often crosses over to share characteristics of tragedy and epic. *Don Quixote* can be considered a satire on the epic with knights, quests, and heroic feats. Molière's comedies, such as *The Miser*, can evoke tragic emotions like pity. The plays of Anton Chekhov are difficult to label tragedy or comedy because the characters live absurd and pointless lives. Great comedy, then, is not simply a string of gags but can exhibit as much or more poetry and philosophy as any other form of high art.

### Case Study: The Road Comedy

Road films depict a group that travels together usually for a common geographical goal. They often take the form of comedies or adventures or both. Their narrative type is episodic, meaning they contain segments that are more independent and loosely connected. As such, they belong to the epic poem tradition of *The Epic of Gilgamesh, The Odyssey,* and *The Divine Comedy. O Brother, Where Art Thou?* (2000) by the Cohen brothers stated in the credits that Homer's *Odyssey* was the basis for the film. Yet, the influence of the *Odyssey* is so pervasive in our culture that any travelogue type narrative owes its existence to Homer, satire or not. *Odyssey* is a kind of comedy, especially in relation to the more tragic and serious *Iliad*. Road films, however, are not always comedies (e.g., *Easy Rider*). But if there is a category in popular culture that best fits great comedy, it is the road film.

*(continued)*

The road comedy can take on elements of tragedy as shown in the 1963 epic *It's a Mad, Mad, Mad, Mad, World.* Stanley Kramer, who normally directs bold dramas like *Inherit the Wind* (1960) and *Guess Who's Coming to Dinner?* (1967), applied his serious talent to this influential comedy. The film shows a police captain (played by Spencer Tracy) following a group of people who learn where a stash of stolen money is buried. Most of the film deals with the farcical way in which the greedy suspects lose any sense of civility in their struggle to be the first to find the stash. The tragedy occurs when the police captain's family unravels while he is about to close the case. In addition, he is denied a pension raise despite his spotless record and years of selfless service to the force. When the disappointments become too much, he decides to take the stash for himself and escape to Mexico. Right after his decision to take the cash, the police chief blackmails the politicians in order to get the captain's pension tripled. Therefore, tragic timing brings a sense of pathos as he is, of course, caught; had he just waited and remained clean for a few more moments, his reward would have arrived. The laughter produced by the mishaps, is, thus, a guilty pleasure in the context of the captain's tragedy.

Most often road comedies deal with human relationships, and the characters learn the values of friendship despite their differences. Two films best show this emphasis on human bonding: *Planes, Trains, and Automobiles* (1987) and *Little Miss Sunshine* (2006). In *Planes, Trains, and Automobiles* two different businessmen end up sharing their misfortunes when their flight is diverted from their Chicago destination to Wichita before Thanksgiving. Steve Martin plays Neal Page, a rich, big-shot marketer, and John Candy plays Del Griffith, a charismatic albeit poorer traveling salesman. Neal is conservative, refined, and used to fine things. Del is just the opposite: talkative, impulsive, and a slob. At first, Neal wants nothing to do with Del, but slowly learns to appreciate his human qualities. Eventually, Neal learns that Del is a lonely widower and will be spending Thanksgiving alone. Neal brings Del to spend Thanksgiving with his family even though Del put him through hell on their journey. The farcical accidents produce the humor, but the characters and their interactions make the film more meaningful. This does not mean that the comical aspect is less important. The film succeeds because of a careful balance between the drama and the farce.

The same careful balance between drama and farce appears in *Little Miss Sunshine*. In this film, a dysfunctional Arizona family is thrown together in a malfunctioning VW bus in order to take a seven-year-old girl named Olive to southern California for the "Little Miss Sunshine" girl beauty pageant. Olive has a close relationship to her drug addict grandfather (played by

*(continued)*

Alan Arkin), who coaches her to do a suggestive burlesque dance for the pageant. Olive's teenage brother is a follower of Nietzsche and has taken a vow of silence until his Air Force matriculation. Olive's gay uncle (played by Steve Carell) failed in a suicide attempt and is under the watchful eye of his sister. Olive's father is an idealistic motivational speaker whose life does not mirror his teachings.

As in *Planes, Trains, and Automobiles,* the characters learn to accept each other and their differences, and they become united in helping Olive achieve her goal. When Olive starts doing her dance, the snobby pageant authorities are

© Fox Searchlight/Photofest

Abigail Breslin in *Little Miss Sunshine*

outraged. In order to protect Olive from embarrassment, the other members of the family join her in the dance, including her idealistic father. Although she loses the pageant and is banned from all future southern California pageants, Olive's family shows her their pride, admiration, and love. There is much in *Little Miss Sunshine* that is critical comedy and even dark comedy, but it is the powerful human and family relationships that make the film qualify as a great comedy.

## Dark Comedy: When Humor Becomes Disturbing

The goal of most humor is to produce pleasure. So when a comedy does just the opposite and unsettles us, it produces a reversal or negative effect. Dark comedy (also called black comedy) is the term that describes when comedy makes us laugh while disturbing us at the same time. It is a relatively recent type of comedy as most comedies were restricted to Aristotle's theory of human behavior below the norm, but without pain. Perhaps one of the first writers to employ dark comedy was the Renaissance author Niccolò Machiavelli. One of his short stories called "Belfagor" tells of a demon from hell that is sent up to Earth by Satan in order to find out if marriage is worse than hell. Belfagor marries and over the years discovers that hell is much more preferable than marriage. In order to get sent back home, he has himself declared a witch and is burned at the stake, rejoicing while he is executed. Where critical comedy seeks to expose the flaws of characters and organizations, dark comedy exposes life experiences and often life itself as a pathetic joke. Likewise, Machiavelli's play *Mandragola* is a comedy that shows how prone human nature is to corruption and how morals and laws are illusions. Machiavelli's pessimism is reflected in his most famous work called *The Prince*. This is a political treatise

Machiavelli

that stresses that a prince needs to be strong and to maintain control because human nature is selfish. According to Machiavelli, we generally act out in self-interest rather than according to our dedication to law and justice.

In 1924, the Surrealist author André Breton published an anthology of Dark Comedy.[11] It begins with Jonathan Swift and includes other authors such as the Marquis De Sade, Edgar Allan Poe, and Franz Kafka. Breton originally considered it to be a work that explains the concept of humor from the Surrealist's standpoint. Curiously, Machiavelli is not given any representation, and it recklessly concludes that Swift was joking in his "Modest Proposal."[12] Nevertheless, Breton's anthology shows that the Surrealists and Dadaists had a fascination for dark comedy. Many of the Surrealists and Dadaists, especially in Germany, had seen lots of death and suffering. They were not just trying to get attention when they called for a complete overthrow of all existing institutions. When the Russians proved that a people could stop a world war by overthrowing the government, Breton and his group were watching. In order to undermine the prevailing institutions, they used the most caustic form of comedy available, dark comedy.

Due to its disturbing and nihilistic nature, dark comedy is used less in popular culture than it is in art and literature. This stands to reason as the forces that produce popular art and entertainment make enough money to care about stability and thus are not interested in cutting their own throats. It can be argued, however, that the films of Robert Rodriguez, Quentin Tarantino, and Tim Burton are good examples of dark comedy. A major exception to television being exempt from featuring dark comedy is the 1950's series *Alfred Hitchcock Presents,* which, in many ways, paved the way to his masterpiece *Psycho.*

## Case Study: Monty Python

Perhaps the most effective use of dark comedy in popular culture came from the British comedy group Monty Python. Their television series called *Monty Python's Flying Circus* included skits that would have rivaled the Dadaists in absurdity. Often the skits can become dark. For example, one skit shows an Olympics for idiots. The idiots do a series of easy tasks like taking bras off mannequins. The final skit is committing suicide, which they also struggle at doing, not out of feelings of self-preservation, but out of idiocy.

Their film, *Monty Python and the Holy Grail* (1974), became an international hit and remains a cult classic. One of the gags involves a black knight whom Arthur dismembers to a stump in order to cross a bridge. Another episode shows a collection of dead bodies in a village. One of the villagers talks the body collector into taking an old man who is still alive. The collector looks around and hits the old man on the head, allowing the other person to place him on the cart of dead bodies. At one point, Sir Lancelot slaughters dozens of peaceful wedding guests because he thinks the castle is a prison for a damsel in distress. In addition to these violent moments, the film is loaded with blasphemy. When Arthur has a vision of God in the heavens, the vision is a low-budget cartoon made from clip art of medieval and Renaissance Christian imagery. At times God gets impatient with Arthur's sycophantic praises, telling him to stop averting his eyes and complaining about the "miserable songs they sing."

The blasphemy humor of *Holy Grail* pales in comparison to Monty Python's next two major films: *The Life of Brian* (1979) and *The Meaning of Life* (1983). *The Life of Brian* follows the character Brian as a kind of parallel to Jesus Christ. Brian, however, is forced into messiah-ship by circumstances beyond his control. The brutality of life during this time, such as stoning and crucifixion, are treated in a humorous manner. At the beginning of the film, a public stoning is treated with frivolity. The victim had

*(continued)*

taken the Lord's name in vain by saying aloud "Jehovah." Now that he is condemned, he dances around repeating "Jehovah" over and over again to the crowd's outrage. When the person overseeing the event inadvertently says "Jehovah" as well, the crowd stones him with a huge boulder. At the end of the film, Brian is part of a group of rebels who are crucified. While they are hanging on their crosses, they start singing and whistling "Always Look on the Bright Side of Life." This ending chorus is one of the best examples of dark comedy by combining frivolity with mass torture taken from real history. It is shocking and funny at the same time. The Python team had a difficult time finding a producer who would be brave enough to risk offending the religious public until ex-Beatles George Harrison agreed to put up the funds. Once the film appeared, it became a lightning rod for criticism from religious officials. On their talk show tour, members of the team were forced to defend the film from angry priests who had no patience for this type of humor.

*The Meaning of Life* has a looser focus than the other two films, but shows no fear of offending sensibilities. Toward the beginning of the film, two births are contrasted with each other. One shows a high-class mother and father surrounded by doctors and the latest technology. The other is a woman from "the Third World" who has her child while also doing dishes. Because they are Catholic and birth control is prohibited, their poverty-stricken home is overrun with children. Following this scene is a lavish musical number called "Sperm is Sacred." Monty Python's no-holds-barred brand of humor would go on to influence the creators of *South Park,* Trey Parker and Matt Stone.

## ☐ THE ETHICS OF COMEDY: TO LAUGH OR NOT TO LAUGH

The relationship of comedy to society reveals a paradox. On one hand it is not taken seriously at awards ceremonies and in general academia; on the other hand, a simple bad joke can be serious enough to get a person fired from their job. About 30 years ago, "Polock jokes," jokes aimed at the Polish, were popular. Few people actually believed that the Polish jokes were expressions of scorn against the Polish. If there was any nation that the United States would benefit in attacking with humor at this time, it would have been the Soviet Union or Cuba. The Polish were not considered enemies, and a person would have to be a complete idiot himself if he truly believed that the Polish were that stupid. Yet, if asked why Polish jokes were considered okay while racist jokes is were not, most people would have struggled for an explanation.

Just as most people would not believe that being Polish meant being an idiot, even the most racist person would admit that most racist jokes were exaggerations and not a realistic representation of the targeted race. However, this is the common complaint against racist or sexist jokes, that they exaggerate reality. Morreall recalls that in 2002 the British MP Ann Winterton lost her job in Parliament because she told the following joke:

> There were an Englishman, a Cuban, a Japanese man, and a Pakistani on a train. The Cuban throws a cigar out the window, saying they are ten-a-penny in his country. The Japanese man throws a Nikon camera out, saying they are ten-a-penny in his country. Then the Englishman throws the Pakistani out the window. (Morreall, 99)

This is dark comedy to be sure, and on the surface it appears racist at worst, insensitive at best. However, at a closer look the joke is not racist at all. The joke does not put down Pakistani people or even stereotype them. If anything, it puts down the Englishman as racist for murdering the Pakistani. As Morreall notes, there are multiple interpretations to a single joke. Does the fact that jokes rely on different interpretations and are clearly distortions of reality mean that any joke is okay, even racist and sexist jokes? The answer to this is definitely no.

## The Ethical Hazards and Benefits of Comedy

There are three hazards or harmful effects that humor can cause (Morreall, 102–110). The first one is that laughter can suppress real concerns. Morreall notes: "In our daily lives, we sometimes 'laugh off' a problem or criticism instead of taking appropriate action.... if my friend needs my help in controlling his alcoholism, and the next time he gets drunk I laugh at his antics instead of helping him restore self-discipline, then my humor is also irresponsible" (102). Thus, comedy can lead to negligence.

The second hazard Morreall notes is that comedy can "block compassion." History is full of examples where comedy provided a numbing effect on compassion and sensitivity. People suffering from mental retardation, physical deformities, or birth defects were frequently the subject of scornful humor in times past:

> In ancient Roman slave markets, deformed and idiotic children often brought high prices because buyers found them amusing…In fifteenth-century Paris, burning cats was a form of home entertainment. Before the French Revolution, members of the nobility would visit insane asylums to taunt the inmates, by clanking their canes across the bars.…Idi Amin is said to have cut off the limbs of one of his wives and sewn them onto the opposite sides of her body, for his own amusement. A more recent example of sadistic humor is the humiliation of prisoners by Americans in Abu Ghraib prison in Iraq. When asked why they made the men pile on top of one another naked, soldiers said that it was a joke, "just for fun." (Morreall, 104)

The numbing hazard helps us understand the nature of dark comedy as well. Much of dark comedy is meant to expose the callousness of human nature. Now the above-mentioned examples were reality examples of dark comedy. However, the artists can use imitated forms of dark comedy to expose the reality of cruel behavior. Thus, when the German Dadaists used dark comedy, it was a way to attack the real cruelty of Nazism.

Comedy can sponsor racism, which is the third hazard. This hazard is related to the other two, especially the numbing effect. Racist and sexist jokes are unethical because they disengage "us cognitively from the object of amusement" (Morreall, 105). Even though the jokes may reflect exaggerations, they reinforce prejudice by making the offence seem inoffensive. When we laugh, our critical judgment regarding the possible harm is put on hold because it would ruin the joke. Therefore, it is wrong to laugh at a sexist joke because the laughing makes the harmful effect permissible: "Putting a 'play frame' around stereotypes in a joke aestheticizes them removing them at least temporarily, from moral scrutiny. As listeners enjoy sexist and racist jokes, they let harmful stereotypes in under their moral radar. A straightforward assertion might quickly draw criticism, but an exaggerated version of a stereotype presented in a clever way will probably be simply enjoyed" (Morreall, 107).

Sacha Baron Cohen's *Borat* (2007) is a mockumentary somewhat in the manner of Christopher Guest, but uses real people for interviews. Borat

Sagdiyev is a racist journalist from Kazakhstan. We are led to believe that his uncouth behaviors and racist views are an extension of the whole country. However, rather than exposing real racism, the film presents a false history and culture of Kazakhstan. All of Cohen's research focused on southern Russia rather than Kazakhstan. In fact, most of the stereotypes presented in the film were taken from Russian propaganda and their vilification of the country. The film's racism is painful considering the violence which the country went through under the Stalinist occupation. Over a million Kazakhs were killed for their resistance. Morreall notes that by the 1970s, "Kazakhstan was the only Soviet republic in which the native people were in the minority" (107). Of course, most people watching the film would not have known this, making the burden of guilt on the filmmakers. Even though viewers would have recognized the stereotypes, *Borat* is a racist film because it makes it okay to laugh at an oppressed people. Oppression is an important distinction to make when considering comedy that singles out a group of people. Lawyer jokes are not racist because lawyers are not nor have been oppressed. Usually children do not get beat up or teased at school because their fathers are lawyers. The same could be said about doctors, Polish people, or even "rednecks."[13]

Comedy also has qualities that benefit society. Comedy enables one to keep an open mind. One may reconsider supporting a political figure because of the critical comedy waged against them. This is beneficial because the comedy allows us the freedom to criticize people in authority in a manner that direct criticism cannot do. This is one of the reasons why kings had their jesters. They were able to hear and judge the criticism without being degraded. Shakespeare gives a good example of this in *King Lear*. Studies have shown that comedy promotes creativity as well (Morreall, 112–113). Comedy can also diffuse conflict and block negative emotions.

## ☐ SUMMARY

Taking comedy seriously should not be limited to condemning the politically incorrect. Comedy is an art that warrants study as much as any other art form. The creators of entertainment in popular culture know how well comedy sells. Comedies in film are made far more often than other genres, and yet they are more misunderstood or even ignored by critics. Just as there is more to horror than being scared, there is more to comedy than laughter. The best comedies not only make us laugh, they make us think about the irony. Or they shock us into an awareness regarding the dark areas of human nature and history. Most importantly, comedy, like music, is universal to every culture. And, as such, can be an important tool for finding common ground.

---

[1] Cited in John Morreall *Comic Relief* (Massachusetts: Wiley-Blackwell, 2009), 119–124.

[2] Thomas Hobbes, "from *Leviathan*" in *The Philosophy of Laughter and Humor*. Edited by John Morreall (New York: State University of New York Press, 1987), 19.

[3] See Henri Bergson "from *Laughter*" in *The Philosophy of Laughter and Humor*. Edited by John Morreall (New York: State University of New York Press, 1987): 117–126.

[4] Arthur Schopenhauer, "from *The World As Will and Idea*" in *The Philosophy of Laughter and Humor*. Edited by John Morreall (New York: State University of New York Press, 1987), 52.

[5] William Hazlitt, "From *Lectures on the English Comic Writers*" in *The Philosophy of Laughter and Humor*. Edited by John Morreall (New York: State of New York Press, 1987), 68.

[6] Sigmund Freud, *The Basic Writings of Sigmund Freud*, trans. A. A. Brill (New York: Modern Library, 1995), 725.

[7] http://books.google.com/books?id=7vEDAAAAMBAJ&pg=PA41&dq=%22Karl+Welker%22&hl=en&sa=X&ei=_ZEVT7bWK4PZgQfToYXPAw&ed=0CDgQ6AEwAA#v=onepage&q=%22Karl%20Welker%22&f=false

[8] I am using Bonamy Dobrée's article "Comedy" in *Eight Great Comedies* (New York: Meridian, 1996): 453–456 as a model for these subgenres, with the exception of dark comedy as it is not included in the article.

[9] My classics and humanities professor Leon Golden at Florida State University came up with the phrase.

[10] Miguel De Cervantes, *Don Quixote,* trans. Samuel Putman (New York: Modern Library, 1998), 95.

[11] André Breton, *Anthology of Black Humor*, trans. Mark Polizzotti (San Francisco: City Lights, 1997).

[12] Swift makes it perfectly clear that his idea of harvesting infants for food in order to stop poverty is deadly serious. See Jonathan Swift "A Modest Proposal" in *The Norton Reader: An Anthology of Expository Prose* (New York: Norton, 1973), 694. It is interesting that Breton omits the concluding paragraph in his anthology in which Swift claims that he is sincere. One should also note that although the essay is ironic, it is not funny. It could be, therefore, argued that Swift was serious, at least in his attempt to rub a rich and complacent society's nose in the stink of its own moral hypocrisy.

[13] See Morreall's discussion (108–110).

# CHAPTER 5

# Sports and Popular Culture

With the advancement of technology providing humanity an increased op-portunity for leisure and free time, one of the ways that we have devoted a large portion of that time is to the participation in and the viewing of sports, which become no longer just the purview of the rich and powerful. Baseball, which would come to be recognized as America's pastime in the twentieth century, has its roots in the mid-1850s. With the invention of modern rules for college football near the turn of the century, sports—both played and wit-nessed, rapidly became a defining characteristic of human experience. Sports have continued to evolve, but its place as a central component of popular culture remains unquestioned. Modern media have only served to crystallize the hallowed place of sports in our public consciousness, with 24-hour sports channels now numbering in the dozens on television.

Thinking critically about sports, at least as a philosophical undertaking, has its contemporary roots in the work of the late Paul Weiss. His book on the subject, titled *Sport: A Philosophical Inquiry,* was published in 1969 and it ushered in an era when critical examination of sports as a social and politi-cal phenomenon could meaningfully take place. Weiss asked basic questions about what motivates athletes to compete and improve as well as grand ques-tions about the contributions made by sports to civilization as a whole. With this text, Weiss helped elevate sports to a level worthy of serious academic consideration, and since then two central avenues of inquiry have come to the forefront. First, we can examine the ways in which critical inquiry can help us think more clearly about sports. For example, one can use Marxist social theory to discuss the various labor issues that currently exist in professional sports between labor and ownership. Second, we can examine what our actions and interests in sports say about ourselves and our society. For example, what does our interest in fighting in hockey or crashes in auto racing say about us as spectators or our culture in general.

There are times when both areas of critical examination collide. Sports has served as a representation of social change, such as Jackie Robinson breaking the color barrier in baseball in 1947, and has presented a new form of role model to America's youth (regardless of Charles Barkley's famous claim to not hold such a position). While many youth still dream of growing up to be an astronaut, a fireperson or a police officer, the number of children, both male and female, with aspirations to one day play a professional sport continues to grow. This number is only exceeded by the number of parents watching their children play little league games with visions of college scholarship 'and pro contracts danncing in their heads. The role of sports figures as cultural icons is further entrenched by mass media, and this influence goes beyond the sports channels to business and politics. When LeBron James announced on ESPN in the summer of 2010 that he would be playing basketball in Miami during the next year (not actually playing—just announcing where he would play) nearly 10 million Americans tuned in to watch "The Decision."

Where sport plays perhaps its most important role, however, is in the ways in which it helps us to shape our individual and cultural identities. When Barkley stated in his famous Nike commercial that he was not a role-model, he was trying to emphasize the point that the tens of thousands of inner-city children hoping that their proficiency at a particular sport was going to be their ticket out of the projects were operating on false assumptions. In the National Basketball Association there are only a few hundred playing positions across all of its teams, with maybe two dozen positions opening up every year to draftees and free-agent signings. Barkley wanted these children to not dream of being him—becoming a sports icon—but instead to dream about their education and where that could take them.

Yet sports is a place that provides icons, and the way that our favorite players approach their sport offers us lessons that can translate to how we approach our own lives. As Josef Pieper points out in the forward to his *Leisure: The Basis of Culture*, "Culture depends for its very existence on leisure, and leisure, in its turn, is not possible unless it has a durable and consequently living link with the *cultus,* with divine worship," (15). For many of us, sports is not about a game, but about a religion, complete with worshipped heroes, even if those heroes all too often expose themselves as mortal and failing creatures (Tiger Woods comes to mind). Regardless, when our favorite player puts on the jersey for our favorite team, they can take on a mythical status in our hearts and minds. It is this status that perhaps somewhat justifies the obscene salaries that many sports superstars earn, sometimes exceeding tens of millions of dollars per year in all four major sports, as well as in soccer and auto racing. With increased salaries comes a need to increase revenue, and from stadium naming rights to exclusive television deals to higher ticket prices, sports has increasingly become big business.

Still, sports also offers moments of inspiration. Tennis star Billie Jean King serves as one great example of a pioneer who transcends the sports arena. When *Life* magazine compiled a list of the 100 most important Americans of the 20th century, King was one of only four athletes on that list (alongside Robinson, Muhammad Ali and Babe Ruth). Other magazine polls have mirrored this result, as *Seventeen* magazine listed her as the single most admired woman in the world in 1975. Her famous Battle of the Sexes match with Bobby Riggs offered evidence for the claim that women deserved an opportunity to compete, and given that opportunity could compete successfully. LPGA great Annika Sörenstam serves as another reminder of this point, as her appearance in a PGA event in 2003 was the first time a woman had competed with the men since the 1940s and Babe Zaharias. While Sörenstam missed the cut, her 96th place finish put her ahead of 15 of her fellow male competitors. What can we learn from the examples of King and Sörenstam about being role models as athletes and as people?

The sheer number and variety of sports and other games of leisure on the world stage forces us in this chapter to select a representative sample for deeper consideration. The sports we will discuss include American football, soccer, baseball, golf, and hockey. To do justice to the topic of sports as an important contributor to popular culture, this chapter would need to be greatly lengthened and the number of sports and topics discussed within those sports would need to be increased. That being said, we offer these sports, and the topics covered within each sport, as a representative sample of the kinds of issues and questions that deserve to be raised. Because of this approach, this chapter is organized not around theories as themes, but around the sports themselves. Within each section, questions and examples are raised to at-tempt to jump start our reflection, with the hope that your prior knowledge of theories and concepts covered in this textbook's early chapters will offer opportunities to go beyond the text.

## ☐ FOOTBALL

Football has steadily become the most popular sport in the United States, seemingly surpassing even baseball as the sport at the forefront of public consciousness. The NFL's showcase, the Super Bowl, is always a greatly an-ticipated event which draws a huge television audience, massive advertising revenue, and exorbitant ticket prices. Football has long been seen as a bastion of masculinity and testosterone. While a handful of women have attempted to play the game at little league, high school, college, and professional levels (including a short-lived National Women's Football League in the 1970s) the vast majority of people still believe that the game is simply too violent for women to participate in. It was not until 1997 that Liz Heaston became the first woman to play and score in a college football game, kicking two extra points for Willamette University. Other young women had attempted the game, including Frankie Groves at Stinnett High School in Texas, whose play in 1947 led to the governing body of Texas high school sports creating a rule that banned girls from playing high school football. This ban would remain on the books until 1993. Why was a ban necessary if girls are incapable of playing the game? Why would someone not want women to play football?

The famous passage of Title IX in 1972 helped to change the atmosphere of women in sports, stating in part that "No person in the United States shall, on the basis of sex, be excluded from participation in, be denied the benefits of, or be subjected to discrimination under any education program or activity receiving Federal financial assistance . . ." In the aftermath of Title IX, mas-sive growth of women participating in sports occurred, with the number of women playing college sports increasing by 450 percent and the numbers in high school sports estimated by some to have increased by 900 percent. This growth, however, has been primarily within sports such as softball, volleyball, soccer and basketball. Football remains taboo, even though conventional wisdom might argue that young girls, because of their earlier growth spurts, could be important members of little league football teams. If young girls

© Erich Schlegel/Corbis

Cowboy's Stadium

were given a chance to pick up the game and grow up playing the game, there is no reason to think that more women would not find themselves on the field in college and even professional levels. As the situation stands now, social closure (which involves processes and institutions where one group excludes another from certain positions) prevents the overwhelming majority of women from seeing football as a viable athletic opportunity.

Perhaps the most famous example of a woman playing big time football involved Katie Hnida, who played as a placekicker for the University of New Mexico. In 2003, Hnida became the first woman to score in an NCAA Division I-A game, the highest level of college football. Before playing for New Mexico, she had attended the University of Colorado at Boulder, making the football team as a walk-on but never playing. Before her graduation in 2004, Hnida joined a group of women accusing other members of the Colorado football team of sexual harassment and rape. She never pressed charges, but her 2006 book *Still Kicking: My Journey as the First Woman to Play Division One College Football,* discusses her experiences trying to break the testosterone ceiling.

The sheer violence of football has caused many parents, both of little boys and little girls, to persuade their children into directions other than the gridiron. Medical science has increasingly become more and more concerned about the effects on health and well-being caused by concussions received during play. The June 2011 issue of *Pediatrics* released the results of a study covering thirty years of trauma-related sports deaths among young athletes in 22 sports, with 57 percent of those deaths coming in football, with a shocking 14 percent of the deaths involving concussions received prior to the fatal injury. The National Football League has taken action to protect their current workforce, outlawing headhunting and handing out harsh fines to repeat offenders. The current rule changes, however, do not help the retired football players. Over the last five years, HBO's "Real Sports" program has covered the on-going research connecting concussions with a wide array of illness, including dementia, depression, and Lou Gehrig's disease. These stories also depict the NFL's skepticism of these connections and resistance to cover the healthcare costs that result from these illnesses.[1]

The issue of violence in football is only highlighted by the recent New Orleans Saints bounty scandal. This scandal saw defensive players earning bonuses as bounties for hits that involved injuring other players, including increased bonuses for knocking a player out of the game or forcing them to be carried off the field on a cart or a stretcher. The highest bounty appears to have been placed on Brett Favre's head, with Saints linebacker Jonathan Vilma reportedly offering.

© Duomo/Corbis

Youth football players

The health of NFL players has also been at the forefront of an ongoing debate regarding the length of the regular season. Owners have been proposing to extend the season by two games, yet players have argued that the season is already too long and physically demanding as it is, believing that more games will result in more serious injuries. The length of the season has $10,000 to any player who knocked Favre out of a playoff game. Why do you think a program like this might pose a problem for the NFL? grown in the past, going from twelve games to fourteen in 1961, and then to the current sixteen in 1978. The number of games in the playoffs has increased as well, going from eight teams playing a maximum of three rounds to the current twelve teams playing a maximum of four playoff rounds. This trend has mirrored the expansion of the regular season and playoffs in nearly every other major sport, with the baseball season going from 154 regular season games and one playoff round to 162 games in the regular season and three rounds of playoffs. Hockey has also seen expansion, with the four-team two-round best-of-seven playoffs replaced by sixteen teams playing four rounds. One of the emblems of hockey's Detroit Red Wings, the octopus, is made antiquated by this change, as its eight legs represented the eight wins the team used to need to win the NHL championship, Lord Stanley's Cup. Some players, however, might argue that you really can have too much of a good thing, and that additional economic profit for the owners should not be earned by further exploitation of players.

Whether expansion is exploitation or not, fans remain hungry for more. Football in particular stands as an interesting example of the modern sports fan's psychological passion for a game. Football has truly become a year around sport, as the college game offers spring practices and rankings of recruiting classes, and the professional level obsessed with interest in the draft (including which team is on the clock), as well as optional offseason training activities, or OTAs. Fantasy leagues, an increasing presence surrounding all major league sports, seem to have a particular frenzy in football and offers additional fuel to the football fan's fire. Over twenty million Americans are involved in some form of fantasy football, with businesses dedicated to advising or managing these leagues turning into an $800 million industry. We must ask ourselves if this obsession is a good thing.

College football represents the most popular and highest money maker in college sports, yet its growth in popularity and prosperity has come with a host of new problems. One issue that has plagued the game for years is the way in which a national champion is named. For years the champion was named via the Associated Press based off of a poll of news media conducted at the end of the season. The AP poll was first held in 1936, and it was joined in the 1950s by the Coaches' Poll, which is made up of select members of the American Football Coaches Association. Most times the two polls are in agreement, but eleven times they have disagreed, effectively splitting the national championship. Since 1998, the Bowl Championship Series, or BCS has attempted to offer a system that would put the top two teams in the country against each other in a national championship game. The BCS is a combination of polls (including the Coaches' poll mentioned above) as well as an average of computer rankings. The BCS is a highly debated topic among fans and sports talk radio pundits, as the top two teams picked by the process are not always the only two teams that may make a valid claim to deserving an opportunity. Many compare the BCS process unfavorably to the NCAA basketball tournament, where 68 teams compete in a single elimination tournament to find the best team in the nation. Does having more teams involved in deciding a national championship a good thing or an economic thing?

Another problem facing college football, and other college sports as well, centers around the ways in which high school players are recruited to some schools (involving violations of the NCAA rulebook). Recent scandals have seen once highly regarded programs such as the University of Southern California face NCAA punishment, with star running back Reggie Bush and his family receiving improper benefits from agents while in school, basically forfeiting his amateur status. Bush gave up his claim to the 2005 Heisman Trophy, and the USC program was stripped of wins during their 2004 season as well as the BCS national championship. Ohio State University was also sanctioned by the NCAA over violations involving football players, including star quarterback Terrelle Pryor, exchanging autographs and team memorabilia for tattoos. The resulting cover-up cost their coach, Jim Tressel, his job, and Ohio State vacated all of their victories from the 2010 season. NCAA investigators also examined the circumstances surrounding Heisman trophy winning quarterback Cam Newton and his play for Auburn University during their national championship season in 2010, particularly questioning the degree to which Newton's father was involved in soliciting funds in exchange for influence in helping his son choose a school. These scandals pale in comparison to events such as those that surrounded Joe Paterno and Penn State, where the issues are more serious than winning and losing. Still, is it fair that NCAA athletes make big money for their schools, but receive little more than a scholarship?

## ☐ BASEBALL

Baseball, a game that for decades was recognized as America's pastime, has become a worldwide phenomenon, with the Little League World Series seeing teams from every corner of the globe attempting to be recognized as the best. The popularity of the game has had its ups and downs over the last twenty years, with a work stoppage in 1994 due to a player strike costing baseball it's postseason and fan support. The popularity of the game suffered when the game resumed in 1995, with drops in attendance and television ratings almost across the board. This downturn was reversed during the great homerun chase of 1998, as Mark McGwire and Sammy Sosa sought the single season homerun record held by Roger Maris since 1961. Fans flocked back to the

Barry Bonds

stadium to watch the increasing number of moon shots leaving the field of play, and baseball was back in the hearts and minds of many Americans.

During the growth spurt in homerun numbers that occurred in the 1990s, little was said about what might have been behind those gaudy numbers. A record that had stood unchallenged for almost forty years, was broken in quick succession by three men (including McGwire, Sosa and Barry Bonds, who would set the current mark of 73 homeruns in a single season in 2001). Once revelations of performance enhancing drugs began to surface, including a set of hearings on Capitol Hill involving past and current ball players, people began to look at these celebrated new records in a different light. Now it is clear that the widespread cheating that occurred during the steroid era, beginning in the late 80s and early 90s, did a great deal of damage to a sport that has long viewed its history and its records as sacred artifacts. As homerun numbers soared and records fell (including Maris' record and Hank Aaron's career number of dingers), baseball fans found themselves cheering these acts of mammoth strength and later bemoaning the shortcuts that were made to achieve them. It is interesting to note that baseball was saved from economic ruin after a strike by players that were cheating. Were people or baseball itself willfully turning a blind eye because the ends justified the means?

At the forefront of this controversy was Barry Bonds, whose seven Most Valuable Player awards stand as testament to how respected he was at the height of his career. In 2006, however, Lance Williams and Mark Fainaru-Wada published their book *Game of Shadows,* which alleged that Bonds' great achievements were due to his use of performance enhancing drugs. It is in large part because of that book that Bonds went from being a sports icon to a rogue character who besmirched the game. He would stand trial in 2011 on perjury and obstruction of justice charges for allegedly lying to a grand jury investigation of BALCO, the Bay Area Laboratory Co-Operative founded by Victor Conte that was at the forefront of the performance enhancing scandal stretching from baseball to track and field to football. Bonds would be found guilty on the obstruction of justice charge.

Bonds was not alone in his actions, as further reports and revelations were either leaked to the press or presented as part of official enquiries. For example, the Mitchell Report, named for former Senator George Mitchell who served as the chair of the year-and-a-half investigation initiated by the Commissioner of baseball, was released in 2007. The report named dozens

of players, including Roger Clemens, who allegedly used performance enhancing drugs, including steroids, during their careers. Certainly it cannot
be denied that other sports have had difficulties with cheating or tampering
within their games. One need look no further than the widespread doping
that has occurred in professional cycling, and the allegations that continue to
swirl around Lance Armstrong, for evidence of this. Baseball, furthermore,
has always had a love/hate relationship with its rules, with practices such as
the spitball and bat corking remaining a part of baseball lore. The very entertaining book by Dan Gutman, *It Ain't Cheating If You Don't Get Caught:
Scuffing, Corking, Spitting, Gunking, Razzing and Other Fundamentals of Our
National Pastime,* chronicles this history of rule bending and breaking. Hall
of Fame pitcher Gaylord Perry, long suspected of using the spitball during
his lengthy career, went so far as to title his autobiography *Me and the Spit-
ter: An Autobiographical Confession.* The steroid and performance enhancing
controversy, however, introduces new problems ranging from the health of
the players involved to concerns about the ethics of shortcuts and the example
set for young ballplayers. It was these issues that led the U.S. Congress to hold
hearings in March of 2005 (where Mark McGwire famously and repeatedly
asserted during his testimony that "I'm not here to talk about the past"), and
it is the label of cheater that continues to keep many of the players under suspicion of using these substances from the games' Hall of Fame. Is all cheating
the same? Why do we laugh at a spitball, but demonize Bonds and Clemens?

Baseball is also a sport that perhaps more than any other has a negative
relationship with its officials. Screams questioning the vision of baseball officials to catcalls demanding to "kill the umpire" are almost embedded in the
fabric of baseball. Referees make mistakes in every sport, but in baseball these
mistakes almost seem to take on a life of their own. Take as just one example
the infamous call by Don Denkinger in the 1985 World Series between the
St. Louis Cardinals and the Kansas City Royals. The Cardinals had the lead
in what would have been a title clinching game six, when Denkinger's call at
first allowed the game-tying run on base, giving the Royals an extra out. They
took advantage of that call to take the lead and win both game six and seven
and claim the World Series.

A more recent example saw Detroit Tigers pitcher Armando Galarraga
clearly robbed of a perfect game during the 2010 season by a blown call at
first by Jim Joyce. The out would have been the last out of the game, had the

correct call been made, a point verified by super-slow motion instant replay. Joyce had once been voted the best overall umpire in baseball after *ESPN the Magazine* conducted an anonymous poll of current major league players, but that honor did not cover up the fact that Joyce had simply made the wrong call, a fact that even he admitted after the game, stating that he "just cost that kid a perfect game." While both Galarraga and Joyce were praised for their sportsmanship and candor, increased television coverage, broadcasting nearly every major league game played in all major sports, along with 24/7 television and radio commentary, have placed ever-increasing strain on the umpire. High definition television, with its multiple camera angles and instant replays, now allow every fan to scrutinize calls in every sport. While golf has a history of players calling penalties on themselves for rules violations, the fans have become umpires via television and call in to report rules violations that the golfers themselves are unaware of many sports, such as football and hockey, have embraced new technologies and mechanisms to review close calls and get the call right, but baseball still resists instant replay save for specific homerun situations. Perhaps it is baseball's dedication to its history and traditions that causes it to drag its feet regarding reviews using instant replay, but it is unclear whether this dogmatism should be lauded or criticized.

One change that baseball was forced to embrace surrounded the reserve clause, which tied baseball players to the teams that drafted them until they retired, were traded, or were given their unconditional release. Curt Flood, then of the St. Louis Cardinals, challenged this practice in court, and although he lost the resulting U.S. Supreme Court decision in 1972, his actions help galvanize the players' union and would eventually lead to the creation of free agency in the 1970s. Free agency would go on to allow veteran players to test the market and control their futures, and henceforth average salaries would skyrocket, going from $24,909 in 1969, before the Flood case, to $512,804 by 1989, to $3,340,133 in 2010. As baseball salaries grew and only a handful of teams such as the New York Yankees had the deep pockets to continue to sign nearly everyone they wanted, other general managers would attempt to find ways to keep costs down. Some teams simply ceased being competitive, while others, such as Oakland Athletics and their general manager Billy Bean, would adopt new statistical philosophies to find players who could produce but were overlooked by other teams. This philosophy, which would be chronicled in a 2003 book by Michael Lewis called *Moneyball: The Art of*

*Winning an Unfair Game* (and a 2011 film staring Brad Pitt), would led to a revolution in baseball statistics. These new statisticians were proponents of Sabermetrics, which was derived from the acronym SABR for the Society for American Baseball Research. This new research, which ran contrary to old school methods that focused on intangibles like heart and grit, focused on new numbers such as VORP (value over replacement player) and would replace more traditional numbers such as batting average with BABIP, or batting average on balls in play. Whether or not this new emphasis on objective numbers as the sole basis for determining a player's worth is here to stay is an open question that raises the issue of what makes great baseball players truly great. Regardless, we need to consider if the era of free agency, which is obviously better from the players' perspective, is actually better for the game itself.

Another area of controversy related to baseball involves the collectibles that fans purchase in order to feel a closer connection to the game they love. Baseball cards have been a component of the fans appreciation for the game of baseball since the late 1800s, where they were designed and including in packaging to lure consumers into buying products ranging from tobacco to caramels to dog food, and most recently chewing gum. Today, baseball cards are a multi-million dollar industry, with some collectibles rising to the status

© Tannen Maury/epa/Corbis

Wrigley Field in Chicago

of investments. For example, a high grade copy of the very rare 1909 Honus Wagner tobacco card sold in a 2007 auction for $2.35 million. As current card makers continue to find ways to increase name recognition and generate hype around their new products, various gimmicks have been tried, including ultra rare serial numbered cards as well as cards autographed by the player. Card manufacturers attracted controversy, however, when they began taking apart vintage sports memorabilia (including game used bats and jerseys) to include small half-inch swatches embedded within the cards themselves. Early examples of these memorabilia cards were released by card manufacturer Upper Deck in the late 1990s. In 1998 Upper Deck sliced a Babe Ruth bat into hundreds of small pieces and embedded them onto cards as part of their "Pieces of History" promotion. The player jerseys used include rare items worn by Willie Mays, Mickey Mantle, Lou Gehrig, as well as Ruth. Some question whether or not these rare historical artifacts should be destroyed to create baseball cards, but the phenomenon appears here to stay, as cards from all major sports now feature examples such as these in their products.

## ☐ GOLF

Golf has often found itself as a focal point for discussions of racism and sexism, as the game has traditionally been seen as a sport for the upper and middle class white male. In the December 23, 1996 issue of *Sports Illustrated,* Gary Smith wrote in "The Chosen One" that the world of golf is a "white canvas ... the moneyed, mature and almost minority-less world." The last twenty years has ushered in the era of the Ladies Professional Golf Association as well as the singular athletic genius of Tiger Woods. Much has been made about these developments, comparing them to the progress that our society has seen in the awareness of and work to eliminate racism and sexism in the United States. While changes have certainly not happened overnight, today nearly every sport contains numerous minorities at every level, from the field to the highest levels of management. Some suggest that golf be held up as a model for equality because it is one of the few sports that has allowed for women and men to compete against each other at the highest level. Even amongst recreational golfers, the handicap system as well as the use of multiple tees to even out various skill levels is said to allow anyone to play anyone else on a fair and even level regardless of age or sex. As for race, some might point out that the recognition of Tiger Woods, whose ethnic heritage is black, Chinese,

Photofest

Tiger Woods

American Indian, Thai, and white, as the greatest player of his generation is evidence of a changing of mindsets regarding race in organized golf. After all, the number of African Americans, as well as Asian and Hispanic American and other minorities playing golf in the United States have increased in large amounts over the last fifteen years, with a recent study by the National Golf Federation estimating that one in seven golfers (combining professional and amateur ranks) in the United States is a minority.

While much has changed, much more remains the same. Racism and sexism still exist in and around golf, so again we see social closure, with both women and minorities facing what some call "interactional barriers" to their participation in golf.[2] In recent history, much of our discussion of race and sex in golf has centered on the famed Augusta National Golf Club, home of the Masters Golf Tournament. For starters, Augusta National went without a single African-American member until the 1990s, and many still believe that the private club membership's view on minorities mirrored that of Clifford Roberts, co-founder and longtime Chairman of the club and tournament, who remarked that "as long as I'm alive, golfers will be white, and caddies will be black."[3] This attitude was certainly not isolated to Augusta GA, however, as the PGA of America added a provision to their Constitution in 1943 mandating that only "professional golfers of the Caucasian Race...shall be eligible for membership." This clause remained part of the PGA Constitution until 1961.[4] Furthermore, Augusta National was the site of protests in 2003 by Martha Burk, chairwoman of the National Council of Women's Organizations (NCWO). Hootie Johnson, then

Bobby Jones

chairman of Augusta National, responded to pressure from both Burk and some advertisers by stating that the club had a private membership process and that he saw no need "to radically change our membership." Johnson added that while the club might one day allow women members, "that timetable will be ours and not at the point of a bayonet."[5]

One reason offered by Alan Shipnuck, author of *The Battle for Augusta National,* for the phrasing of Johnson's response was the controversy that had surrounded another private club in 1990—Shoal Creek Golf Club in Alabama, and its attitude towards minorities. Hall Thompson, founder of Shoal Creek and member of Augusta National, responded to that controversy by saying that the club had the freedom to associate with whoever they desired, adding that "I think we've said we don't discriminate in every other area except the blacks." Shipnuck asserted that the idea of inviting an African-American to join a country club in Birmingham, Alabama was an amazing rarity. With seven clubs with over 6,000 members in Birmingham, there were only two African Americans. Nine days before the PGA Championship was scheduled to be played there that year, the club buckled under the pressure of protest and admitted its first minority member, a move that was followed at other clubs around the country as the PGA instituted a policy requiring that clubs hosting PGA tournaments not discriminate. Does one minority included in the club actually signify a change in racial policy?

The specific language of the new policy stated that potential tournament hosts must guarantee "that the membership practices and policies do not discriminate on the basis of race, sex, religion or national origin." Augusta National and the Masters are exempt from this requirement because the PGA considers this tournament, as well as the other three majors, non-PGA Tour co-sponsored events, so this non-discrimination policy does not apply.[6] While the actual protest spearheaded by Burk at Augusta National failed to lead to changes in the club's policies, general concerns regarding how these private clubs are viewed and the degree to which that reflects on the game of golf are still worthy of serious consideration, especially given that as many as one third of all golf courses are private, choosing to not give specific information about their membership breakdowns.[7] Harry Edwards, renowned Sociology Professor Emeritus at the University of California, believes that the reason these clubs are so reluctant to open up about the gender and racial breakdowns of their clubs is because the facts of the matter do not match their non-discriminatory rhetoric. Edwards states that "when it comes time to ante up, to show their policies are working, that they've opened up, they don't have the numbers."

It is certainly true that social/cultural background impacts one's recreation possibilities, as Washington and Karen point out in their essay "Sport and Society." They remark that "social class is a key component of our understanding of sports. It is important to understand what connects particular groups of people to particular sports activities and what role these play in the reproduction of inequality in a given society."[8] Still, if one looks past the cost involved in playing golf as a dominant factor in deciding who does and does not play, then other factors need to be considered. Focusing on issues of sexism, according to McGinnis, McQuillan and Chapple one of the key ways in which women are made to feel unwelcome on the golf course is through the ways in which golf courses are defined "as men's spaces." Their research centered around a series of interviews with female recreational golfers with various levels of experience, skills and seriousness about the game. Many of these women felt that they were singled out and felt stereotyped as being poor or slow players. As a result, these women said that they either felt pressured to "play similarly to men" to deserve to be on the course (including a large concern for driving distance), or the occurrence of "role entrapment" which "translated into emphasizing the femininity of golf and exaggerating differences between men and women on the golf course," leading to conscious attempts to not appear masculine—not too aggressive or intense.

It is this concern that led LPGA commissioner Ty Votaw to emphasize the "five points of celebrity" (performance, appearance, passion, relevance and approachability) to the players on tour. The degree to which sex appeal, long a controversial element of the marketing of women's golf, plays in this conception of celebrity is not clear, but what is clear is that Votaw wants the LPGA players to be more than just great golfers.[9] As a result, current professional golfers such as Michelle Wie, Paula Creamer and Natalie Gulbis are recognized as much for their physical look as their physical accomplishments on the golf course. *Sport Illustrated's* online website even contains links to stories and blog posts ranking "The 50 Hottest Female Golfers of All Time." Should inclusion on this list be seen as a compliment or an insult?

Michelle Wie

This form of role entrapment regarding how women should play golf is amplified by the classification of the red tees as the women's tees. McGinnis references R. W. Connell's work in this area, particularly the concept of "hegemonic masculinity." According to Connell, the hegemonic masculine concept (in the current case, the big hitting driver), "is always constructed in relation to various subordinated masculinities as well as in relation to women." The blue tees (the manly tees) are in contrast to the white tees (for seniors and lower-skilled men), and are entirely separate from the red (women's) tee box. McGinnis adds that "according to the rules at many courses, people should select tees according to ability; however...the unwritten, gendered rules regarding 'men's tees' and 'women's tees' usually prevail." Instead of letting skill decide where one should play from, there is an added stigma to playing from the forward tees. In fact, many male players have heard the threat of having to play their next shot with their pants around their ankles and prove their manhood if their drive does not go past "the women's tees." To take one more example of how the tee confusion makes certain gender roles manifest, male members of some handicap scoring systems are only allowed to enter scores from the back and middle tees and are not even given the option of registering a score from the forward tees.[10] Still, we should ask ourselves whether or not it matters if we call the red tees the forward tees or the ladies' tees.

One of the key elements mentioned in discussions of the social closure amongst a golfing community resistant towards the inclusion of women and minorities is the make-up of the role models within that community—the membership of the PGA of America. Professional golfers, the teachers and stewards of the game, are underwhelmingly female (3 percent) and lacking African Americans (with on some accounts only 44 Class A certified professional among the nearly 20,000 in the U.S.). Regarding the lack of female PGA instructors or women in upper management positions, McGinnis argues that "it takes extreme courage for women to enter golf professionally when there is little gender-specific social support." This lack of female role models for other women is similar to the lack of minority role-models, especially when Tiger Woods is taken out of the equation.[11] Even though the growth of golf has seen an influx of players from a variety of nationalities and backgrounds, golf at both the professional and amateur levels remains primarily white and male. If golf truly wants to turn over a new leaf and escape its racist and sexist past, then clubs and golf professionals will need to do more to celebrate their changing views to have a real impact on altering past impressions, felt by many women and minorities, of not being wanted. This process can begin by an increased level of transparency on the part of golf's leading institutions, including openly discussing how many women and/or minorities are in their clubs, and why the numbers are what they are.[12] What else could or should be done to address sexism and racism on the golf course?

Beyond a discussion of race and gender, golf also provides an opportunity to reflect on the ways in which sports impact our environment. While most major sports structures are placed within or very close to metropolitan areas, golf courses take up large amounts of space and require large amounts of resources around the globe. Most golfers may be said to hold a view of the game as a good walk spoiled in which mankind, with golf club in hand, can commune with his or her natural surroundings. In fact, many golf clubs advertise the natural splendor and scenic wonder of their courses as prime selling points. For example, a simple Google search found over 80,000 websites touting the "natural scenic beauty" of a golf course. However, environmental ethicist Aldo Leopold wrote that we lack "an intense consciousness of land…separated from the land by many middlemen, and by innumerable physical gadgets," (pg. 261 in *A Sand County Almanac*). To what degree should the casual golfer, while enjoying the intensely manicured fairways and greens of the world's golf courses, be aware of the resources that go into maintaining the course, or the impact that the creation of the course itself has on its environment?

While high profile and controversial examples such as Donald Trump's building the "Greatest Golf Course in the World" along an ecologically sensitive stretch of Scottish dunes might temporarily grab our attention, the same questions might be raised concerning the majority of courses, yet remains unspoken. Golf, rather than allowing an opportunity for environmental reflection, may do more harm than good by giving the golfer an inauthentic or false sense of environmental awareness. In fact, some could assert that golf, often far from being a game of serene natural isolation, is a sport that works within a constructed social and ethical code that often has run contrary to a concern for environmental ethics. What can be done to make the game more environmentally friendly?

## ☐ HOCKEY

The sport of ice hockey has a peculiar place in American history. In many polls ranking the greatest sports moments in history, the Miracle on Ice, when the 1980 U.S. hockey team beat the mighty Soviet Union in the Olympic semifinals, comes out at or near the top of the list. Beyond the Olympics, however, hockey is often identified as the least of the four major team sports. This is in stark contrast with Canada, which holds the game to the status of almost being a religion. The question of how it is possible that two countries that share the longest undefended border in the world could have such a different perspective to the same game is one of the items worthy of our consideration. This is especially true when one considers that the overwhelming majority of NHL teams are located in the United States, with only seven of the thirty teams currently residing in Canada. In the states, hockey has continued to have a smaller and smaller portion of the media stage.

When the game is viewed, we see that fighting holds an important place in the fabric of hockey. There are many reasons why a fight might occur, including retaliation for a previous play, as an intimidation tool to deter plays against established stars before they even occur, or simply to try to shift the momentum during a game. Most hockey fights occur between specialists, or enforcers, who hold the specific role of defending the honor of the team when necessary. There are efforts afoot, however, to ban the practice. For example, the Canadian Academy of Sport Medicine has said that fighting is responsible for numerous unnecessary injuries and "is an endemic and ritual-ized blot on the reputation of the North American game." The commissioner of the NHL, Gary Bettman, downplays such positions, asserting there is no need to consider banning fighting from the game, adding that "Fighting has always had a role in the game and the amount of fighting is determined by how the game is played."[13] Concerns about the role of the enforcer in hockey increased during the 2011 off-season, as three current and former enforcers (Derek Boogaard, Rick Rypien and Georges Laraque) died with at least one of these deaths self-inflicted. A 1997 *Sports Illustrated* article on the role of the enforcer called that position "the worst job in sports."[14]

Still, one of the highlights of any player's career is their first Gordie Howe hat trick—a goal, an assist and a fight in the same game. There is a great deal of orchestration that surrounds most fights in the game, with unwritten rules dictating the behavior of the players, coaches and the officials. In fact, most hockey fights are pre-meditated, with the combatants discussing whether or

© Tony Ding/Icon SMI/Corbis

Patrick Kane of the Chicago Blackhawks

© EXPA/Sportida/NewSport/Corbis

A fight breaks out during a hockey game

not to enter into the altercation before the gloves are dropped, with cheap shots and altercations with injured players seen as dishonorable behavior. Ross Bernstein discusses this phenomenon in his *The Code: The Unwritten Rules of Fighting and Retaliation in the NHL*. Should fighting be banned from hockey or is this element essential to the character of the game? Why is a behavior that is illegal and immoral off the ice acceptable on the ice?

## ☐ SOCCER

Soccer, or football as the rest of the world knows the game, is by far the most popular team sport in the world. Soccer is believed to date back in one form or another to ancient Greek and Roman games, as well as to ancient China, and it is played and watched on every corner of the globe. The World Cup, the signature soccer event which occurs every four years, saw an estimated three quarters of a billion people tune in to watch the 2010 tournament. Yet for whatever reason, the game has never taken hold of the United States psyche, although the MLS (Major League Soccer) league is on the rise, expanding to a total of 18 teams in North America during its 2011 season. Furthermore, increased coverage in the United States of professional leagues from other countries, including the creation of cable channels devoted exclusively to the game (Fox Soccer Channel, for example) has exposed American fans to soccer at its highest levels. Some say that this lack of American interest in soccer is due to the slower pace of play, the lower scores, or the simple fact that traditionally the United States' men's team has not been particularly good (with the skilled U.S. Women's team standing in stark contrast). Why do you think America is not as in love with soccer as the rest of the world?

Regardless, this increased exposure to quality soccer as well as the growth in quality of American play, fits in line with the claims made by Raymond Boyle and Richard Haynes in their *Power Play: Sport, Media & Popular Culture,* who discuss the connection between the ways in which television dictates how sporting events are seen and understood, taking a crucial role in "what we call the sporting triangle of media sport: the relationship between television, sponsorship and sport… The key drivers which have shaped and continually reshaped sport as a cultural and ideological form as a commercial/business entity"[15] This phenomenon transforms sports into media events, and media events have the opportunity to capture the imagination and interest of the casual observer as well as the next generation of athletes. The added fact that more and more big name stars come to play in the United States, including David Beckham, translates into more media exposure. While it is true that other big name players have attempted to spark soccer excitement in the United States in the past, most famously Pelé with the New York Cosmos in the mid-1970s, the explosion of media outlets and consumer sports possibilities might mean that the current uptick in soccer interest in the U.S. could be a permanent one. The degree to which this increased media exposure is responding to a prior growth in viewer interest or is creating that interest is the classic chicken or the egg question that may never be answered. Regardless, the game's simplicity, including the fact that only a single ball is needed to play the game, might explain the world-wide popularity of soccer, due in large part to the economic viability of the game compared with games like American football, hockey or golf that require more specialized and expensive equipment.

In the international game, soccer has unfortunately remained an arena that contains large amounts of racist and anti-Semitic behavior, with some stadiums having sections dominated by groups such as white supremacists, whose behavior ranges from jungle chants to codes such as "88." According to the article "Fighting Racism in Soccer Stadium", "the number 8 [is] the numerical equivalent of the letter 'H,' and '88' being skinhead code for 'Heil Hitler.'"[16]

Youth soccer players

Teams playing against the Netherlands' Ajax team (which identifies itself with a Jewish heritage) have cat-called them with "Jews into the gas" and hissing sounds to imitate the flow of gas in a gas chamber. Chants of "dirty ape," and "black shit," have accompanied the monkey and gorilla sounds and the throwing of

bananas onto the soccer field during professional games in Europe. Soccer star Thierry Henry heard these and similar chants during his time with the Spanish national team, and this in part motivating him to start a campaign against racism called "Stand Up Speak Up" which is dedicated to awareness of and resistance to these racist actions. The campaign is symbolized by two interlocking wristbands, with one white and one black.

As for the play on the field, in sharp contrast to the renowned toughness of hockey players, soccer has had to deal with an epidemic of diving, where players who have barely been touched (if touched at all) by an opponent flail about the ground as if they had been mortally wounded in an attempted mugging. Diving is designed to receive free or penalty kicks from the official or even trick the official into giving the opposition an unwarranted yellow or red card.[17] Many sports have some variation of the soccer dive, such as flops in basketball (usually done by defensive players trying to draw a foul on the offensive player) or hockey, but soccer players are notorious for taking the dive to ludicrous levels. Attempts are currently being made by the governing bodies of soccer to try and limit diving, with an increasing number of penalties being given for this unsportsmanlike conduct. Is diving unsportmanlike or simply part of the game? Why do certain players dive while others reject the practice?

Women's soccer is becoming more and more popular around the world, with the Women's World Cup increasing the visibility of the game. Just as many Americans instantly think of the Miracle on Ice when the word hockey is mentioned, women's soccer also has a similar singular moment in the U.S., but for perhaps very different reasons. In July of 1999 the United States faced China in the final of the Women's World Cup, and Brandi Chastain launched the fifth and final kick of the penalty shootout into the back of the net to secure the title. Chastain spontaneously took off her jersey and fell to her knees. This celebratory photo found its way to the covers of *Time, Newsweek* and *Sports Illustrated.* Had her jersey remained on, we might wonder if that moment would have received the media attention that it did.

## ☐ CONCLUSION

*The Pop Culture Zone,* another text that focuses on getting students to write critically about popular culture, lists 89 different individual sports, team sports, and leisure activities in its attempt to illustrate the breadth of possibilities we have to choose from. When looking at these possibilities, including the sports focused on in this chapter, we should be aware of what these sports/leisure choices say about us, and try to examine what influences the choices that we make. We do not operate in a vacuum, as family, class, national/cultural identity, gender, race and sexuality all can impact which options appear to us as live options and which areas are either closed or so unappetizing as to be untenable.

Regardless of the sport, however, we continue to be amazed at the aesthetic beauty of sports and the athletes themselves, as they continue to push the boundaries of what is physically possible. Just as the idea of the four-minute mile was seen as scientifically impossible before Roger Bannister proved the experts wrong on the 6th of May 1954, sports continues to find new and amazing ways to drive us and delight. Whether the games are little league games between seven-year-olds, over-the-hill adult softball or beer leagues, or the pinnacle of professional leagues, sports maintain an honored place in our life and leisure.

---

[1] Chris Nowinski, former Harvard University football player and professional wrestler, was featured in these Real Sports stories, and is the author of *Head Games: Football's Concussion Crisis.*

[2] Lee McGinnis, Julia McQuillan, and Constance L. Chapple, "I Just Want to Play," *Journal of Sport and Social Issues*,29, No. 3: 313–337.

[3] Rick Reilly, "Strokes of Genius," *Sports Illustrated* 86, no. 16, April 21, 1997: 30–49.

[4] Alan Shipnuck, *The Battle for Augusta National: Hootie, Martha, and the Masters of the Universe*, (New York, NY: Simon and Schuster, 2004), 25. Also *see* John H. Kennedy, *A Course of Their Own: A History of African American Golfers*, (Lincoln,NE: Univ. of Nebraska Press, 2005).

[5] "Burk Fails to Make Cut at Masters," *Washington Times*, March 21, 2004. Shipnuck, *Battle for Augusta*, 6, 9–10.

[6] Shipnuck, *Battle for Augusta*, 26. Jill Lieber, "Golf's host clubs have open-and-shut policies on discrimination," *USA Today*, April 9, 2003.

[7] See Marcia Chambers' *The Unplayable Lie: The Untold Story of Women and Discrimination in American Golf* (New York, NY: Pocket Books, 1996) and her essay "Ladies Need Not Apply," *Golf For Women*, May/June 2002.

[8] Robert E. Washington and David Karen, "Sport and Society," *Annual Review of Sociology*, Vol. 27 (2001): 187–212. The Nine Core Values are honesty, integrity, sportsmanship, respect, confidence, responsibility, perseverance, courtesy and judgment (www.thefirsttee.org, accessed May 6, 2008).

[9] McGinnis, "I Just Want to Play," 324.

[10] R.W. Connell, *Gender and Power: Society, the Person, and Sexual Politics* (Stanford, CA: Stanford Univ. Press, 1987), 183. McGinnis, "I Just Want to Play," 325. The Golf Association of Michigan can be found at www.gam.org.

[11] McGinnis, "I Just Want to Play," 327.

[12] These questions are not new, and I have touched on some of them myself in a chapter in *Golf and Philosophy: Lessons from the Links*, edited by Andy Wible.

[13] "Fighting not up for debate: Bettman," CBC News, March 26, 2007.

[14] Michael Farber, "The Worst Job in Sports," *Sports Illustrated*, March 24, 1997.

[15] pg. 16.

[16] Andreas Tzortzis, "Fighting Racism in the Soccer Stadium," DW-World.de, March 6, 2003.

[17] See P. H. Morris and D. Lewis, "Tackling Diving: The Perception of Deceptive Intentions in Association Football (Soccer),"*Journal of Nonverbal Behavior*, Vol. 34, no. 1.

# CHAPTER 6

# Technology and Popular Culture

Popular culture has delighted and entertained us, enriched our lives in numerous ways. Technology, however, more so than many of the other areas covered throughout this book, may be most responsible for impacting our evolutional progression into the future, because in this arena the progress made in advancing technological popular culture also clearly parallels and even drives our changing society as a whole. The twenty-first century has seen a continuation in technological jumps that serve as markers for human progress. From the printing press to the electric light bulb to the airplane to the personal computer, our technology has made our lives easier by making once arduous tasks easily achievable, while also changing the way we think and interact. Technology is not just a tool for entertainment (although it is certainly that) but drives the very progress of humanity as a species.

Twentieth-century German philosopher Martin Heidegger also recognized that for humanity today technology plays a huge part in our understanding of self and the world around us. As Heidegger explains in his *The Question Concerning Technology*:

> The essence of technology is by no means anything technological. Thus we shall never experience our relationship to the essence of technology so long as we merely conceive and push forward the technological, put up with it, or evade it. Everywhere we remain unfree and chained to technology, whether we passionately affirm or deny it. But we are delivered over to it in the worst possible way when we regard it as

something neutral; for this conception of it, to which today
we particularly like to pay homage, makes us utterly blind
to the essence of technology...(4).

What Heidegger is asking us to do is not simply absorb passively the pleasures that the objects of technology have to offer, but to engage with these creations and actively investigate the way we feel about them, what they do for us, and how they may even be changing us. Because of the central place that technology plays in both our culture and our popular culture, ranging from cooking our food and warming our homes to playing computer games and chatting online with friends, technology's presence in our lives is nearly all encompassing, and its ever-present existence can sometimes hinder our ability to stop and reflect seriously on technology as a phenomena in our collective existence.

This chapter will offer a sampling of some of the more common and pervasive monuments from technology today that is impacting our culture, including Facebook and iPods, as well as flash forward to what the near future might have to offer, including programmable sex robots. This list is by no means exhaustive, but only provides a starting point for further examinations, and the purpose of this sampling is to provide an opportunity for a further reflection on elements of our lives that we take for granted. We also must remember that technology offers a moving target, as older technologies become extinct and are replaced with innovative ideas. Regardless of the era of technology in consideration, much work can and should be done to try and understand the values and meanings that come with our cultural choices, and perhaps it is looking at why certain things reach a tipping point to becoming popular and others are relegated to junkyards and landfills where we can find the most enlightenment about ourselves and our world.

## ☐ FACEBOOK

One of the most pervasive new developments occurring in technology that is changing the ways that we interact and entertain is the creation of social media. At the forefront of the social media revolution is Facebook. The friends I have on Facebook represent every element of my life story, stretching from my first-grade class through former students from classes I had taught years ago, to current coworkers. One could *almost* get a picture of the person I am and the life I have lived by reviewing the profiles of my 222 friends. I am not alone in this regard, as some estimates assert that the usage of social networking sites has quadrupled in the last five years (Correa, et al.: 2009). This being said, we need to consider how as Facebook becomes a larger and more expansive part of our culture, it has transformed the ways in which people view themselves as well as their relationships. What does your profile information say about you, and how accurately do you think this information represents who you are?

This analysis of personal identity is important because of the degree to which Facebook is providing a new platform for creating and displaying our new sense of self as well as our understanding of our relationships to others. In particular, the technology of Facebook is changing the way we understand our relationship with others, including our expression and understanding of intimacy. As we become more conscious of the number of friends we have (or in some people's case, do not have) or about whether or not a new relationship is going to become Facebook official, we begin to see ourselves taking on a new status. According to Facebook, the average number of friends for each user is 130, yet numbers like this might serve as an artificial measure on which to judge our self-worth. Facebook itself may just be the latest incarnation of

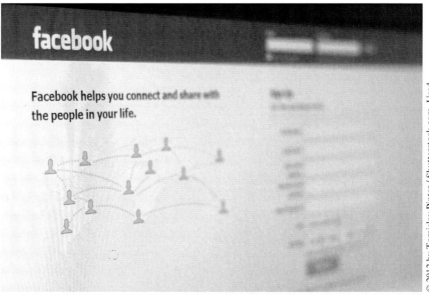

© 2012 by Tomislav Pinter / Shutterstock.com. Used under license of Shutterstock, Inc.

Facebook Homepage

a pattern dating back to the start of the computer age with networking on Prodigy through more recent phenomena like MySpace, but the sheer number of members and followers behind current sites Facebook and Twitter indicate a depth and degree of use unseen in the past.

Facebook currently claims over 400 million users, and according to Mark Zuckerberg, chief executive of the site, their core values remain the same. "If we give people control over what they share, they will want to share more. If people share more, the world will become more open and connected. And a world that's more open and connected is a better world."[1] Our world may be more connected, but are all of the connections equally valuable, or are some connections deeper and more significant than others? By putting all of my friends on the same list and broadcasting status updates to them all at once, am I sacrificing a level of intimacy that might exist between one or more of them if that same exchange of information had occurred on the face-to-face level? By using Facebook as my main tool for staying connected, I have to recognize that I might be losing the ability to appreciate the singular relationships that exist relative to that list, as well as my particular duties to those individuals. This is not to say that achieving this balance is impossible, only that it can be much more difficult and personally confusing.

From the perspective of a pragmatist philosopher such as John Dewey, we should endeavor to consider the degree to which these social networks become tools that we use to define ourselves without consciously reflecting on their roles or the meaning they assume in re-creating who we are. As noted Dewey scholar Larry Hickman points out in his book *John Dewey's Pragmatic Technology*, Dewey "warned of the dangers of technologically induced uniformity, mediocrity, and domination," (176), and a nonreflective acceptance of the values of Facebook may be doing more harm than good. While Facebook helps us maintain friendships and build communities that may have been lost in the past, we should consider the possibility that this new form of relating to others sacrifices a physical intimacy with a few for a technologically artificial and lesser form of emotional intimacy with a larger community.

Serious work has been invested on both sides of the discussion. Some, such as Dean Cocking and Steve Matthews in their article "Unreal Friends," have argued that it is psychologically impossible for relationships based solely on nonvideo Internet exchanges to become close friendships. They assert that the virtual friendships lack the human goods commonly understood as existing in friendship because of how the process of posting ideas and opinions on the Internet takes place within the context of a distorting filter that prevents us from revealing our true self to our friends. In these Internet-based friendships, "what is lacking here is not merely a partial, or marginal set of factors, but a significant global loss and distortion of the real case" (231). Others, such as Zygmunt Bauman, have affirmed that the barriers of the virtual world help bring to fruition the shallow nature of our online relationships, pointing out that these online text exchanges we take part in often only remain at the level of the online messages and do not develop along further lines.

The other hand, represented by Adam Briggle in his "Real Friends: How the Internet Can Foster Friendship," argues directly against the position held by Cocking and Matthews, insisting that "mediated indicators can be richer and more accurate than offline indicators...for the cultivation of relational identity via interpretation" (73). One reason offered for this is the belief that writing can require a certain level of deliberateness, and that this purposefulness can arise in the crafting of written correspondence, both in handwritten letters as well as in virtual Internet correspondence. Briggle admits that the offline world may provide a richer and more extensive set of cues in our relationships with others, but politeness or political correctness might constrain us "from working with them to do the important interpretative effort of building close friendships" (75). Are there differences in the way we communicate with our face to face friends, versus online or in texts, versus letters that are particularly important (such as letters of application for jobs or college)?

One important consideration about social networking websites that was not focused on by either Cocking and Matthews or Briggle is the degree to which the friendships found there are often rooted in preexisting offline relationships. Recent studies, including one conducted at Georgetown University and published in the *Journal of Applied Developmental Psychology*, indicate that the main reason for being interested in using Facebook is a desire to reconnect with people from our pasts [Pempek, Yermolayeva, and Calvert (233)]. However, one must also recognize the ways in which Facebook connections sometimes lead to the formulation of new friendships (I personally have Facebook friends that only met through conversations tied to my status updates). Also, services like eHarmony and other online dating sites attempt to use the internet as the basis for finding new love connections. A simple Internet search reveals that there are hundreds of different social networking sites that service a wide range of communities from Jewish singles to numerous book clubs.

Technological advances and the creation of Computer Mediated Communication (CMC) help to enable us to get and stay connected, representing a massive evolution in communication, both in terms of time, ease of use, and sheer volume. Even the telephone, hailed as a technological breakthrough in communication, still allows for such signals as a tone of voice or the depth of a sigh to add to and dictate the progression of the conversation. What is important about the advances in CMC such as those found in social media such as Facebook are the ways in which it is changing the rules for how we interact with each other by placing our friendships in a virtual context. By sacrificing physical interactions for virtual messages, we lose some possibilities for physical intimacy and greatly hinder our ability to create emotional intimacy.

While existing personality theories mostly focus on physical interaction, what are the consequences of using Facebook as our primary tool of social interaction? The degree to which individuals consciously place certain pieces of information on their profiles or on their status walls, or self-censure certain things out, is different from the ways in which unconscious and nonreflective choices are made. Regardless, we must remember that a person is more than a checklist of likes and dislikes. When a person is granted access to our profile as a friend, the entirety of our online self can be revealed all at once. This runs contrary to social penetration theory, a psychological and communication theory developed by Irwin Altman and Dalmas Taylor that argues that friendship is rooted in the gradual process of disclosure over time. This perspective asserts that deeper levels of intimacy between two people begins on the surface and deepens after vulnerability, particularly through mutual self-disclosure. Friendships that are rooted online in Facebook interaction lack developing layers of personal self-disclosure to other particular persons and hence stagnate intimacy, an element crucial to deeper levels of friendship. Understanding people is hard enough when we have the full use of all of our senses in our interactions with others, but when that full sensory context is removed in the movement to a computer interface, our ability to make meaningful conclusions is greatly reduced. When people reach the point where they have several hundred Facebook friends, there is a risk that there will be a muddying of the lines of intimacy between a real friend and a mere acquaintance or pseudofriend. How much time to you spend thinking about every friend past and present who might read a post or see a picture you post online before carrying through with that post?

Various accounts of friendship, and human interaction in general, discuss the ways in which we attempt to create a concept of identity for the consumption of others as well as the ways in which the opinions of others enable us to reevaluate our selves. Cocking and Matthews discuss three senses of friendship, the mirror view, the secrets view, and the drawing view. The mirror view of friendship, rooted in ancient Greek philosopher Aristotle's conception of the term, asserts that we tend to seek friends very similar to ourselves, so that our choice in friends can be said to self-disclose how we view ourselves. This concept of friendship, for example, might dictate choices regarding friend requests, particularly if someone might feel resistance about confirming an accidental acquaintance like a work colleague, or resist Facebook suggestions regarding friends of friends. The secrets view, as Cocking and Matthews explain, is different because this "account focuses not on disclosure of self *in* the other, but of disclosure of self *to* the other" (226). The amount of information I am willing to reveal to someone—the degree of vulnerability I am willing to allow—determines the degree to which someone can be called a friend. Applying this view to Facebook, we can think about how when one posts a status update they have to be cognizant of their friends list. Since in most cases all of their Facebook friends are on equal footing in the virtual world, a wise person might reflect on the fact that everyone, both close friends and casual acquaintances, will be made aware of a newly updated status. When forgotten, this fact can lead to uncomfortable situations, such as a student posting about how unfair a particular exam might have been, forgetting that their friends list includes that very professor.

The drawing view of friendship both denies and combines the other two perspectives. According to Cocking and Matthews:

> According to this view, neither similarity nor secret-sharing
> is important or distinctive of close friendship. Rather what
> is central to the nature of friendship is that one's identity is,
> in part, drawn, or shaped, by the relations one bears to one's
> close friends, and in turn this process of drawing further
> structures the relationship. (226)

The drawing that occurs in this relationship can involve our being motivated by our friend to try something new out of respect for our friend's interests (indicating a certain level of trust) or can involve the process of interpretation (recognition of an aspect of our friend's character and how that recognition impacts our interaction with that friend and the environment around them). When a friend posts a video to their wall of a band the friend enjoys, we might find ourselves willing to give that song a listen because of our respect of our friend's taste. Which view of friendship do you think is most accurate for the online world? Does a different view seem more accurate for offline relationships?

All three of these conceptions of friendship are rooted in the basic principle that who we associate with plays a tremendous role in the formation of personal identity. Because Facebook lacks the multilayered complexity of real-world interactions, it runs the risk of making a three-dimensional relationship one-dimensional. Unless someone chooses to send a private note through the Facebook interface or go out of their way to limit which friends receive a status update or can view an image, all revelations are for all ears on one's friends list, preventing an opportunity for conscious and deliberate sharing of intimate information between particular friends, and perhaps creating an environment of isolation and alienation. This isolation is what drives the increasing use of social networking as a tool to help us to once again feel connected in a meaningful way to those around us, even if we are not. What if, however, our new tools for social connection, while working, are not working as well as they could or should? What if we are using these new tools in an inauthentic or incorrect way (or we are allowing them to change the way we live in an inauthentic or incorrect way)? We should also recognize how Facebook, by turning the noun friend into a verb (friending), has enabled us to degrade the meaning of the noun itself.

We can allow Facebook to merely rise to the depth of the mundane or serve as an opportunity for increased levels of self-conscious introspection and meaningful communication. Briggle, in his defense of CMC, argues that the element of writing is the beneficial element that websites such as Facebook can provide, for writing, be it in a journal or letter, provides an opportunity for increased levels of introspection. At the same time, Briggle admits that "e-mail and instant messaging are so casually used and not well suited to the long-exchanges more frequently found in handwritten letters," adding that short and truncated messages squeezed in-between other deadlines hinders their ability to create an opportunity for serious self-examination ( 76). For Briggle, what must be done to make our virtual communication more beneficial and allow for deep and significant online friendships is that we must seek sincerity in what we say and emphasize deliberateness in the crafting of our electronic messages. We must be called upon to consider what the various faces and names on our friends list mean to us, remain cognizant of the various roles that they play in our lives, and focus our attention toward making sure that we are aware of why we call these people friends. Facebook may help us reconnect with friends and family separated by time or space, but those connections are valuable relationships that must be fostered in ways beyond status updates and its related comments or likes. Facebook may make us feel connected in an intimate way when we are not, but a careful and deliberate consideration of each of those relationships on an individual level helps us maintain the singular and unique relationships that are hidden by our friends list. We must remember that Facebook is not who I am, nor is it even a complete and accurate representation of who I am (as if such a thing existed).

Even if Facebook should drop in popularity and users in the near future, it cannot be denied that these social networks appear to be making a significant change in human relationships. The richness of our human relationships, and the true possibility for these relationships and the people in them to develop, requires that they not remain virtual and one dimensional. Moving forward from our virtual worlds and our virtual selves, we have to ask ourselves some important questions. First, are we using Facebook in a healthy and self-affirming way or are we using Facebook in a way that undermines our ability to have authentic relationships with people or warps our sense of self-identity? Also, is this a technology that makes us better, makes us healthier and happier, or is it something that is becoming an increasing distraction and interruption to a different way of living and interacting—the world before computer-mediated communication? Both questions indicate a need to log off from our Facebook pages and other CMC networks and log back into making a greater effort to instantiate intimate and direct face-to-face relationships with the people that matter in our lives.

## ☐ THE IPAD AND THE KINDLE: MAKING COMPUTING MORE PERSONAL

With its April 2010 launch, Apple's iPad in particular, and slate/tablet computers in general, have served as all-in-one revolutionary inventions that brought a new mixture of portability and power into the hands of users around the world; so much so that some commentators remark that they represent a paradigm shift in our interaction with information. While smartphones have been pushing the boundaries of portable computing power for years, the tablet format offers a technological tool whose real-world applications appear to be limitless. While some have criticized the tablet revolution as being overblown, calling the iPad nothing more than a miniature laptop, these new tablets offer competitive performance, longer battery life, and faster and easier use both for work and play. One review marveled at the speed with which presentations and spreadsheets could be created using the touchscreen on an iPad, and another review by CNN trumpeted the iPad design for consuming media from books, blogs and video to portable gaming. A 2011 *ABC News* story highlighted the five most significant ways that the iPad had become a valuable tool. These uses included it serving as a tool for medical doctors to access medical records and record data, with some doctors going so far as to use the iPad during surgery. Another way that the iPad is proving itself to be a useful tool is in law enforcement. Police officers are using the iPad to access maps, view photos identifying stolen property, and file

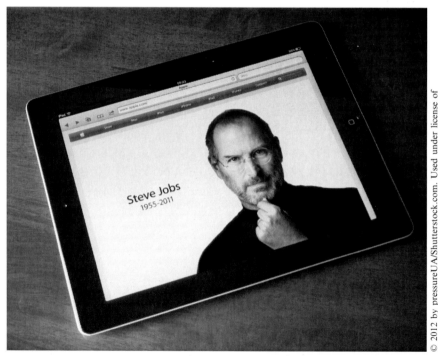

© 2012 by pressureUA/Shutterstock.com. Used under license of Shutterstock, Inc.

Steve Jobs and the iPad

reports from the scene of the crime. One might even envision a time in which people would be able to vote in elections using their iPads or iPhones, texting their vote instead of traveling to a polling center.

Another place that has seen tablet computers having an impact is in education. They have become an increasingly present tool in the classroom, with many instructors and students making the product a required element. For example, Seton Hill University in Pennsylvania recently provided an iPad to every incoming freshman. Case studies are beginning to be done looking at the educational uses of iPads, and many of these have emphasized the strength of the iPad for finding quick and easy information, as well as its ability to provide opportunities for collaboration, including examples such as musical collaborations in which a class of students contribute to the group writing and performing of a song using their individual iPads. In essence, the iPad gives students the ability to learn any time they choose. Negatives, however, include the degree to which students can easily become distracted, with teachers commonly finding students using applications or accessing web pages not relevant to the class assignment at hand. Teachers will need to continue to innovate and find ways to manage the environments in which the iPad is used. Are laptops or tablets present in the classroom? How are they being used in the classroom setting?

An obvious spin-off from the tablet computers we have discussed so far is the e-reader. Few could deny that our society runs at a faster pace now than it did in past decades, and in no place is this more obvious than in the communication of ideas. As Jeff Gomez points out in his book *Print is Dead: Books in our Digital Age*, our reality is "[a] society that used to communicate via the postal service, expecting someone to respond to a letter in a number of days, now expects a response to an email in a matter of seconds" (2008: 4). Gomez sees the youth of today as bored by the idea of reading books, choosing to Google rather than go to the library. He sees this simply as a technological evolution, going so far as to jokingly mock traditional book lovers who can be seen clutching printed tomes to their chests. He asserts that the love one shows when hugging a book is not toward the book, just as kissing the photograph of a lover is not worshipping the photo itself, but what the photo represents. What matters in our books, says Gomez, is the subject, for "it's a writer's words that touch us, not the paper those words were printed on" (20). Gomez concludes that electronic reading is catching on, simply put, because the experience and features are superior in e-texts than in print, and all that is really changing is the apparatuses of reading. Even if you are or are not an avid reader, how do you think the two versions compare? How might this book be different or even improved if placed into an electronic format?

Sociologists Griswold, McDonnell, and Wright might very well agree with Gomez. They refer to the last few decades, with large-scale reading groups and high print volumes, as an anomaly, concluding that "the reading class" is actually a smaller and self-perpetuating minority of our population. While Nicholas Carr believes this is perhaps an overstatement, his *The Shallows: What the Internet is Doing to Our Brains* does assert that the computer age in general and the creation of e-readers in particular are changing the way our brains read. With sky-rocketing e-reader sales occurring in the last couple of years, more and more people are turning to devices like the Amazon Kindle to read books and other formerly printed media such as magazines and newspapers. According to Carr, "The Kindle's most radical feature…is its incorporation of links into the text it displays. The Kindle turns the words of books into hypertext. You can click on a word or a phrase and be taken to a related dictionary entry, Wikipedia article, or a list of Google search results" (102). On the one hand this kind of technological innovation seems to be an invaluable tool for helping people to get beyond the text to search for deeper meaning and connections, but Carr sees a downside in how the distractions of the Internet undermine deep reading. This is in large part due to a shift in thought processes that occur when reading a text that includes links. When readers come to a link in a reading, they have to pause and allow their prefrontal cortex to evaluate that link and decide whether or not they want to pursue it. This subtle shift in brain activity "may be imperceptible to us—our brains are quick—but it's been shown to impede comprehension and retention, particularly when it's repeated frequently" (22). With each shift, our focus and attention are undermined. These shifts can be subtle, but can you remember a time when you were working on a project for a class and got into a groove that was broken by an unwanted interruption? Does the fact that the interruption was unwanted at the time versus a choice on our part make a difference in our view of the brain shift?

This process of shifting brain activity has also been studied by Duke University professor Katherine Hayles, whose article "Hyper and Deep Attention: The Generational Divide in Cognitive Modes" lays out the distinctions between hyper attention and deep attention. The former displays symptoms that tend

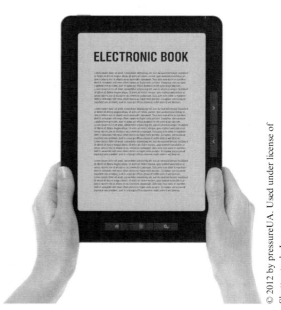

to switch focus rapidly and include a shorter attention span and higher needs for sensory stimulation found in networked forms of media. Deep attention, on the other hand, features a tendency to concentrate on a single subject, such as a book, for long periods of time, ignoring the surrounding environment in the process. Evolutionarily speaking, the hyper attention came first, as deep concentration is a luxury

© 2012 by pressureUA. Used under license of Shutterstock, Inc.

A Thousand Books at Your Fingertips

that only became manifest within the context of the protection that occurs with law and society. Hayles sees the current shift back to hyper attention as characteristic of a generational shift in cognitive styles that are away from the print and toward the digital, with ramifications that stretch throughout our society. She concludes that educators will need to be sensitive to ways in which the two cognitive modes can enhance each other, such as using interactive fiction (half literary narrative and half video game), Google-jockeying of presentations (when the class searches the Internet for content to display on screens behind the speaker that support the speech itself), and encouraging real-world connections (such as using identity creation on Facebook in relation to a novel such as *The Education of Henry Adams*). In what ways might the class you are currently taking be improved by plugging into digital media and your natural abilities at hyper attention?

Attempts to manage the differences and bridge the divide between these two thought processes aside, however, we have to recognize that hyper attention, and its perceived roots in the multitasking rage, might be less valuable than we are led to believe. Many multitaskers see themselves as masters of the universe who run at a higher level of efficiency than others, but recent studies have indicated that this belief may be far from the truth. A Stanford study of multitasking found that people who claimed to be good at juggling multiple activities actually performed worse than nonmultitaskers in completing basic assignments. One part of the Stanford study flashed two red rectangles on a screen twice, asking the subjects to determine if the red rectangles had changed their position. Surrounding the red rectangles were blue shapes that the participants were asked to ignore. The self-proclaimed multitaskers were much less likely to correctly respond to the question, in part because they could not ignore the irrelevant information.[2] However, it is not just that we have a difficult time separating the important from the insubstantial, but that we live much of our lives simply distracted as our minds feel pulled in multiple directions. Studies of office workers who work with computers show that they are constantly trying to balance separate tasks with their emails, checking their inbox 30 to 40 times per hour (much more often than they believe, incidentally). We have to acknowledge the degree to which our mobile technologies, including the tablet computers, e-readers, and smartphones are creating greater opportunities for distracted multitasking that undermines our remaining ability to focus.

According to Carr, changes in the ways in which people read will also impact writing styles. As one example, Carr discusses the phenomenon of Japanese novels being composed on mobile phones. In 2007, the three best-selling novels in Japan were all written on cell phones. These novels reflect the medium on which they are created—with many of these being love stories written primarily in short sentences that have the characteristics of tweets or text messages. According to one of these text-message-based authors, this new format is more palatable to young readers because traditional books are done "by professional writers…their sentences are too difficult to understand, their expressions are intentionally wordy" (105). The issue is not only a lack of depth that these new formats tend to encourage, but also the degree to which the malleability of the electronic word will alter the perspectives of other authors. Carr asserts that as the things that we read become more modular in their presentation, along with the provisional structure of the Net itself, we will find authors being more cavalier with their writing. A printed book is permanent in ink and paper, but the writings of the Internet age lend themselves to constant revision, with publication being less of an end goal and more of an indefinite and ongoing process.

Another way in which the mobile revolution is impacting our society in a significant way is within education, particularly online classes. We already touched on ways in which the iPad was revolutionizing the classroom, but we also have to recognize that online classes, which have existed for many years, are becoming more pervasive, with more and more students taking classes in the virtual world. Mobile computing makes it so easy for students to complete reading assignments, view class-related media, and submit assignments from places far afield of the classroom such as their dorm room or an exotic beach. The degree to which these online classes enable student learning compared to traditional face-to-face courses is a question that must be more clearly addressed. A study spearheaded by Don Krug in the education department at the University of British Columbia, titled "Student Achievement in Online Distance Education Compared to Face-to-Face Education," admits:

> Regarding the quality of learning through ODE [Online Distance Education], much of the research has concluded that learning in ODE is as good as the learning in face-to-face education (F2FE) (Hong, 2002; Kleinman & Entin, 2002; Rovai, 2002). On the other hand, contradictory findings from individual studies have reported on student achievement between the two settings. Even the quantitative and qualitative reviews of synthesizing the individual experimental studies have reported inconsistent results.[3]

The U.S. Department of Education had conducted a meta-analysis of studies such as the one listed above.[4] Focusing on 51 of the most rigorous and statistically significant studies, they concluded that online education has definite advantages over face-to-face learning, but that blended classes (part face to face and part online) had the best likelihood of achieving the highest student learning. Positives for online education included giving students more control of their interactions while also letting students operate as individuals in the completion of assignments on their own schedule. An interesting caveat, however, was that one of the reasons for why this analysis believed students did better online is that students online were spending more time on their assignments. At the end of the day, pedagogies must be developed that allows for the maximization of both traditional methods as well as our increasing number of online courses.

## ☐ THE IPOD AND FILE SHARING

Before the iPad and the iPhone, however, our world was first changed by the creation of the iPod mobile digital device in 2001. Michael Bull, a lecturer at the University of Sussex, writes on the impact of the iPod as part of his book

*Sound Moves: iPod Culture and Urban Experience*. He calls the product the first consumer cultural icon of the new millennium, pointing out how its use is habitual in that it has become a large part of how people move through the world (in particular, its presence on runners and walkers on city streets as well as by commuters to and from work). With the aesthetic of the vinyl record cover being replaced by the style of the iPod, as well as the fact that half of the nearly 1,000 people Bull interviewed for his study had illegally downloaded music, indicates to Bull that the market is moving toward the artifact that holds the music rather than the music itself. According to Bull, one of the reasons that the iPod is so popular, beyond its ease of use and transportability, is the way in which it allows you to control your environment. An example of how you can control your interactions with others is the idea of nonreciprocal looking. In this scenario you look at those around you in public, but at the same time, you are able to control the degree of interaction by distancing yourself from other people. If and when they look up at you, the earplugs clearly indicate that you are otherwise engaged. In this sense, the MP3 player is not entirely about entertainment, but about control. We might ask ourselves why we have or don't have an iPod, and if we feel certain

An Apple Store, Home of iPad, iPod and iPhone

© 2012 by michael rubin/Shutterstock.com. Used under license of Shutterstock, Inc.

places are appropriate places to use it (the gym) while others might not (the classroom or the family dinner table).

One book in the Open Court "Pop Culture and Philosophy" series is dedicated to the increasing importance of the iPod. *iPod and Philosophy: iCon of an ePoch*, edited by D. E. Wittkower, is made up of 19 essays that examine the ways in which the iPod impacts our thoughts, our actions, and our sense of community. Of these essays, one of the most interesting, by Matthew Dewey, places the iPod within the context of a historical process that date back decades, seeing the device less as iNew and more as simply the iNow. The iPod is not a wholly new device says Dewey, but part of a tradition that dates back to the boom box, the Walkman, and portable CD and DVD players. Our downloading of music was not a new creation of Napster but dates back to making mixed tapes or even recording music off the radio. Music, in particular, has seen numerous "revolutions" in format, ranging from phonograph albums of various sizes and speeds, to eight-tracks and cassettes, to the compact disc and now the MP3 file. Why do we seek the newest formats? According to Dewey:

> The apparent physical need to have new things, this *arousal*, so to speak, contrived by an appealing idea or object, doesn't require that the idea or object be significantly "new." People don't buy new cars because the new cars are terribly different from the older ones, or because driving specifically requires new vehicles. There are other more deductive and culturally-influenced reasons for the insistence on new things, and the hyper-accumulation of material objects can reach a significantly addictive quality when it highjacks the sensation of "now." (188)

Dewey does not just see the iPod as a possible example of a Marxist creation of material want where it did not perhaps exist in the past (although this is an issue we would certainly be justified to ask). What is important here, says Dewey, is the iPod is not just a vehicle for playing music, but is primarily one of our first portable extensions of the Internet that helps "us to elevate and acclimate ourselves to an ongoing digitization. The digital I, the individual, and the iPod together can now work…to mediate a new experience and sense of identity," (189). It is the digital future for humanity as a whole that Dewey sees being introduced through the iPod.

This digital future includes the phenomenon of file sharing. The sharing of music files over the Internet dates back to the early 1990s, with the creation of the MP3 file format making music files much smaller and manageable. It was the creation of Napster in June 1999, however, that brought file sharing to the masses. Although Napster itself as a file-sharing entity would last only a couple of years before the *A&M Records v. Napster* decision of July 2001 forced its shutdown, the public interest in file-sharing of various forms of entertainment media remains, with Gnutella, LimeWire, and the Pirate Bay serving as other popular examples that have come and gone. Moral and economic questions surround file sharing as a practice, with one core question involving the degree to which file sharing impacts legitimate music sales. A 2008 *Chronicle of Higher Education* story by David Glenn discussed the conflicted evidence on this point, concluding that the majority of economic studies show that file sharing hurts sales, especially for artists who are already established. That being said, a great deal of reflection should take place about whether or not file sharing and illegal downloading is a legitimate problem or simply a nuisance for music executives and artists.

Regardless of the cause for the iPod and MP3 player revolution, one cannot deny their pervasiveness. I, for one, am amazed at the percentage of students walking around college campuses that are carrying MP3 players and wearing headphones. These students are examples of beings who are in a real sense disconnected from their immediate sensory surroundings. This isolation into an audio cocoon is a double-edged sword, according to Wittkower, in that "we isolate ourselves; and yet, we isolate ourselves within a world of culture, expression, and individual and social meanings," (xii). We identify ourselves, in large part, by the kind of media that we enjoy, adopting a social identity that may include labels such as punk, hippie, or metal head. This social identification into a culture, however, takes place within the context of isolation that may best be characterized by Martin Heidegger's concept of homelessness. Craig Condella discusses Heidegger's concept when contrasting the difference between calculative and meditative thought. The former kind of thought is interested in results and manipulating the environment to get those results, while meditative thought requires silent concentration and introspectively reflects on the nature of the meaning of existence itself, a kind of thought that Heidegger asserted was essential to our authentic existence. This is because the trick in meditative thought is that it includes a careful consideration of who one is within the context of where one is. With the iPod it does not really matter where we are because our music allows us to ignore our surroundings, and in doing so alienating ourselves from where we are.[5] Do we find ourselves using our headphones to disconnect from the world, and to what degree are we successful when we do this?

The conclusion of this chapter discusses the ways in which technological advances are impacting not just what we think but how we think, but for now within the specific context of the iPod we must recognize concerns raised by some critics who have compared the iPod to the drug soma from Aldous Huxley's *Brave New World*. According to Joseph C. Pitt's essay "Don't Talk to Me," iPod users "avoid eye-contact. They don't want to engage in conversation. They want to listen to their music. Their entire body language signals avoidance of human interaction," (162 in *iPod and Philosophy*). The iPod, according to Pitt, has become an escape mechanism that each person can program on their own to create the environment that they feel comfortable in, and he wonders if the consequences of this practice will eventually undermine our ability to socially interact in a productive fashion.

## ☐ SEX AND TECHNOLOGY

January 2010 saw the unveiling of what is believed to be the first interactive robotic sex doll at the AVN Adult Entertainment Expo in Las Vegas. While blow-up sex dolls have existed as frat-party staples for decades, this new item comes with a price tag that can reach as high as $10,000 and comes preloaded with five different personalities, ranging from Frigid Farrah, who is reserved and shy, to S&M Susan, who specializes in fulfilling pain/pleasure fantasies. The robot is designed to respond to its owner's statements and actions, saying things like "I love holding hands with you" when it senses you touching its hand. According to the creator, Douglas Hines with True Companion LLC, this is much more than a sex doll because "Sex only goes so far—then you want to be able to talk to the person." This product can be updated through a Wi-Fi connection, responds to the likes and dislikes of its owner, has the appearance of a heartbeat that is actually a circulatory system that heats its body, and can even simulate an orgasm. A Huffington Post blog asserted that at this stage, however, Roxxxy's "level of sophistication demonstrated was not beyond that of a child's talking toy... it can't move on its own, not even to turn its head or move its lips."[6] Still, this new arena of product asks us to rethink what it is that we want from our relationships, and if the answer is primarily sex and someone to tell us how great we are, this might do the trick. Can we think of positives and negatives that might come from choosing a robotic mate over another human being? If you're in a relationship, are there times that you wish your mate was a robot?

True Companion's website states that sex robots will become commonplace in the future, asserting that most adults never share their deepest fantasies with their partners. They see Roxxxy and the companion male robot Rocky as sexual aids no different from a vibrator, but clearly the possibilities here for the creation of pseudo relationships are worthy of our attention. The Steven Spielberg movie *A.I.: Artificial Intelligence* featured a character played by Jude Law named Gigolo Joe, who was a male prostitute mechanical robot (or mecha) that was specifically created and programmed to mimic love and desire, right down to his ability to play romantic music to set the mood. While Roxxxy is a far cry from Gigolo Joe, scientists recognize that robots will play an increasing role in our futures, completing tasks that are too dangerous (firefighting, for example) or time consuming (24-hour elder care) for many people today. According to a recent *Newsweek* article by Dan Lyons, "Don't Be Scared, It's Only a Robot," nearly 300 researchers worldwide are currently involved in a new field of studies known as human-robot interaction. This field examines not how robots can be programmed or operated, but instead the way in which people respond to robots. The key goal in these studies is to make robots less the object of sci-fi horror stories like *Terminator* and less intimidating.

One example of this involves a treat called "readability." When we approach a new obstacle, such as a door or wall, our heads move as we take in the situation via a rudimentary scan. When a robot is placed in a similar situation, such as trying to figure out how to open a door, it "will simply stand in front of the door, not moving, just scanning the surface with its cameras. To a human, the machine seems to be stuck in one place." Simply having the robot move its head from side to side and up and down while sizing up the door (movements that are totally unnecessary to the robot's assessment of the situation) helps communicate to humans the robot's process of figuring out how to get through the door. Studies seem to indicate that extra actions such as these help people feel more comfortable in the presence of robots and allows them to feel that they can "relate" to the robot's situation. Still, sociologist Sherry Turkle is concerned about how allowing robots into our lives, and even sometimes preferring robots over human interaction, may have its downside.

While Turkle focuses much of her book *Alone Together: Why We Expect More from Technology and Less from Each Other* on the ways in which we are changing the way we relate to each other, she does discuss Roxxxy, saying that these inventions open us up to relationships without demands, because "[r]obotic companionship may seem a sweet deal, but it consigns us to a closed world—the loveable as safe and made to measure" (66). This closed world of robots lacks the authenticity of human relations, demeaning what it means to be in a

© Blutgruppe/Corbis

Is This the Droid We Are Looking For?

relationship. Robots, as well as our increasing Internet lives, try to create new ways of thinking about and being intimate, but as Turkle points out "when technology engineers intimacy, relationships can be reduced to mere connections. And then, easy connection becomes redefined as intimacy. Put otherwise, cyberintimacies slide into cybersolitudes" (16). The trick here is that in a time when we already have plenty of reasons to be insecure about ourselves and our relationships, we find ourselves turning to technology for comfort, and for Turkle that comfort could quickly become an emotional crutch.[7]

While sex robots might still be a futuristic oddity for most people, the bottom line is technology has already had a great impact on our romantic and sexual lives. Just as some conservative preachers nearly a hundred years ago bemoaned the ability of the telephone to allow a lover's voice to be heard on a pillow at night (and created an opportunity for phone sex), the smartphone and the computer age have brought us sexting and sex-skyping. A cover story in newsmagazine *The Week* in June 2011 reexamined the question "Is Sexting Infidelity?" This story, which was published in the wake of former-Congressman Anthony Weiner's sexting scandal, points out, "In a brave new world of online porn and instant Internet connectivity, millions of other men, and yes, women are exploring the 'countless new avenues' for extramarital adventures" (June 24, 2011, p. 6). This new world has been confirmed by a study appearing in the academic journal *Sexuality & Culture* by Diane Wysocki and Cheryl Childers. Their article, "'Let My Fingers do the Talking': Sexting and Infidelity in Cyberspace," talks about how online relationships are changing the standard dating culture paradigms. Studies have shown that those who turn to online sexual relations (ranging from real-time cameras to looking at sexually explicit photographs) do so for reasons that include its place as a benign outlet for sexual frustrations, its opportunities for sexual experimentation with likeminded people, and its promotion of safe sex.

Websites like AshleyMadison.com were created in the last 10 years primarily as a service for married people and people in long-term relationships. The website, which claims to have over 13 million members, promotes itself with the motto: "Life is short. Have an affair." The study by Wysocki and Childers found that this service was primarily male (61 percent), with the largest percentage of users in their 40s. Respondents to a survey reported that more than two-thirds of people had met people face to face after first meeting online, with females being much more likely to engage in this behavior. "Females were much more likely than males to have met someone in person that they first met online. Given that our female respondents were much less likely to be married than were males, females may see the Internet as an unthreatening way to find potential real-life partners... to 'weed out' the undesirables" (235). More members of the site reported using the site for real life sexual hookups (74.9 percent female and 77.2 percent male) than even for merely cybersex (60.0 percent female and 53.5 percent male). Clearly, the members of AshleyMadison.com prefer the real to the virtual, although the study revealed that cybersex was a significant predictor of future behavior, because previous cybersex activity "tripled the odds of females cheating online and quintupled the odds for males" (236). Wysocki and Childers conclude that their research shows that as technology changes, those changes will not just be for the generations that grew up with that new technology, but that, regardless of age, they will impact the way people find potential partners. The fact that so many people are seeking out partners outside marriage might cause us to reflect on the meaning of marriage and how that institution itself might be changing. Compare the stories of your dating experience with older siblings, your parents, and your grandparents, and notice ways in which dating has changed over the years. Are these changes positive or negative, and to what degree do you believe technology has spearheaded these changes? Could you imagine your grandmother sexting?

## ▢ VIDEO GAMES

One of the side effects that have come with our increasing computer technologies and programming skills is our ability to use these tools for our entertainment with the creation of games. Video games have existed in one form or another since 1947, when the first video game was created using cathode ray tubes to simulate the display of a missile on a radar screen. They have been popular since the 1970s, and whether the discussion focuses on early efforts like Pong, where the gamer endeavored in a computer tennis game to keep the ball on the screen, or current massive multiple-player role-playing games like World of Warcraft or SecondLife, we have gained immeasurable amounts of joy and excitement. Children have been playing games for years, but the physical outdoor games such as freeze-tag and Cowboys and Indians gave way to board games such as Risk and Connect 4 to computer game systems, including Atari, Nintendo, and PlayStation. Some games have educational lessons, and others are purely for fun. Some are even going so far as to elevate the video game to the level of art recognition, with the Smithsonian American Art Museum offering its patrons a new exhibit, "The Art of Video Games."

© 2012 by Sean D. Used under license of Shutterstock, Inc.

Kids Enjoying Some Harmless Fun?

One video game industry study asserted that the percentage of kids aged 2 to 17 in the United States who play video games is 91 percent. A 2011 *Frontline* episode titled "Digital Nation" discussed some of the pitfalls of a gaming society. Excessive video game use is being seen by some as akin to an addiction. In World of Warcraft, the average player spends 10 hours a week within that gaming environment. This pales in comparison to the gaming that can be seen in places like South Korea, where popular computer cafés, or PC Bombs as they refer to them, offer rows and rows of computers, primarily for gaming. Inside these establishments, gamers play in marathons that often can stretch over 24 hours. In the extreme, *Frontline* reported a story of a 28-year-old gamer named Lee Seung Seop, who actually died after over 50 hours of playing the game StarCraft without breaks for food or water. There is so much concern about video gaming in South Korea that there is a program called "The Internet Rescue School," a two-week program that attempts to get teens to disconnect from the Internet and stop obsessing with video games.[8] How much time do you spend playing video games, and do you sometimes choose playing over doing other things you need or want to do? Does the choice to play a game over completing necessary tasks mean there is an addiction or problem with gaming?

Much of the debate surrounding video games has centered on the violence depicted within games, as well as the degree to which that violence translates into violent behavior in gamers. Studies on the effects of gaming are varied in their results, with some arguing that video games model aggression and alter the participant's perspective on acts of violence, making them more likely to participate in aggressive acts like bullying than they would have otherwise. It is this view that has led to several games being censored or banned, starting with the 1976 video game Death Race, where players drove cars and ran over gremlins. Other views, such as the catalyst model, argue that aggression is due to a combination of factors, including genetic risk factors. Henceforth it may be that children with a predisposition to violence are drawn to that type of game instead of the game somehow creating a disposition to violence. Attempts to standardize a code for rating video games have served to calm some of these concerns, making it easier for parents to make judgments about what level of game they are comfortable with their children playing. Other concerns remain, however, including the depictions of women, minorities, and gay and lesbian characters, where stereotypes still invoke criticism from many.

The story is not all negative however, as some are using virtual games as a form of immersion therapy to help people with mental disorders work through their problems. An example of this phenomenon involves the treatment of military soldiers dealing with posttraumatic stress disorder by replaying some of the scenarios that they experienced in combat and working through their responses to those situations. Others point out that video games can serve as a way of helping children deal with feelings of stress and aggression, and some assert that multiplayer games can help people learn to become a more effective member of a team. Perhaps most interesting is the degree to which game play improves hand-eye coordination and dexterity. While it is no surprise that video game experience might help a soldier be more adept at operating an unmanned drone, researchers are finding improvements in other areas. For example, "A study of 33 laparoscopic surgeons found that those who played video games were 27 percent faster at advanced surgical procedures and made 37 percent fewer errors compared to those who did not play video games."[9] If findings like this can be confirmed, we might find ourselves looking less at a doctor's advanced degrees and more at the high score records.

© 2012 by Berci. Used under license of Shutterstock, Inc.

Atari 2600

## ☐ CHANGING THE WAY WE LIVE

As discussed in the numerous examples above, technological advances in the last few years have changed the ways in which we interact with others, express ourselves, and engage with the world around us. This last section will try to draw some points of comparison from among the previous sections, highlighting an overarching concern that some have about the general direction of our technology as a whole.

A new Columbia University study found that the use of Google and other Internet search engines to access information ranging from research projects to trivial facts may be changing the way our brains store information. In part, the study included experiments analyzing the ways in which students answered trivia questions, looking at their ability to recall information in a variety of scenarios. The research was headed by Betsy Sparrow and published in *Science*. In essence, our brains are more likely to forget things that it believes can easily be rediscovered through the Internet, and furthermore that we often are able to remember where information is located on the web rather than the actual information itself. The most obvious example of this phenomenon can be seen in our increasing inability to remember phone numbers and addresses that we believe can easily be looked up using our smartphones.

The general discussion of how our new technologies are impacting our thought processes is best encapsulated in a text we mentioned earlier, Nicholas Carr's excellent book *The Shallows: What the Internet is Doing to Our Brains*. Carr discusses the idea of neuroplasticity, the view that sees our brains not as processors that become fixed in their ways as we age, but as continually changing and with every sensory input we provide it, reprogramming itself along the way. As Carr correctly points out, the Internet is now widely used for shopping and banking, for researching and booking travel, for watching video and listening to music, and for reading and writing everything from brief correspondence to the electronic books discussed above. The main difference that Carr articulates between the world before the Net and the world after its creation is the way in which the Internet presents information and how the mind adjusts to match. "Whether I'm online or not, my mind now expects to take in information the way the Net distributes it: in a swiftly moving stream of particles. Once I was a scuba diver in the sea of words. Now I zip along the surface like a guy on a Jet Ski" (6–7). The Columbia

University study mentioned above indicated this same phenomenon; that we become what we think, or at least that we can change our brain structure by the ways in which we think about the world. Neuroplasticity may have benefitted our species in the past as we learned how to incorporate tools into our daily tasks, but this evolutionary benefit, however, may have a downside. As Carr explains the research: "The paradox of neuroplasticity...is that, for all the mental flexibility it grants us, it can end up locking us...The chemically triggered synapses that link our neurons program us, in effect, to want to keep exercising the circuits they've formed" (34). The brain reprograms itself on the fly, and one example of this can be found in the brains of London cab drivers, in that "the longer a cab driver had been on the job, the larger his posterior hippocampus tended to be," which is the part of the brain that helps the driver store and manipulate mental representations of his or her surroundings (33). Another example is seen when someone loses one of their senses such as vision. The brain rewires itself and uses the brain capacity that once was used for sight in other more meaningful ways, such as reprocessing the sense of touch used for reading braille. For Carr, this neuroplasticity is impacted by the addictive nature of the Internet, which he asserts teaches us to not see the forest or the trees, but instead focus on leaves and twigs.

Another example of the way in which our changing technologies are impacting the way our brains work can be found in our automobiles. The use of global positioning systems (GPS) to find our way from point A to B seems on its surface to be an amazingly useful tool with little to no downside. Now we can avoid getting lost or needing to ask a stranger for directions, as our programmable GPS cannot only help us get home but also help us find our favorite shopping outlets and restaurants along the way. The convenience, however, appears to come at a price, as studies are indicating that the users of GPS actually lower their IQs with extensive use. The idea is that reliance on GPS undermines our mind's ability to think of problems in three-dimensional space, as we do when we are looking at a map and trying to figure out where we are relative to where we want to go, and then have to visualize how to get from A to B. A map does not tell you to turn left, so you have to figure out each turn on your own after visualizing your position. With the aid of GPS and its turn-by-turn instructions, this kind of advanced problem solving is no longer necessary, and our brains no longer get the benefit of this kind of workout.

Unless you are of a religious order that practices a reluctance to adopt new technologies, such as Amish or Mennonite, advances in technology are going to have a clear and distinct impact on you and your quality of life. Instead of merely being a passive consumer who merely absorbs and uses these advances, I hope this chapter has given you reason to be more thoughtful and reflective regarding the ways in which you choose to let technology into your lives, and more aware of the ways in which those choices might be affecting who you are and how you think.

---

[1] As quoted in the *Washington Post*, May 24, 2010.

[2] Adam Gorlick, "Media multitaskers pay mental price, Stanford study shows," *Stanford Report*, August 24, 2009. http://news.stanford.edu/news/2009/august24/multitask-research-study-082409.html. See also Ryan Hamilton and Kathleen D Vohs, Being of Two Minds: Switching Mindsets Impairs Subsequent Functioning of Mind, *Organizational Behavior and Human Decision Processes*, December 2010.

[3] *European Journal of Open, Distance and E-Learning*, Vol. 2007, No. 1. (2007)

[4] Scott Jaschik, "The Evidence on Online Education." *Inside Higher Ed*, June 29, 2009. http://www.insidehighered.com/news/2009/06/29/online

[5] Craig Condella, "iPod Therefore iAm." *iPod and Philosophy: iCon of an ePoch*. (Open Court Press, Chicago), 2008.

[6] For the Huffington Post story, complete with pictures, go to http://www.huffingtonpost.com/2010/01/10/roxxxy-sex-robot-photo-wo_n_417976.html.

[7] See David Levy's *Love and Sex with Robots* for an opposing view that argues that robots can help make us better friends and lovers because of our ability to practice with them.

[8] See Martin Fackler, "In Korea, A Boot Camp Cure for the Web Obsession." *New York Times*, November 18, 2007.

[9] http://en.wikipedia.org/wiki/Video_game

CHAPTER 7

# Comparative Popular Culture

We now turn to the international perspective. The intent of this chapter is to give the student a brief comparative view of popular culture outside the US by examining the popular culture of China, Japan and India. While this chapter cannot aim for completeness, it will help the student get acquainted with the interpretation of three important cultures outside of the US. Because of globalization, it is no longer acceptable to study national cultures in isolation. The core set of comparisons in this book will be limited to the US, India, China and Japan. There is much more to our world, but space considerations require us to restrict our gaze. India and China are obvious candidates because of their recent economic growth, but they have also been the cultural centers of gravity in Asia for millennia. The ideas of these countries dominated the countries near them for a long period of history. Thus Chinese Confucianism and Chinese versions of Buddhism make their way into Korea, Japan and Viet Nam, while Burma, Thailand and Cambodia have more of an Indian Hindu and Buddhist cultural character. Between the two of them, China and India are responsible for much of the culture of Asia. The post-Cold War world seems to be developing into a world in which the US, India, China will be the primary generators of popular culture, although many other countries will make significant contributions. The US, China and India will also be the dominant economic, political and military forces in the world, which is not surprising given what we already know about the connections between culture, economics and politics. While Japan's influence is likely to wane in the future, its culture was the first Asian culture to successfully challenge the West. So while Japanese culture is heavily influenced by China in

Japanese culture's formative years, it made a powerful historical statement in its heyday, and it will still be highly influential for years to come. Therefore our focus in this chapter on popular culture outside the US will be on China, India and Japan. This is in no way to belittle the contributions of other countries. Two particularly serious omissions are the neglect of Spanish-speaking culture and Islamic culture, but there is simply no way to cover all parts of the world with adequacy. In future editions we will remedy these omissions.

## ☐ CHINA

The rise of China is probably the single most important phenomenon in current world history. The demographic forecast indicates that China will be the largest economy in the world in a relatively short time. This is bound to have significant ramifications for the nature and direction of world popular culture. It is also the case that China formerly held a dominant a position in the world, and this dominance is reflected in the extent to which Chinese culture has affected all of East Asia. China was the dominant military and cultural force in Asia and most probably the world for much of world history. This should make it clear that China is not just the most recent contender for world dominance, but a structural fact of world culture. China is not only a dominant economic force in the world, it is building on a long-established cultural dominance of Asia. It thus arrives at economic dominance armed with a strong set of cultural symbols to propel its ideological influence on the world.

This means that it is absolutely crucial to understand basic cultural facts about Chinese history and culture. Chinese culture is fundamentally a combination of ancient Confucian, Daoist and Buddhist ideas with a more recent strong dose of

© CHINA DAILY/Reuters/Corbis

Confucius

Marxism. Although this is a vast oversimplification since many other religions are present in the vast area we call China, one could do worse than focusing on Confucius as the seminal thinker of China. He is certainly China's equivalent to Plato in providing the first and most influential set of answers to the questions the Chinese asked themselves about life and the world. One could even argue that Confucius had a greater effect on Chinese thinking than Plato or even Christ did on Western thinking because Confucius' ideas permeate Chinese social structure, while neither Jesus' nor Plato's ideas have ever determined the structure of Western social institutions. Further, Confucius' ideas extend well beyond China into Japan, Korea, Viet Nam and elsewhere in Southeast Asia.

Confucius' influence on Chinese society is profound. Confucius' principles of Ren (gentlemanliness), Li (propriety/order) and Hsiao (filial piety) still govern Chinese behavior in spite of over fifty years of Communist rule. The Confucian gentleman was a man (Chinese society, like most ancient societies, was sexist) who was well-educated, cultured in a variety of the arts, obedient to his elders and superiors, and who followed the prescribed moral rules and rituals to the letter. Thus Chinese society prior to 1949 was hierarchical, highly ordered, ritualized, traditional and conservative, and these characteristics can be traced back to the philosophy of Confucius.

The Confucian personality type—obedient, obsequious, hard-working and respectful, still prevails in East Asia—probably more in Japan, Taiwan and Korea than in mainland China, but even there as well. Americans cannot help but notice that East Asians, in general, have these qualities to a greater extent than typical Americans. Americans are much more individualistic than East Asians. The communist revolution reinforced this aspect of Chinese personality with its emphasis on the collective, the family and the state, over the individual person. We will see this exemplified in much Chinese popular culture.

The Chinese state is very old—Chinese dynasties are traced back almost 4000 years. Imperial China endured for millennia for many reasons, not least of which was the belief in the mandate of heaven. The mandate of heaven was the idea that if a person managed to take over the state then it must have been the case that they were supposed to do so, that it was "in the cards" so to speak. Heaven sides with the winners in Chinese history, and so it is not surprising that the emperor would be called the "son of heaven." This notion gave China a stability never matched in any other part of the world. This stability, however, would end up keeping China from modernizing, so that when change finally did come to China it came as a complete rejection of its past. Revolutions are never pleasant, but the Chinese revolution was as complete a rejection of its past as it could be. But for most of its history, China was very stable in overall structure. Dynasties changed, but the structure of society rarely did.

The Chinese imperial order was very strong both internally and externally. Internally, Chinese society was administered by a group known as "scholar-officials," who were the agents of imperial power outside the capital. This centralized administration of the empire helped to prevent the accumulation of too much power by nobles, who were the main contenders to power in China. The scholar-officials, unlike the nobles, attained their position meritocratically, by passing a difficult civil-service exam. But the royalty, nobles, eunuchs and scholar-officials all together made up a very small percentage of the population, which was made up largely of peasants, for Imperial China was an agrarian society. The vast majority of China's people (80–90%) lived off the land, and this generally agrarian character holds true even today in spite of the massive modernization and urbanization of contemporary Chinese society.

Externally, China was the dominant power in East Asia, and this is reflected in its foreign relations in which other countries were forced to accept subordinate status to the "son of heaven." Both Japan and Korea accepted this subordinate status, and both felt the immense influence of their larger neighbor. Japan and Korea both borrowed heavily from Chinese tradition, embracing Confucianism and later, Buddhism as well as literary, artistic and musical styles. China was thus a cultural center for much of East Asia.

Chinese history is a sequence of dynasties going back to the Shang or possibly the Hsia, and reaching all the way into the 20th century, in which the last gasps of the last imperial dynasty, the Manchu, were breathed. The most important dynasties were those of the Han (206 BCE to 220 CE), the Tang (618–907 CE), the Ming (1368–1644) and the Qing (Manchu, 1644–1911), each lasting around three hundred years (notice that all of American history, by comparison, constitutes a little over 200 years). The Tang dynasty is often regarded as the cultural highpoint in spite of being a relatively weak dynasty.

Xian, the Tang capital, was the terminal point of the Silk Road and therefore the recipient of all the ideas passed along the Silk Road. In Xian one could find all the major religions of the world. Christianity, Islam, and Buddhism were all significant presences in Xian, and many more obscure religions such as Zoroastrianism and Manichaeism.

The Chinese Revolution came about for many reasons, and this not the place to rehearse them all, but there are a few points that are especially important for understanding contemporary Chinese culture. There are really two stages to the Chinese Revolution. First there is the overthrow of the Imperial Order in 1911. After forty more years and a fourway contest between the Republican government, the Warlords, the Communists and Japanese, the Communists emerge triumphant. The key arguments to understanding any revolution are economic, political, cultural and military, and this is true of China's 1911 revolution. Militarily the Chinese were weak in comparison to the Western powers and Japan (who invaded China in 1894 and didn't leave until the end of World War II) but they also were unable to maintain order against peasant protest movements, which we see in the twenty one year long Taiping Rebellion (1850–1871). The Western powers used their military superiority to set up zones of influence in economic concessions obtained in unequal treaties. It was also a time in which there was dynastic restlessness as anti-Manchu feeling was increasing. The Qing Dynasty never completely resolved the issue of Manchu "Chineseness," of being an outside group usurping the rightfully Chinese throne. There is the important role of the Empress Dowager, who some believe mismanaged the changes brought by the modern world. It certainly did not help that she was a woman at the head of a sexist society, but her decisions were generally too conservative to bring China into the 20th century. Droughts, famines and floods also exacerbated the social tensions already present in Chinese society. Finally, Western social, political and scientific ideas were beginning to permeate Chinese society. For all these reasons China, which had been the dominant power in Asia for thousands of years, finally fell apart.

Now imagine the blow to the Chinese psyche when they are made to submit after regarding themselves as the dominant race for as long as they could remember. It is no surprise that it took from 1911 to 1949 for China to regain independence, and the group that took power, Mao's communists, was determined to completely remake Chinese society according to the Marxist model. As you should recall from our discussion of Marxism, Marx thought that the transition from Capitalism to Communism would involve a change in what had been thought to be human nature. Economic philosophers before Marx had assumed self-interest and greed to be the major predictors of human behavior. Marx rejected this idea, that people are naturally greedy, as mere ideological justification for the capitalist system. Marx thought greediness would fade naturally over time with a change in the economic system. Mao believed

Mao Zedong

Photofest

that China could not wait for the normal evolution of human nature. For one, Mao considered China still a feudal country, which Marx would say had to first go through a capitalist revolution in order to build the industrial base and social conditions for the transition to communism. Mao rejected this limitation on the theory. Mao felt that the Chinese revolution could skip the capitalist step and go straight to communism from feudalism. Clearly, Mao thought that China required some wrenching changes.

The question that arises at this point is whether the attempt to create a new communist person would be consistent with a thriving popular culture. Creating the new communist man required strict control of media messages, and this was not going to give any room for a mass culture independent of party propaganda.

When Mao's first attempt at economic management, the "Great Leap Forward," failed spectacularly in producing economic growth or stability—it produced instead famine and the deaths of an estimated twenty million people, Mao's power declined. While the new leadership thought the mistakes were the result of bad economic theory, Mao blamed the result on a lack of true communist consciousness and recommended a cultural revolution to root out the remnants of the old capitalist thinking that he believe was still holding back China. By 1966, Mao had enough support to launch the cultural revolution.

The Chinese Cultural Revolution was the logical outcome of Mao's thinking, and these ideas led to millions of deaths in China and, exported to Cambodia, they led to the Killing Fields, where between 1/4 and 1/3 of the population of Cambodia was killed. The Cultural Revolution that lasted from 1966 to 1976, the year of Mao's death, was an attempt to create a new kind of person in a short time. Like its antecedent, the French Revolution, the Chinese Cultural Revolution ends in terror. This is a case in which an inexorable logic seems to move from political principles of equality to the arbitrary killing of millions. Mao decided that the revolution had not gone deep enough into the mentality of the new Chinese people, so he advocated that they go even farther in rooting out capitalist influence. Anything that implicated the old order was condemned as counter-revolutionary. The "Red Guard," a group of young people dedicated to ideological purity, was allowed to engage in harassment and even killing of those people it determined to be insufficiently communist. Many educated people were determined to be ideological impure and were sent to re-education camps or killed. Anyone involved in ancient Chinese arts was suspect, as was any business owner or former business owner. Popular culture was now completely under the command of the propaganda departments of the Communist Party. This terror did not end until after Mao's death, after which his followers, the "Gang of Four," lost their battle with the reformists led by Deng Xiaoping.

Deng Xiaoping was the decisive figure in turning the communist revolution in an economically sound direction. Deng began to allow more private business activity and eased up on the censorship of the arts. Popular culture was no longer merely an appendage of the propaganda effort, although there is still significant Party propaganda to this day. Many ostracized people were rehabilitated. Deng himself had spent time working in a factory as part of his own "re-education" during the cultural revolution. Once the markets were freed enough to encourage business activity, China's economic potential was allowed to flourish, and flourish it did. China became an economic powerhouse in short order. Popular culture followed in the wake of economic liberalization. However, economic prosperity also brought a yearning for political change, which resulted in the Tiananmen Square episode of 1989. In 1989 a protest developed on the occasion of the death of Hu Yaobang, who had been considered a friend of the democracy movement. The protestors wanted less censorship and greater democracy in China. The protest gave us a profound lasting image when a student blocked the progress of some tanks merely by refusing to move out of the way. This image, caught in both photograph and video has become iconic of the freedom movement in China and freedom movements generally. But China's leadership was determined to avoid the fate of the Soviet Union and Eastern Europe. Remember, this was the year that the Berlin Wall came down, signifying the end of Communism in Europe. China's leadership saw that things could easily get out of hand. The Chinese leadership decided to hold the line and not let Tiananmen turn into something bigger. So they cracked down and used force to end the student protest. But they did not leave it at that. They knew they could not keep down all the aspirations of the Chinese people, so they offered to permit more and more economic freedom. The result of the whole affair was a crackdown on political freedoms and the establishment of what we will call "the Grand Bargain." The "grand Bargain" was a tacit agreement that the people would be allowed to engage in significant economic freedom, but that they must refrain from questioning the decisions of the Communist Party.

© Bettmann/CORBIS

Deng Xiaoping

"Tankman" facing down tanks in Tiananmen Square

The irony that results from this Grand Bargain is that we have a "dictatorship of the proletariat," which Marx thought of as an unfortunate transition mechanism necessary to defend communism from capitalist plots or ideas, turned into a dictatorship that facilitates capitalism. For China is now capitalist in everything but name. Ultimate control of the economy lies in the hands of the Communist Party, but the Chinese Communist Party has learned how to allow significant private enterprise and even encourage it. The Chinese are even engaging in industrial policy, encouraging companies to locate within its borders, and though they have achieved a different consensus about the role of govt and private enterprise they still with the same kind of juggling of incentives we see in Western capitalist countries. China now has more millionaires than the U.K. or France. But political control will remain strong in China for the foreseeable future. So the current picture of China is one of a country that controls the political discussion with some rigor, but also permits a significant part of its economy to run on its own. Popular culture in China exists in a context of political restrictions but economic freedom.

Popular culture in China is circumscribed by Communist party censorship, but that still leaves a great deal of room for a vigorous popular culture. We begin our discussion of contemporary Chinese popular culture by looking at Chinese popular music.

Music in China consists of two types: Tongsu (Party approved patriotic rock music) and Yaogun, or non-official rock music. Tongsu lyrics are generally in praise of the Chinese Communist Party leadership and in praise of Mao in particular. Tongsu songs are written by a small group of writers for a variety of singers, often chosen for looks rather than singing ability, and sound like soft pop music of the West. Tongsu is generally disseminated via television. For example, the song, "The Great Undertaking," (anonymous) describes Chinese' oil workers' patriotic love of the Party. The Communist Party used the song as propaganda to get people to feel positive about the Party and the ideas of the Party. They did this by writing a song that expressed love, or at least some kind of deep emotion toward the Party and expected that people hearing the song would emulate the emotion.

Then the song turns to an appreciation of Chairman Mao. One cannot overestimate the personality cult surrounding Mao, and such songs are examples of propaganda meant to solidify the cult. Tongsu songs want the workers

© Fritz Hoffmann/In Pictures/Corbis

Chinese rocker Cui Jian

to believe that suffering for Mao is actually a pleasant experience. The Party realized their policies entailed suffering, so the Tongsu songs attempt to make the suffering easier to take by turning it into a kind of economic martyrdom, sacrificing oneself for the sake of the Party. The corollary of martyrdom is heroism, thus the workers become heroes, so doing their duty for the party, especially in difficult circumstances brings prestige. Tongsu songs offer praise to the workers for battling the elements in a harsh land often end with a final homage to Mao.

From a Western point of view this sugary kind of praise is a bit off-putting. No one in the US would be comfortable replacing the name Mao with Obama, Bush or Clinton. But the first purpose of this song is not aesthetic, it is political. The Communist Party felt that the best way to sell the party line was to embody it in the person of Mao. And it was, of course, in the interest of Chairman Mao to acquire this kind of uncritical adulation.

Yaogun rock music in China is interesting because, like most rock music, it draws on the adolescent rage of youth, but this rage cannot become overtly political. Musicians such as Cui Jian use hard rock's rhythms and harmonic structures, which is typical of Chinese rock music, but what is most interesting about Cui Jian is how he moves at the edge of political acceptability. He rages against life and society generally rather than the government, which means his criticisms stay just inside the realm of acceptable lyrics. Let's look at his song, "Slackers, the lyrics of which are easily found on the internet. It begins with a request that he not be pampered."

Cui Jian's generation grew up in better circumstances than those first generations who endured the Great Leap Forward and the Cultural Revolution, but they were not without their own anxieties. The wish not to be fussed over is a reference to the one child policy. Because of overpopulation, China instituted a one-child only policy, which alleviated population pressures but also led to parents spoiling their children.

Cui Jian bemoans the fact that the older generations regard the present generation as slackers, and he basically agrees with the assessment, embracing "slackerhood," but still argues that he must "save face."

The reference to "saving face" is interesting since it refers to a Confucian notion of propriety in which maintaining one's respect in society is absolutely crucial. Oddly enough, this notion of keeping face is combined with a nihilism in which only the mundane matters. Behind this nihilism is a disdain for money, which, because of the Grand Bargain, is now the focus of most Chinese lives. He believes Chinese people only think about making more and more money.

Make more money, make more money.

He even seems to embrace the inevitable and defends the money-oriented life. Cui Jian's music shows that he believes there is pervasive corruption. But Cui Jian always returns to the personal and reveals a vulnerability: he despairs of being able to commit to anything. and embraces the coddling of his parents and the care free attitude that results. Qui Jian is thus embracing a carefree nihilism. Cui Jian does admit to caring for other people, however, it is not a patriotic feeling, but a more basic feeling of solidarity in spite of attacking his contemporaries notions of what is cool. Cui Jian sees the way popular culture is homogenizing Chinese life, but he suggests that Chinese should refrain from being too critical or contrary, which we can imagine ultimately makes his music palatable enough for the communist authorities to accept without censorship.

It is interesting that China's political circumstances have produced this prognosis of the kind of ennui. We could have almost predicted such ennui would be likely to result from China's manner of regulating discussion and behavior. Every political system has its corresponding form of existential angst and Cui Jian, even if not representative of Chinese psychology, still presents a very interesting kind of nihilist response. It also tells us what to expect in the way of creativity in the Chinese context. We should look for all the standard ideas common to all civilizations, such as lost love, the quest, revenge, betrayal etc., but we should expect what, from the point of view of our own culture, what would be unexpected. The lament of the powerless has a certain poignancy in the case of Chinese artists since they are barred from some kinds of criticism. But even with this sort of restriction, Chinese pop artists have a wide latitude of expression, and this will allow for some (but as with all pop culture, a small percentage) to reach a high level of aesthetic quality. This happened in other communist countries, such as the Soviet Union and Cuba. The political restrictions were problematic, but they did not stop high level creativity.

Television did not really begin to be a fact of Chinese life until the 1970s, and even then it was mostly political programming to support the government. It was not until the 1980s that the ordinary Chinese had regular daily access to television programming. The 1980s, however, saw an explosion in television ownership as well as in the number of stations. The number of households with a television went from two percent in the late 1970s to just under fifty percent by the 1980s, and by the 1990s it was up to eighty percent.

*Yearnings* was a serial television show that remade Chinese viewing habits. Watching this weekly show became a habit that was not required, it was a genuine fad. Mass numbers, in some cities as much as 90% watched it weekly. The origin of Yearnings is instructive. Prior to this series China imported much of its television soap opera content from Hong Kong. Chinese writers found this unacceptable and determined to rectify the matter and took up the task of writing soap operas. They saw that writing soap operas was different than writing sophisticated literature, and so they intentionally dumbed down the material and used obvious clichés to capture the audience. Wang Shuo, one of the writers, has been quoted as saying, "Make somebody as good as possible and then have them done over really badly." (Latham, 63) The writers knew how to pull on the heartstrings of the common Chinese person, and they used this knowledge to engineer their own success. They succeeded beyond their wildest dreams. The series was a big hit, and even the Party officials thought it was good communist art. They thought that the series portrayal of ordinary Chinese people was flattering and presented good role models for the people. The writers were surprised and a bit embarrassed by their success since they had all produced better work without receiving popular acclaim, but now having intentionally produced weaker work they become successful. On the other hand, they were accused by the intellectuals of selling out, of bastardizing their art. The logic of writing for the mass market had reached China with *Yearnings*, and it was there to stay. Now it is standard practice to produce inferior work for the masses, just like in the rest of the world. Thus China has joined the capitalist world in producing culture that sells rather than culture that is good. In fact, the line up of Chinese television channels is not much different than the line up elsewhere in the world. The main difference, of course, is that China does not have the free-wheeling political discourse we see in the West.

China today has sixteen China Central television (CCTV) channels:

CCTV1: the main news and entertainment channel

CCTV2: the economic channel

CCTV3: general arts and information channel

CCTV4: the international Chinese language channel, aimed principally at overseas Chinese viewers

CCTV5: sports

CCTV6: movies

CCTV7: youth, agriculture and military affairs channel

CCTV8: TV dramas

CCTV9: English language channel, aimed at overseas viewers

CCTV10: Science and Education

CCTV11: theatre, opera and traditional music

CCTV12: legal affairs

CCTV13: International and National News

CCTV14: Childrens' programming

CCTV15: Music Channel

CCTV16: French and Spanish language channel, aimed at overseas viewers. (Latham, 54)

The above are the national channels, and they give the nation a certain unity of popular culture. On the other hand, there are also regional and local channels, and while these are also monitored for political correctness, they do provide a certain amount of linguistic and cultural diversity. There is a limit to this diversity, however. While the Chinese leadership will allow cultural differences to be aired, they are not willing to permit political differences to be aired. For this reason, DTH (direct to home) satellites are banned except for special cases. All satellite transmission are channeled through cable, which the Chinese government controls. Recently China has loosened up on satellite transmissions, and there are something like forty million illegal satellites in use, so the Chinese are not as strict about satellite as official rules would indicate. Further, the Chinese government has begun allowing DTH satellites in rural areas in order to bring news to areas without access to news.

China has all the kinds of television entertainment we find in the US. They have game shows, reality tv, quiz shows, variety shows, karaoke, fashion, comedy, virtually all the genres of television programming available in the west. So for the most part, the general look of Chinese television is very similar to television in the West. The primary difference is in the amount of censorship. The Chinese Communist Party keeps close tabs on all cultural activities. This follows from the ideology of Maoism, which felt it was crucial to root out anti-communist influences. While censorship has relaxed a great deal in recent years, political speech is still highly regulated.

Chinese News is strictly controlled, particularly the national news outlets of CCTV. The Chinese people have become accustomed to "reading between the lines" of television news, but there are limits to this skill, and thus the Chinese people's access to news will always be circumscribed. This kind of restriction makes news much less of a player in Chinese politics. Chinese news has the appearance of informing the public, and it does a reasonable job with non-political stories, but otherwise it keeps the Chinese people ignorant of politics with the exception of the official line of the Communist Party. The other parts of the news, such as book or movie reviews, are often part of a bribery system. Want a good review for your book, play or film? Give money to the reviewer.

The Internet in China presents both an opportunity and a danger to China. The internet has vast economic potential, but it also has powerful political potential. While China wants the economic gains that come from a freely operating internet, it does not want the political power of the internet in the hands of people outside the government. China's response to this dilemma has been to allow most non-political internet traffic to proceed, but to block any sites it finds politically problematic. What counts as politically problematic is interesting. We would expect explicitly political websites critical of the government to be blocked, but it is more surprising to find sites like Facebook blocked. Apparently the reason for blocking Facebook is its potential for organizing protest very quickly. It is also interesting which political sites get blocked. Some conservative political websites are allowed, but Huffington Post, a liberal website is blocked. China does not say why they block any given site, or even that they are doing it, so we can only speculate. In the case of Huffington Post it could be that they have posted articles critical of the Chinese treatment of Tibet, but we will probably never really know. Internet pornography is available in China, but it is officially outlawed. Clever Chinese can bypass the restrictions on pornography, but Chinese law keeps pornography from being the massive presence it is in the West. But the Chinese leadership is not terribly worried about pornography, and it flourishes in the big cities like Shanghai. Pornography is not political, so it from the Party's point of view, letting a bit of pornography slip though is no danger to the system.

While China's film industry has some distance to go before it can claim to have anywhere near the influence of Hollywood or Bollywood, Chinese film is in something of a golden age. Chinese actors and actresses, such as Gong Li, have international fame. Recent Chinese films show real greatness. Chinese films are playing internationally, and some have been nominated for Oscars with *Crouching Tiger, Hidden Dragon* winning the Oscar for best foreign language film in 2001. The films of Zhang Yimou and Chen Kaige are high quality and play to world-wide audiences. Films like *Hero* and *House of Flying Daggers* by Zhang Yimou are both critical and popular successes. Chen has done great work, possibly the greatest, but Zhang has had more commercial success and has the better overall record.

Zhang and Chen are the most popular and important members of what is called the Fifth Generation of Chinese filmmakers, and were members of the first class to graduate from the Beijing Film Academy, which was re-opened in 1978 after being shut down during the Cultural Revolution. The career of Zhang Yimou is instructive. Early in his career he made art films like *To Live*, and *Raise the Red Lantern*. *To Live* was praised by critics, but Zhang did not endear himself to the authorities with his implicit criticism of the Great Leap Forward and Cultural Revolution. But as Zhang turned to more popular fare like *Hero* and

Gong Li

Photofest

Gong Li

*House of Flying Daggers*, and which, not coincidently, were more to the liking of the communist authorities, Zhang became a favorite of the Chinese leadership, and he was given the prestigious job of producing the Beijing Olympic Games in 2008. Some have accused Zhang of selling out, but whether he has sold out or not, he has produced excellent films, and the Beijing Olympics were a great success.

*Hero* and *House of Flying Daggers* are instructive for understanding Chinese popular self-consciousness. These films created a space for a sophisticated and noble self-understanding of both Chinese historical identity and the nature of current Chinese rule. When the assassin in *Hero* realizes that the Chinese Emperor might in the final analysis be correct to unify the whole country under his rule, the hero sacrifices himself for the system. This idea works to legitimate the sacrifices the current leadership of China asks of its people today. Whatever we think of the message, it is a powerful film and effective piece of ideological justification for the Chinese regime. *House of Flying Daggers* is not as political as *Hero*, but it is a masterpiece of film making. Rarely has such beauty been displayed in a film. *House of Flying Daggers* revels in the beauty of Chinese spaces, costuming and people. The film is a veritable tutorial in the use of color and the cinematography (Zhang started out as a cinematographer) is unfailingly majestic and profound.

Chen Kaige has similarly been in and out of the Chinese government's good graces. His film, *Farewell My Concubine*, may be the greatest Chinese film ever made and one of the greatest from any country. Following the careers of two Opera actors, Kaige takes us on an historical tour of horrors of 20th century Chinese history while delving deeply into gender and psychological issues. It is also a very personal film for he has the main characters all commit unforgivable betrayals just as he himself denounced his own father during the Cultural Revolution. *Farewell My Concubine* contains several episodes quite amenable to the use of the theories we use in this book. To point to just one, in the beginning of the film a prostitute takes her son to an Opera training school for children but is refused because he has an extra finger. In a horrifying scene she cuts his finger off and returns to the school where he is now accepted. The cutting off of the finger is clearly a Freudian metaphor for castration, and since the actor ends up playing female roles (women were not allowed to participate in Chinese Opera until recently) and becomes homosexual as he matures, the symbolism is clear. But what is most interesting about the film is how it traces the ups and downs in the fortunes of the two actors as they attempt to pursue their art during the many political upheavals in 20th century Chinese history. In the end they are brought low by the Cultural Revolution, which has no place for decadent opera stars who just want to pursue their art.

© Bai Xiao Yan/Sony Pictures Classics/Bureau L.A. Collection/Corbis

Ziyi Zhang in *House of Flying Daggers*

Leslie Cheung and Fengyi Zhang in *Farewell My Concubine*

Because China is fairly new to capitalism it has not built up the legal frameworks to govern it. (The same is true of the former Soviet Union. As they turned to capitalism they also became very corrupt.) Thus there are many sectors of Chinese life victimized by corruption. Party functionaries often take advantage of their positions to exact bribes or direct funds in ways beneficial to themselves and their families. Opportunities for officials have only increased with economic liberalization. Officials in charge of some sector of the economy will often create hybrid private/profit entities that skate between the laws of commerce. The Chinese realize this, and Chinese officials are always launching campaigns against corruption, and anti-corruption is a common theme in both officially sanctioned culture as well as independently produced popular and high culture. Polls show that corruption is high on the list of the publics concerns.

China is not very respectful of copyright laws. Software piracy is rampant. Western movies are quickly bootlegged and sold without any royalties for the producers of the work. It is thought that as much as 93% of all films sold in China are bootlegs. As much as 90% of all music sales in China are unauthorized. Several lawsuits are ongoing, and it is likely that as China becomes more integrated into the international economy it will begin to get more serious about copyright infringement. It is also more likely they will become more respectful of copyright as indigenous Chinese authors, composers and filmmakers become interested in their own royalties.

Sports in China follows neither the amateur nor the market models of organization of sport in the West, but rather adheres to the old Communist model developed by Soviet Russia. Promising athletes are identified early in life and routed into special sports schools, where their lives revolve around their training. The Chinese have come in for some criticism for burning out or injuring young athletes with overly rigorous training methods, but their performance in international sports competitions show the effectiveness of Chinese methods, which were used by Soviet Russia to good effect, and is still utilized by Cuba, always a power player in international sport. Interestingly, if the Soviet Union had remained united, they would have the highest overall medal count in the Beijing Olympics with 118 (The US had 110 and China 100). The recent introduction of professional athletes into the Olympic Games was largely a response to the perceived unfairness of amateurs from other countries competing with government supported athletes from China, the former Soviet Union and Cuba (12th in the Beijing Games). Even though the communist model for the general economy has been rejected around the world, the communist model for sport is thriving and obviously very effective as China's performance in the Beijing Games, the most numbers of gold medals and 2nd overall to the US, shows that China is really in the argument for greatest sport nation.

The history of Chinese performance in the Olympic Games linked to the political history of China. Before Deng Xiao Ping, China won few medals compared to its size. By 1992 in Barcelona, however, the medal count for China hits 50, and goes no higher than 63 until the Beijing Olympics, when it contended for first with the US (110) with 100. If this trajectory holds, China should be the overall champion in both numbers of medals as well as gold medals.

Yao Ming is probably the biggest star in Chinese international sport. Yao's size, at 7'6" is a symbol of the power of China, and the Chinese are immensely proud of their sports tradition. Yao is the biggest player in the NBA just as China has the largest population. Basketball was introduced very early by Christian missionaries and has since been at least a small presence in Chinese life, but during the Cultural Revolution sports organizations

| Year | Gold | Silver | Bronze | Total |
|------|------|--------|--------|-------|
| 1984 | 15 | 8 | 9 | 32 |
| 1988 | 5 | 11 | 12 | 28 |
| 1992 | 16 | 22 | 16 | 54 |
| 1996 | 16 | 22 | 12 | 50 |
| 2000 | 28 | 16 | 15 | 59 |
| 2004 | 32 | 17 | 14 | 63 |
| 2008 | 51 | 21 | 28 | 100 |

were disrupted. Only with the reforms of Deng Xiaping has sport reemerged in China. It is remarkable that China has done so well after having to rebuild its sports organization after 1978.

Conclusion: The Chinese government believes it can continue to have a flourishing economy and culture without popular political participation. They may be right. Many authoritarian countries are looking at the Chinese model as an alternative path to modernization, one without democracy. This may work while the economy is humming along with 8–10% growth, but that will not go on forever, and that will be the real test of the staying power of the communist party. China is facing several large problems in its future. First, there is a demographic time bomb caused by the one-child policy. The younger generations are much smaller than the older generations, so there will be fewer young to take care of the old. Since China does not have the social safety net that we find in Western countries this could be very problematic. This is why the New York Times opinion writer, Tom Freidman, says that China is in a race

Yao Ming

© Qi Heng/Xinhua Press/Corbis

to get rich before it gets old. They need to build up a surplus for the time when the population of supported older people is larger than the population of younger people doing the supporting. Second, China is experiencing uncontrolled growth without much regard for the pollution they are causing. Eventually the Chinese will have to get greener than they are now. To be fair, China is doing more to address environmental concerns, but their efforts fall far short in the face of the growth we see in Chinese industry and development. Third, China is trying to have a flourishing economy and culture while maintaining control of the internet. They may be able to pull it off, but they are more likely to face a choice between having to give up on economic and cultural progress or opening up the political sphere.

## ☐ JAPAN

If any country constituted a rival for American influence in the world of popular culture, it is Japan. In spite of Japan's current economic and cultural malaise, it has been a major contributor to world popular culture. Japanese films, manga, anime, cars, toys, electronics, fashion and karaoke are all world-wide in their presence. There was a period in the 1970s in which many in the US felt that Japan was passing or at least drawing even with the US economically and culturally. Like all cultures, there are religious components to Japan's cultural sensibility, so we begin with some of the key myths of Japan's Shinto religion.

Although Buddhism is more popular in Japan than Shinto, Shinto provides more of the mythological foundation of Japanese popular culture. Confucianism, imported from China via Korea, with its moral code and focus on ritual is also in the Japanese religious mix. The key myths for our purposes is the Shinto creation myth, the idea of Kami, and the notions of purity and pollution. After five gods were produced in primordial creation, two more came to be, Izanagi and Izanami. They were given a special spear by the elder gods and were told to create an island by using the spear to stir the ocean. Once solid land was created they built a palace for their wedding and a pillar to the heavens. When the god and goddess are ready to procreate it is the result of noticing the complementary nature of their genitalia. This conception of sexuality legitimizes the basic sexual urge. But the next part of the narrative gives sexuality a set of boundaries.

Izanagi and Izanami perform a ritual of walking two different directions around the pillar, but, unfortunately, Izanami performs the ritual incorrectly and speaks first upon meeting Izanagi behind the pillar. Because of this mistake they give birth to a leech-child, which they discard. They perform the ritual again, this time having Izanagi speak first, and so Izanami gives birth to the Japanese islands as well as several deities, including a fire deity, whose birth causes the death of Izanami. Thus, transgressing the ritual requirements of rigid sex roles causes tragedy.

Izanami goes to the underworld to find Izanami, but he finds her in a state of decomposition and covered in maggots. Appalled and fearing that he will be spiritually polluted by her dead body, he runs away from her and back to the upper world. Izanami sends various demons after Izanagi, but he closes the opening between the worlds with a boulder. Izanami then vows to kill one thousand people every day. Izanagi responds that he will create fifteen hundred each day, and that is where the relative balance of birth and death was established. Izanagi then purifies himself by bathing in water. His bath creates more deities, including the ancestors of the people of Japan. The Japanese creation myth thus establishes sexual hierarchy, the importance of ritual and doctrine of purity and pollution. We will see that patriarchal sex roles, descent from the gods, ritual correctness, purity, pollution and cleanliness constitute the foundation of Japanese mentality that then gets rationalized when brought into contact with Westernization and Modernization.

There are conflicting legends about Amaterasu. Amaterasu is the offspring of Isanagi and Izanami, who, in one version, decide to come together in order to provide the earth with a ruler. In the other version of the story, Amaterasu is created when Izanagi purifies himself after the underworld episode. In any case, Amaterasu is thought to be the goddess of the sun and the ancestor of the Japanese ruling family.

The story most associated with Amaterasu has to do with her conflict with her brother, Susanoo, the storm god. After much feuding, Amaterasu retreats to a cave and refuses to leave it. But since she is the goddess of the Sun, her behavior plunges the world into darkness. After several attempts to get her to leave the cave, she is finally coaxed out by Uzume, the goddess (kami) of merriment. Uzume creates lots of noise by dancing naked, and when Amaterasu leaves the cave to see what the commotion is about, she is faced

© 2011 by Dr_Flash. Used under license of Shutterstock, Inc.

Japanese Torii

with a mirror, which shows her great beauty. Drawn into the merriment, the cave is closed off. With Amaterasu back, the light returns to the world. We should notice one structural similarity with the story of Izaname and Izanagi. In both stories a gateway is closed, signaling that keeping boundaries is essential to Japanese norms. The boundary between sacred and profane is the most important boundary in Japanese symbology. This boundary is represented by the ubiquitous Torii Gate, which we often find in front of Shinto and, to a lesser extent, Buddhist temples. The origin, oddly enough given the Torii's association with traditional Japanese culture, is probably Buddhist, and therefore, ultimately of Indian origin, probably the Sanchi Gate. This is a good lesson that traditional symbols need not be indigenous.

Of crucial importance to Japanese thinking is the idea of Kami, which are similar to gods, but what a Westerner might more accurately recognize as a spirit. A Kami is the embodiment of *mononoke*, or life spirit. Kami are found in natural objects and creatures from rocks, to mountains to trees and animals. There are also guardian Kami that protect places or clans. The emperors and other exceptional people are associated with Kami. Even abstract concepts can be Kami. Honoring Kami is one of the "Four Affirmations," which are (1) Family and tradition are to be honored, (2) Nature is sacred,

(3) Ritual purity and general cleanliness are to be maintained, (4) Honor the Kami and ancestral spirits. In addition to these formal aspects of Japanese religion, there is also a more collective sense of identity. There is a sense that the group is more important than the individual, that the individual is submerged. We see all these aspects of Shinto embodied in much Japanese culture, particularly the animation of Murakami, who will be discussed below.

The Japanese history that is important for our purposes begins in the 19th century with Japan embracing modernity, particularly modern armaments, and becoming an imperial power in East Asia. Japan defeats both China (1894–5) and Russia (1904) and asserts its preeminent role in Asian politics. In World War I Japan fights on the side of the victorious allies against Germany and is accorded "big five" status at the Treaty of Versailles. Militarism takes hold in Japan and Japan becomes increasingly more aggressive, invading China and occupying Manchuria in 1937 and joining with Nazi Germany against the US and its allies in World War II. After dominating much of East Asia and the Pacific, Japan is finally defeated when the US drops the atomic bomb on Hiroshima and Nagasaki. Japan's shock over the atomic bomb and defeat was profound and has had lasting effects on Japanese popular culture. Like the Chinese, the Japanese had an exaggerated sense of superiority, so when they are defeated the whole edifice of Japanese self-confidence disappears. They reject militarism and turn entirely to economic and cultural pursuits.

## Godzilla

The atomic bomb became an important symbol for Japanese popular culture. The most obvious example is that of Godzilla. Godzilla is such an interpretively pregnant symbol that it can express many ideas, some of which are contradictory. A list of the possible meanings of Godzilla includes the following:

1. The atomic bomb
2. The US
3. Natural disaster (Japan is located in an earthquake zone)
4. The West
5. Modernity
6. Technology
7. The revenge of nature
8. Death

The interpretation of Godzilla gives us a good opportunity to use structuralist theory. Godzilla represents both sides of some binary relationships, both technology and the revenge of nature against technology. Likewise, Godzilla represents both militarism and anti-militarism. Many powerful symbols overwhelm any one side of a binary relationship and end up representing both. A good example comes from Hindu religion. The god, Shiva, was originally the god of destruction in opposition to Brahma, the god of creation as well as Vishnu, the god of preservation. But as time went on, Shiva took on both his own and Brahma's roles, so now Shiva represents both creation and destruction. Further, Shiva represents both asceticism and eroticism. Godzilla is the same kind of figure. He represents both science and anti-science. He represents both overreaching, and the reaction against it, both

Toho Pictures/Photofest

Godzilla

Japan and the West, both modernity and the rejection of modernity. A survey of the Godzilla films shows this analysis to be correct. In some films Godzilla destroys Japan. In other films he saves it. In some films he does both.

The creation of Godzilla was a result of a Japanese filmmaker trying to think of a Japanese counterpart to King Kong, which was a massive popular success in the West. A comparison of Godzilla and King Kong is illuminating. They are both embodiments of their county's national horror. While Godzilla represents the dropping of the atomic bomb on Japan, King Kong is a symbol of black slavery (Rosen, 2004). He embodies the white American fear of black Americans. At the time of the first King Kong film the US was a country deeply affected by racism. White Americans feared black men and associated black men with a powerful animality. This fit a need to primitivize African Americans, to make white America feel superior, and to justify the differential treatment they gave black Americans. The islanders in the film are African instead of Pacific Islander, as one would expect on such an island. This slip is revealing. Blackness becomes synonymous with primitiveness, with animality.

White American males of the 1930's also feared black sexuality. It is revealing that the sacrifices to King Kong are female, and revealingly in the film, a white woman. There is a fetishization of white women in American culture. With white male fear directed toward black men, white women become the object of the fear of loss. White women come to represent a purity that black men endanger. All this is quite racist, but it was a very real ideology of hate in American history, and it was exemplified in the King Kong film. Notice that this ideology can be expressed without it being an explicit intention of the author. King Kong embodies all these notions. King Kong represents black men and their perceived danger to white women. King Kong is also a moral parable about the failure to contain male sexuality. King Kong represents the loss of control, and his death represents the punishment for the loss of control. Thus does King Kong speak to our national horror, slavery, while Godzilla speaks to the national horror of the Japanese, the atomic bomb. Our monsters reflect our fears.

## Manga

Manga is probably Japan's most important export after cars. The popularity of the manga cannot be overestimated. Large percentages of Japanese read Manga and watch anime. We distinguish three kinds of manga, Shonen

Manga (for boys), Shojo Manga (for girls) and Hentai (for adults). But manga are not just read by the Japanese. Large numbers of Westerners, particularly young boys, read manga. A fair amount of the audience for American comics also reads manga. Manga and comics fit the same niche in the illustrated story market. There are several differences between American comics and Japanese manga. First, while American comics are in color, Manga is typically black and white. While American comics are 17 × 26 cm (6 5/8" × 10 1/4"), manga are typically paperback size at 17.5" × 5". Manga, like all Japanese books, are read from back to front and right to left, while comics are front to back and read left to right.

There are several levels of difficulty in manga. For younger boys, Yugioh and Pokemon often function as entry points for readers. Pokemon and Yugioh manga are both highly integrated with commercial tie-ins: Yugioh cards, action figures, video games, posters, apparel and manga function to lead the consumer from one product to another. Yugioh is particularly interesting because it is a story about a card game, hardly an obvious recipe for action-oriented male adolescents. There is action, but it is action organized via a card game. Yugioh is a young boy, short for his age, who comes upon a puzzle, solves it, and is then possessed by an Egyptian god, who then duels in a card game that has a real counterpart. The cleverness of this story is that it sets up the collecting of cards in a way that reflects the core narrative. It is a narrative deliberately built according to a marketing perspective.

The business and memetic perspective is that there is a market for memes that can be collected. The relationship between markets and memes is an increasingly important one. Companies that are the best at using memes will make the most money. The Konami company, which produces Yugioh, is a master at using memes profitably. The market for collectible cards, as we see with both Yugioh and Pokemon cards, is a case of a market making use of the classificatory impulse in young boys. Boys, or at least most boys, are inclined to organize any group of similar yet different items. Baseball cards, coins, stamps and so on all attest to the power of the classificatory impulse. Yugioh cards, like most non-sports cards, uses colorful and striking images on the cards. The arbitrary power assignment given to each card by the game creates different levels of cards, but also cards that carry out particular functions. So not only must you buy the most powerful cards, you must buy cards that enable the powerful cards to be more successful. Most cards come in

© Courtesy of Warner Bros/Burea L.A. Collection/Corbis

Yugioh

packs of random cards. Again, because they are random, effort and many purchases are involved to be able to adequately run the game. Yugioh is a marvel of marketing.

Pokemon also utilizes a heavy tie-in marketing plan. Pokemon works the memes of its franchise quite well. The Pokemon tournaments of the story contain balls with a distinctive coloring, which can be sold as toys, the characters and creatures of the story can be monetized, virtually everything about the Pokemon phenomenon is monetized and marketed.

Girls are also provided with many choices of manga. Shojo manga is aimed at girls from 10 to 18. *Sailor Moon* and *Fruits Basket* are typical of this sector of the manga market. Sailor Moon is about a color-coded group of super-powered girls who fight evil and negotiate relationships with boys with about equal effort. Each girl is associated with a planet, and all are reborn members of a race of beings that patrolled the solar system. The Sailor uniform was incorporated because of its popularity in girls' fashion. Sailor Mercury is particularly interesting. Sailor Mercury has a very high IQ and is associated with water and mercury. While she intends to follow in her mother's footsteps and become a doctor, she also secretly loves romance novels and popular culture. She is the "techie" of the group, and represents women who cross the gender barrier in occupation. What we see is a working out of some of the issues facing Japanese girls in a traditional but also ultra-modern society. Japanese women wish to maintain their femininity, but they also want to play a larger role in society.

A second level with greater levels of violence consists of manga such as Naruto and Dragonball Z. Naruto is a adolescent ninja warrior who tries to become the Hokage, or the leading village ninja. Naruto has a spirit of kami inside him, the nine-tailed demon fox. The presence of the demon inside of Naruto is the basis for several of the plots of the Naruto series. Naruto is an example of the influence of Shinto on manga with it use of the demon inside him. It is also a morality play in that each character displays distinct virtues that have their counterparts in the vices of the villains. Dragonball Z is very loosely based on (it might be more accurate to say "inspired by") the traditional Chinese epic, *Journey to the West*. The series follows the main character, Son Goku, (who has a monkey's tail) as he attempts to find the seven mystical Dragonballs. Most episodes, however, involve tournaments where the characters battle villains. *Dragon Ball Z* is immensely popular. It has sold 300 million copies worldwide and was made into widely viewed anime episodes as well as a full feature film. It is a good example of Japanese culture with great crossover appeal. Young people growing up in the US are all exposed to *Dragon Ball Z*, and many become regular consumers of each episode.

The third level consists of manga such as *One Piece, Bleach, Death Note* and *Black Cat,* which take the reader from young adult to serious adult manga literature. These works explore more serious themes and have more complex plot lines. *Death Note* is about a star high school student who by chance, stumbles upon and picks up a book left lying on the sidewalk by a shinigami, or death god named Ryuk. The book is a tool for the death gods. They write the name of a person who will die in the book, along with the time and cause of death. If no cause is given, the person will die of a heart attack. The writer must know what the person who is to die looks like, so there can be no mistake. Ryuk leaves the book to be found merely because he is bored and wants to see what will happen. Light, the student who picks it up, quickly figures out the book's power and decides to use it for good, to rid the world of evil. Initially, Light acts for the good of the collective, and there is evidence that he acts as a good family member and student. Soon, though, he begins to act in his own self-interest when he uses the book to cover up his actions. His father is chief of police! The other main character is L, an enigmatic special detective who tries to trap Light. Ryuk sets a nihilistic tone in that rather than taking his duties seriously, he flaunts them by letting a human use the book. He says many times that there is no meaning to anything, so why not see what happens if a human is given the power? Light believes that he was chosen to use the book for some reason, and goes off rail when he likens himself to a god, able to choose who is worthy of life or death. In the end, his own death is meaningless, as is all existence.

The next level is Seinen Manga (and its female version, Josei Manga), which is essentially the level of serious literature. In this group we count works like *Ghost in the Shell* and *Akira,* both of which were made into films. *Ghost in the Shell* is a manga classic in the cyberpunk tradition. It is called "cyberpunk" because its plot lines revolve around issues in artificial intelligence in a dystopian setting in which key characters are social outsiders, punks. Like many manga, this story was turned into a highly successful film. While there are not that many punks in this particular film, there is a substantial treatment of artificial intelligence. The opening credits are generally regarded as one of the highpoints in manga tradition. Kenji Kawai's musical score combines with the construction of a female cyborg to create iconic film. The film's background philosophy is contemporary philosophy of mind, which is a very good source for new ideas about the future. Even the presentation of the names of people involved in the film is significant. From a whirl of numbers each name is formed, almost as if indicating that every one of us is ultimately a set of numbers.

Streamline Pictures/Photofest

*Akira* (1988) by Katshiro Otoro is another manga classic set in a dystopian 2019 Japan that has survived a massive explosion and the world war that followed. Japan is portrayed as decadent,

Poster for Japanese animated film, *Akira*

corrupt and victimized by terrorism. *Akira* began as a popular serial manga, and it was eventually turned into a popular animated film. The film is about children with superpowers that are difficult to control. The film draws on the experience of the atomic bomb and begins with an explosion, which was caused by one of the mutant children, Akira. The story then moves decades into the future where the possibility of a recurrence of mass destruction again rears its head.

The main characters in *Akira* are members of a motorcycle gang. Motorcycle gangs are called *Bososuko*, and the young men spend most of their time acting out in a typical Freudian adolescent rebellion against authority. The main characters, Kaneda and Tetsuo, skip school, engage in petty crimes and fight with other gangs. These boys attempt to gain prestige by gaining the respect of the other boys in the gang and their girlfriends since they are unable to do well in school or attain the other standard forms of respect in Japanese society. As boys from families in lower-level occupations they react against the society that has relegated them to a lesser status. The boys reject the work ethic of previous Japanese generations and prefer to hang out, party and get in trouble. Interestingly, their fights and hooliganism become informal maturity rituals that establish a pecking order among the boys. Thus in spite of the boys' rejection of the traditional pecking order, they find themselves attempting to establish another outside of tradition. This shows the powerful hold biology has on behavior. Most cultures have maintained a version of the mammal hierarchy, and in spite of the Bososu-kuo's efforts to effect a stance outside the structures of polite society, hierarchy rears its head in the interpersonal dynamics of the gang.

The action in the film is frenetic and *hyperreal*. The action is hyperreal in the sense that artificiality has become the real. Horrific fights between the gangs are sometimes played in slow motion to increase the visual impact of a scene. The use of slow motion makes possible an attention to detail that makes the scene more than real, hyperreal. The speed of the motorcycles is dizzying and meant to indicate a flirtation with loss of control. Issues of control often concern teens as they come to terms with bodies in hormonal overdrive. The fear of losing control is a very human fear, and it is particularly clear in Japanese culture.

The irony of the fear of *Bososuko* is that the Japanese have the most conformist society in the world. Only a very small percentage of Japanese youth rebels against the Japanese way of life, at least until very recently. The iconic Japanese worker is the Salaryman. He can be seen every day going to work and coming back again in any large Japanese city. He is dressed in the standard uniform of the Salaryman, the business suit and tie. She is in some conservative short skirt and blouse. But the Japanese miracle of the 1970s and 80's is long past. Japan has been in a recession for decades, so the ordinary Japanese young person has grown up in a society with a sense of increasing limitations, of decline. There is a postmodern anxiety that comes when highly modernized nations find themselves on a long downward trend. This is not to say that Japan is no longer formidable. It is still one of the most economically powerful countries in the world, but the feeling of slippage has certainly infected Japanese social consciousness. From a cultural point of view, however, these more reflective times typically produce more and better culture. And Japan has not disappointed.

Akira also deals with the problem of terrorism, interestingly, long before the events of 9/11. In the structure of the film we see various levels of rejection of the social order. The terrorists represent an even more serious threat than the *bososukuo*. One of the two main characters, Kaneda, befriends a terrorist named Kei and the two of them get drawn into the events surrounding the metamorphosis of Tetsuo, the core plot of the film.

The army, represented by Colonel Shikishima, the person in charge of the mutants in the program, is seen as disgusted with the civilian leadership, conspiring with corrupt politicians and willing to violate rights. The Colonels disgust is rooted in a deeper notion of the necessity for order. The Colonel is nevertheless a somewhat sympathetic character who survives in the end.

The character of Tetsuo is at the center of the film because it is his transformation that disrupts the order that has maintained since the explosion years earlier presented at the beginning of the film. Tetsuo was an orphan who is experimented upon by the government at an early age. Later, as the boy reaches adolescence, he begins to change and manifest powers. Unfortunately, his body starts to transform on its own. The uncontrollable physical transformation causes Tetsuo to become unhinged mentally as he copes with both his new power and lack of control over his power.

The story of Tetsuo is a meditation on power. Tetsuo has an inferiority complex in the gang he is in with Kaneda, yet he looks up to Kaneda. Kaneda befriended him when he was brought to the orphanage. Kaneda has the power in the gang, and Tetsuo resents not having it. Tetsuo resents not having a motorcycle like Kaneda's. Tellingly, Kaneda tells Tetsuo that Kaneda's bike is too powerful for Tetsuo. Tetsuo does, in fact, lose control of the motorcycle when he rides it, which makes it clear that Tetsuo is not equipped psychologically for the use of great power. When Tetsuo manifests his powers he also loses control. The film is issuing a warning to us that controlling great power is difficult, and sometimes best denied to certain individuals or groups. One can easily read this as a reference to Japan's bid for world power status, which ended in disaster. And, of course, it is a reference to the dangers of nuclear science, which Japan felt in a direct fashion.

In spite of supplying the name for the film, the character of Akira only appears at the very end of the film. Akira is highly symbolic character. We eventually find out that he was the cause of the first explosion. He discorporated with the explosion and is then kept in special receptacles, which are broken by a flailing Tetsuo. Once released there is a explosion and Tetsuo and Akira move to a different universe to prevent the Earth from being destroyed. Both Tetsuo and Akira represent unrestrained power and unrestrained youth. They are both representative of the notion of overreaching, which is so central to science fiction.

Japanese religion often has an influence on Japanese popular culture. The best example of this occurs in the films of Miyazaki, who is by far the most important Japanese director of anime. Miyazaki has world wide fame, and there is a museum, the Ghibli Museum, dedicated to his work. Typical of Miyazaki's work is a mythical and magical background against which an ambiguously moral story is played out. Miyazaki's work has produced many beloved characters that have been marketed as toys. It is hard to overestimate the love Miyazaki's fans have for his work, as a visit to the museum will attest.

*Princess Mononoke* is the story of a young man, Ashitaka, who is wounded and poisoned by a wounded boar. Ashitaka goes on a quest to find a cure for the poison. He encounters San, a human girl raised by wolves, who is in conflict with an iron producing town led by Lady Eboshi. Lady Eboshi represents progress, science, capitalism and modernity, while the wolf girl, San, represents nature and religion. We have seen how Japanese religion postulates several kinds of supernatural beings or spirits. The tree spirits and other forest beasts, including the boars, battle to protect the forest from the town. The battle between Lady Eboshi and the forest protectors tends to cast her in a negative light, but we also find out that Lady Eboshi is a benefactor to lepers and former prostitutes, which puts her in a better light. It is this moral ambiguity that makes the film interesting. We are presented with a picture of a world in which the distinction between good and bad is not as clear as we sometimes suppose. The result is an ethic of balance between forces rather than the obliteration of one or the other. Industry and the world of the forest are in conflict, but it does not mean that one or the other is evil or should be eliminated. Miyazaki is no Marxist. Capitalism should not be eliminated; rather, we should work to develop a balance between progress and nature. There are many Shinto elements present in this film. In fact, it could almost be called a "Shinto film." A few examples will have to suffice: the old woman washes Ashitaka's wound, which indicates cleansing and purity, key notions in Shinto. The mother wolf is a Kami, as Miyazaki indicates by giving her three tails (Kami are often revealed by unusual physical features). Next, nature plays an important role in the story, and finally, disaster and disease result from the violation of Shinto values.

Although it was not directed by Miyazaki, the film, *Pompoko,* was made by his production company, Studio Ghibli. *Pompoko* is one of several environmental films by Studio Ghibli in which economic development in Japan is causing damage to nature. In *Pompoko*, economic development is edging out the creatures of the forest. The raccoons, whose Kami status is indicated by their giant testicles and ability to transform, wage a war against the developers and hamper their progress as much as possible. They lose in the end, but accept their loss and integrate with humans instead. The female raccoons play a strong role as the keepers of tradition and peace, as they regulate the men when they war amongst themselves. Pompoko is a bitter-sweet acceptance of loss. Miyazaki's films almost always assert some sort of loss and the need for an acceptance of this inevitable loss. In Miyazaki's view, we will not be able to reverse environmental decline, but we will still probably survive the damage and adjust. Life will be less pleasant, but it will be life.

*Ponyo* is the "Pinocchio" story of a female fish that wishes to become human. In this film it is the liminality that is dangerous. Ponyo's transformation puts nature out of balance, but once she becomes completely human order is restored. The structure of *The Little Mermaid* by Hans Christian Anderson is very similar to *Ponyo*. Ponyo relinquishes her power for love, just like the Little Mermaid. In the Hans Christian Anderson fairy tale, the thing that attracts the prince to her is her beautiful singing voice. She has to give it up in order to grow legs and walk on land, so she has to make the prince love her without the thing that he would recognize as her. A feminist reading will note that the idea that a woman's duty involves so much sacrifice is indicative of a deeply oppressive hierarchy. It can also be read to reflect how women are often asked to sacrifice ties to their own families upon marriage into another. A counter reading would argue that all people must make sacrifices. The necessity of sacrifice is gender neutral on this reading, and Ponyo can then be read as instructive for all sexes. The lesson will then be that part of growing up is learning that sacrifice is required if we are to get the things we truly desire. It is also required if we are to maintain the social order.

*My Neighbor Totoro* is about a small family that is in crisis because of the mother's illness. The social order of the family collective is broken. In order to repair the break, the father and two sisters of the family move to the country so they can be near the mother, who is in a hospital because of her condition. The house that the family rents has spirits who stay until they are convinced that the family is cheerful and balanced. The nearby forest also has spirits. The girls make friends with the spirits, the Totoro, and it helps and protects them throughout the film. Even though the father can't see the Kami, he believes in them and teaches his children to respect them. All of the four affirmations of Shinto are evident in this film; cleanliness, honoring the kami, respect for family and for nature are prominent within the story.

*Nausicaa* is an environmental film about a society formed after an apocalyptic event. It concerns a princess who is inquisitive and talented, and builds alliances while others are fighting. She figures out what is causing the environmental imbalance and sacrifices herself to fix it, and rises again. Here we have a case where a Western religion, Christianity, with its story of Christ's sacrifice and subsequent return from the dead, seems to offer a good parable with which to interpret a Japanese film. There are some lessons and cautions we can take from a Christian reading of *Nausicaa*. First, we should always be careful when applying cultural frameworks from one culture to another. It is possible to seriously misunderstand a text if we set aside the tradition from which it comes in favor of one from the outside of that tradition. It is better to at least start with the traditions from which a text originates before applying other traditions. On the other hand, meaning is a two variable function that depends on both the text and the reader of the text. As Japanese films gain wide popularity in the US and Western Europe, it is probable that the difference in audience will change the meaning of the films. Given the massive popularity of Miyazaki's work, it is likely that his work will be increasingly interpreted through Western lenses. Returning to Shinto, we can see that it provides us with ideas to interpret *Nausicaa* that work quite well. The emphasis on respect for nature comes out very clearly. It is interesting that Shinto cleanliness and respect for nature become intertwined in the theme of pollution. Pollution defiles nature and makes it unclean. Nausicaa's task

Walt Disney/Photofest

Saski and Totoro in bus stop scene in Miyazaki's *Totoro*

is to reestablish the purity of nature, and she does it by bringing antagonistic people and creatures together. Nausicaa therefore draws on the Confucian/Shinto sense of collectivity that characterizes Japanese thinking.

But not all Miyazaki films affirm the need to sacrifice for the collective. *Howl's Moving Castle* is a fairy tale written by British author Diana Wynne Jones about the self-actualization of a young girl. Sofi inadvertently angers an old witch (the Witch of the Waste) by making her jealous of Howl, a magician/wizard who makes his living by selling spells and potions, but also works as an advisor to the King. The witch turns Sofi into an old woman, and Sofi is forced to seek Howl's help. Part of the curse is that she can't say what is wrong with her, so she is forced to work for Howl and hope for the best. As she is more assertive she starts to flip back to her old (young) self, but with white hair. In the end, she helps Howl with a political crisis and turns back into herself completely. Being in love with Howl has something to do with her return to normal, but mostly, it is about her existential journey to become an authentic being. Themes dealing with self-actualization are more common in Western texts, but it is not surprising to see this theme emerging in Japan as it absorbs more and more influences from the West.

*Kiki's Delivery Service* is also about self-actualization. It is about a young girl who, at the age of 11, must go off on her own for a year to discover her talent and true ability. The only thing she can do is fly on her broom, so she forms a delivery service. In the story, she loses confidence and loses the power to fly (and her ability to hear her cat talk). She seeks the advice of an artist who tells her not to give up, regains her power through believing in herself and ends up becoming an accepted and valued member of the town/society she lands in. This film has strong capitalist elements (Kiki worries about money and her talent gets developed because she needs money to buy food). As a shojo film, it is also another self actualization film of this young girl. Between *Howl's Moving Castle* and *Kiki's Delivery Service*, we see that feminist notions of female self-actualization have penetrated Miyazaki's work.

Miyazaki's films are works of genius, and his work has rightly become internationally beloved. The artistry of his films is at least equal to and generally superior to most other animated films, and few Japanese filmmakers are so strongly identified with Japanese mentality as Miyazaki. His work is a good example of popular culture produced for the mass market that is also of high aesthetic quality. But there are many important animated films from Japan that were made by other filmmakers besides Miyazaki.

*Barefoot Gen* offers a very graphic depiction of the detonation and after effects of the atomic bomb. Besides the historical information that is the basis of the film, the story also explores the collective and determined nature of the Japanese people. The story of the bombing of Hiroshima is told by following the life of Gen, a young schoolboy, and his family. At the beginning of the film, Gen and his brother are told by their father that they are much like the wheat that is growing in the field; they are resilient in the face of hardship. After the bomb falls, the hardships and loss are terrible for Gen and his family, but just like the wheat, Gen and some of the family survive. The collective nature of the family and some of their neighbors aid in Gen's survival. In contrast, *Grave of the Fireflies* is a much sadder, pessimistic film. In this film, after the bomb a young boy and his little sister are left to fend for themselves. They try to stay with an aunt, but she turns them out because she can't or doesn't want to share the little food that she has with the children. The sister is very young and many hardships arise that the young boy is simply unequipped to handle. This film is more of an example of the failure of the collectivity during a crisis than of the hopeful message of *Barefoot Gen.*

*Appleseed* is a post-human film because its story centers around a race of synthetic beings whose purpose is to be pleasant and oil the machinery of society. They are equipped with a timer of sorts that they have to recharge periodically. This timer keeps them under human control. The story is about a human who uncovers the unfairness of this situation and helps to remedy it. Technically, the film is interesting because it was one of the first Japanese films to use CG over actors filmed with sensors on their bodies. It is post human in story and in technique.

Finally, there are adult mangas of a more sexual nature, called Hentai. As a developed modern and semi-secular country Japan is going to have a pornography industry, and adult manga cannot help but be drawn into the world of Japanese sexual appetites. When that much money flows into an area of commerce, in this case pornography, there is a tendency for potential entrepreneurs to consider exploiting this part of the market, and manga creators are no different. They will go where the money is. While there is surely significant resistance to going into sexually explicit manga, at least some will not have notions of propriety strong enough to keep them from such a potentially lucrative endeavor.

Manga and anime show the entrepreneurial brilliance of Japanese popular culture producers. Every character is exploited for profit in as many sectors of the economy as possible. The same character will be used to sell manga, anime, playing cards and videogames. This intensive merchandizing of cultural products maximizes the profit one can gain from any given character. In Weberian terms, we can say that the manga and anime industry is quite rationalized. But in spite of the rationalized nature of Japanese popular culture, we have also seen that Japan has produced some very high-quality work.

## Technology in Japan

The Japanese have a well-known love affair with gadgets and technology. Japanese technology initially had a bad reputation in the West. It was regarded as substandard and cheap. The Japanese themselves recognized this fact and spent considerable effort to remedy the situation. And remedy the situation they did. Japanese car companies came to dominate the car market in the 1970s, and Japan has done even better in the entertainment technology areas such as radio, tv, music players and video games. Only recently with the rise of other East Asian economic actors such as South Korea and, of course, China, has Japanese dominance begun to be challenged.

It may surprise American readers, however, that the Japanese access the internet more through their mobile phones (keitai) than through computers. Part of this has to do with the fact that so many Japanese use public transport and thus prefer a telephone with internet access over a heavier and larger computer. There is also the matter of limited space in Japanese households and the expense of personal computers, particularly for young people.

The iPhone, which is immensely popular in the US, has yet to make major inroads into the Japanese market. This is partly because the Japanese market is very competitive and the iPhone's plans are too expensive. Further, the Japanese are very demanding of their phones. Japanese cell phones have numerous functions, e-mail, tv feeds, youtube, online games, video recording and playback, and many other functions as well. Importantly, Japanese phones never require to be hooked to a computer.

The question whether the pc model or the phone model will win out internationally. The issue is likely to be rendered moot with the advent of the iPad and similar mid-size devices. These devices will probably pull the Japanese and Americans toward a middle point between phone and pc cultures, but the technology is changing so fast it is unclear exactly how things will play out over time.

**Karaoke**

Karaoke is a key part of the social life of Japanese young people. Much of Japanese social life takes place in Karaoke rooms, and business relationships are often cemented through Karaoke. Karaoke is the top cultural activity in Japan. According to the Japan times, 43% of Japanese participated in karaoke, a far higher percentage than any other Japanese activity. When young Japanese people meet to socialize, it is very often at a karaoke room. Participation is expected and non-participation amounts to a social insult. For this reason, most young people in Japan know a least a few songs they can perform when called upon. The quality of the performance is largely irrelevant. No one will criticize another person's performance because expertise is simply not the point. Individuals are expected to have one particular song

Karaoke in Japan

that they associate themselves with, and the group will then link the person with the song. It is also considered to be impolite to sing a song that someone has already sung. Because Karaoke is so popular, advice for how to do it better has spawned a mini-industry of guides, classes and the like to help people with their singing and their stage presence.

Karaoke has spread all over the world. It is very common to see karaoke advertised in the US, Europe and Asia. Why has it turned out to be so popular? Many reasons have been offered, such as a general love of singing, the desire to emulate stars, stress relief, because it offers an opportunity for strategic socializing, and finally, it is a social lubricant for uncomfortable social situations. These explanations offer some validity, but the real overriding appeal, at least in Japan, is to show one's solidarity with the group, which is an important value for all Japanese. After all, singing in front of people is not everyone's cup of tea, and doing so is likely to increase stress for many rather than reduce it. The popularity of karaoke in Japan is linked to the communal nature of Japanese society. Japanese themselves are well aware that they are less individualistic than Americans, and karaoke provides Japanese with the opportunity to show their fidelity to the group. The group can be one's family, one's group of friends, a club, organization or even one's place of employment. Karaoke is even part of business culture. Business in Japan has a distinctive social element, so business in Japan does not end with the business day. Workers are expected to socialize with their fellow workers after hours, and this will often involve visiting a Karaoke room. Even the boss is expected to join in. Karaoke in Japan cuts across the boundaries of class since all classes participate in Karaoke.

## Sumo

Unlike Karaoke, Sumo has not managed to achieve the global reach of Karaoke, Anime or Manga even though it is incredibly popular in Japan. Sumo has been described as a link between Japan's past (specifically the Edo period, from which it derives its fashion) and present. Sumo is deeply connected to Japan's past, and it provides Japan, a country that has made a definitive commitment to modernity, with a sense of tradition and history. Sumo is embedded with heavy symbolism from Japan's Buddhist and Shinto traditions. Sumo is highly ritualized, and the Sumo arena reflects this symbolism.

The Sumo apprentice system is highly hierarchical with beginning and lower level wrestlers subordinate to the older, more successful wrestlers. The wrestlers live together in stables called *heya,* and their behavior is strictly governed. Each *heya* is run by a former wrestler (*oyakata*). Only *oyakata* are allowed to train sumo wrestlers. Wrestlers are ranked according to a system based on six tournaments each year.

In Sumo bouts the wrestler attempts to throw the other wrestler out of the ring, although there are other ways to win (48 ways, to be exact). The bout itself rarely takes more than a few minutes, and sometimes mere seconds. The ring is constructed a new for each tournament. The ring uses the mandala shape, a circle inscribed in a square, which represents a cosmic totality. Yamaguchi Masao argues that there is significant theatricality in Sumo, which is similar in some ways to Kabuki theatre. The ceremonial stamping that occurs prior to the bout happens in both Kabuki and Sumo, and represents the power of the deities. In fact, Sumo has a highly religious dimension. The winning wrestlers are thought to be temporarily inhabited by a god at the moment of victory, and so the match is an enactment of the contest between good and evil. The wrestlers throw a handful of salt to purify the ring at the beginning of the match. The sumo stadium is set up in accordance with Japanese tradition with the emperor sitting at the north end facing south. One can argue that Sumo is almost more ceremony than sport since the majority of the time is taken up with the ritual, with the match itself taking only a few minutes.

The Sumo wrestler has a highly distinctive appearance, which is immediately recognizable. The size and shape of the wrestlers is attained though a special diet. In spite of their rather odd appearance, successful wrestlers are something like pop music stars. Sumo wrestlers sign autographs, and fans collect memorabilia. Prints of Sumo wrestler's hands are popular collectibles. One wrestler, Takanohana, was even engaged to a pop star before the engagement was broken off. So while Sumo is grounded deeply in tradition, it is also very much a modern popular culture phenomenon. One could view Japan in similar terms: grounded in tradition, but very much a modern nation.

## ☐ INDIA

India's rise to world prominence would be the most important fact about the modern world if it was not for China's even more spectacular rise. India's rise, like China's, was a result of major changes in economic policy. Like China, India's economy is poised to overtake the US in the next fifty years. India is also a cultural powerhouse historically and currently. No treatment of global popular culture can justifiably leave out a significant treatment of India.

The history of India can be characterized by seven key stages: the Harappan era, the Vedic era, the Hindu era, the Muslim era, the British era, the Independence Era up to the 1990's and the Manmohan Singh Era. This is not to give each of these eras equal importance; rather, this way of looking at Indian history will help us understand current Indian popular culture. The Harappan era dates back to 2600 BCE, which supports the Indian pride in the antiquity of their culture. The Vedic era dates to just after the Harappan era and extends to the first millennium BCE. This was the crucial era for establishing many of the mythic motifs that would persist in Indian culture to the present. These myths occur in a set of texts called "the Vedas," hence the name, "Vedic." The Hindu era begins with the earliest versions of the two epics, the Ramayana and Mahabarata, and the philosophical works, the Upanishads, around 500 BCE. The epics provide India with many of the stories that are so popular in Indian and Southeast Asian culture. These stories are so infectious that they have spread beyond India into several other countries. One can find episodes from the Ramayana and

Mahabarata on the walls of buildings in Thailand, Cambodia and elsewhere. And like the *Odyssey* and *Iliad* in the West, they provide the foundation myths of the culture of India.

The Muslim invasion in the 12th century marks a major turning point in Indian history. Islam converted a significant part of the Indian population, and to this day Muslims make up ten percent of the population. (The percentage is much higher if we count Pakistan, which was part of India until Partition in 1947.) In fact, India is the second largest Muslim nation after Indonesia even though India is still ninety percent Hindu. The relationship between Hinduism and Islam in India has been a creative but tortured one. It has been creative in that it led to the establishment of a religion that is a synthesis of the two, Sikhism. It is tortured because the two religions have been antagonistic toward each other for most of India's history, culminating with the partition of India and creation of Pakistan.

The British invasion occurred over a period of time. The British East India Company was the primary foreign presence in India after 1617, and the Battle of Plassey left the company the dominant power in India in 1747. The Indian Rebellion of 1857 led to the British government taking over direct control of India. England controlled India until independence in 1947. The independence movement started 90 years earlier in 1857. In the 1920s Mahatma Gandhi convinced the Indian National Congress, a group opposing British rule, to take up non-violence as their tactic. There were several other groups fighting for independence that did not reject violence as a tactic, but it was Gandhi's approach that ultimately brought Indian independence. Much to Gandhi's sorrow, he could not bridge the animosities between Muslims and Hindus. Pakistan separated from India and the two engaged in a series of wars over control of Kashmir.

After Independence, India initially took a protectionist and socialist path that aimed at eliminating hunger in India, and in providing basic living conditions for as many as possible. In Nehru's view, this meant protecting the small craftsmen and guilds from foreign domination. In trying to defend indigenous Indian industries and trades from foreign competition it kept Indian companies from innovating the way they normally would and India fell behind other countries in innovation. This policy prevailed until the 1980's, when Rajiv Gandhi put in reforms to open up the Indian economy, and even more from of what was called the Licence Raj, the vast system of regulations that had built up over years of socialization of many aspects of Indian life. Manmohan Singh's reforms of the 1990's went even further. Through a relaxation of barriers to trade, privatization and other measures aimed at moving from a socialist model to a more capitalist model, Singh was able to energize the Indian economy into a growth trajectory. This growth has led to a newly confident India, not only economically, but culturally. This is not to say that India did not have a vital culture during the socialist years from Nehru up to Rajiv Gandi. It is merely to say that India is now in a particularly vigorous period of economic and cultural growth.

Of all India's cultural production for mass markets, it is Bollywood that is most important. Bollywood is a cultural behemoth. Bollywood is not only the producer of the most films of any country, 800–1000 per year, its films are popular outside of India as well. Bollywood actually reaches an audience of 3.6 billion people. That is larger than the powerhouse of Hollywood, which reaches 2.6 billion people. Bollywood and Hollywood are the twin towers of world film. And it is clear that Bollywood provides most of what Indians want in films since Hollywood has been largely unable to penetrate the Indian market.

Bollywood films also dominate the popular music scene, accounting for up to 66% of the songs in the popular music market. Bollywood is both a film industry and music industry, and dominating two such important parts of popular culture makes it highly influential.

Although Bollywood is taken to refer to Indian cinema generally, and although the term is most associated with Mumbai (formerly Bombay, hence "Bollywood"), there is actually another city, Chennai (formerly Madras) that produces a significant proportion of Indian films, primarily for the non-Hindi speaking Indians. While Mumbai does produce non-Hindi films, the bulk of its output is in Hindi. Chennai produces films in Telugu and Tamil. This restricts the market to around 20% of India's total output, but this still means 150–200 films per year, more than most countries in the world.

For most of Indian film history, family films have been dominant. The reason is that films tend to be attended by whole families. This means that any particular film must have something that will appeal to the various parts of the family. A typical Bollywood film will have a plot that appeals to the various age groups in a family. Following traditions in Indian drama, stories often contained singing and dancing sequences. In Indian film, almost all films are expected to have singing and dancing. Whatever the film is actually about, there is typically a romantic storyline for those of a romantic age, action sequences for men, weddings for women, and comedy, music and dancing for the young. Notice the difference with Hollywood that divides its output into genres that appeal to only a segment of the market.

The family audience also puts restrictions upon how risqué a film can get. Films must be marketed to audiences, and Indian audiences come in families. This meant that Indian directors have to be clever in representing the eroticism that they need to appeal to romantic age groups. Even kissing was prohibited until recently. There is no nudity or profanity, and sexual topics are generally not in any way explicit. While Westerners might find this kind of restrictiveness to be a major flaw aesthetically, we should also notice that the lack of nudity and profanity contributes a great deal to the marketability of Indian films in conservative countries, such as in the Middle East.

Bollywood films are very formulaic. In Weberian terms, Indian films are highly rationalized by market pressures. Because of this market orientation, producers tend to choose a proven formula. But the formula does not have to originate in India. Bollywood has not been shy about borrowing successful formulas or even full plots from Hollywood and elsewhere. The market

Fox Searchlight Pictures/Photofest

Bollywood star Shahrukh Khan

rationality also leads producers to prefer that their ventures involve established stars. The "three Khans," Shahrukh, Aamir and Salman are probably the most famous male Indian actors, and at least one of them seems to be in every important Indian mass market film. We will focus on the most famous of the three, Shahrukh Khan.

To say Shahrukh Khan is an important star is understatement. His fans number in the billions and his net worth is in excess of 500 million dollars. *Newsweek* named him one of the 50 most powerful people in the world. Shahrukh Khan has been in too many films to name, but we can get a sense of his work by looking at four very different films he has done. A testament to Shahrukh Khan's market power, *Dilwale Dulhania Le Jayenge* is the longest running film in Indian history. In fact, it has run continuously since it was made in 1995. *Dilwale Dulhania Le Jayenge* (1995) is in the genre of exotic romance film, a film formula that began to be popular in the 1960s. In this type of film, part of the action takes place in India and part in Europe. Like many Bollywood films there is a love match that is contradicted by arranged marriages. The story begins in London, where the two main characters have grown up. India does not shy away from stories about overseas Indians. True to the formula, the love match involves lovers from different classes. The girl in the love match, Simran, played by Kajol, a superstar actress who has done several films with Shahrukh Khan, decides to go on a European vacation with some friends before she gets married to the man to whom she is promised but to whom she is a stranger. She must also return to India for the rest of her life. Hoping for one last fling in her life, Simran goes on a European adventure. One of students on the trip turns out to be a young man she had previous negative encounters with, played by Sharukh Khan. Shahrukh plays an irresponsible young man on the make for pretty girls. After a rocky start to the relationship, the two young people fall in love and the love triangle is in play. After a climactic fight scene, the girl's father relents and lets his daughter marry her true love. Shahrukh Khan's character becomes more serious and adult by the end of the film. Like all films in the Exotic Romance genre, there are many beautiful locations to provide the exoticism, this time various sites in Europe. In spite of being a mass market product in a well-worn genre, both actors won critical praise for their roles, with Kajol winning the Filmfare Award for Best Actress and Shahrukh Khan winning Best Actor.

*Asoka* (2001) is an historical epic about the Emperor Asoka (304–232 BCE), who became disillusioned with war and became a convert and patron of Buddhism. Historical and religious stories have long been a popular part of Indian cinema and television with several versions of the *Ramayana* and *Mahabarata* being made into films. Asoka could not be any more different from *Dilwale Dulhania Le Jayenge*. Instead of a light-hearted film of romance and travel, Asoka is an epic about an important era in Indian history and religion. The film was a commercial failure in spite of being a serious attempt at an important story in Indian history.

*Veer-Zaara* (2004) was rather more successful. It followed the formula of the star-crossed romance, this time between a Pakistani girl, Zaara, played by Preity Zinta, and an Indian Airforce Squadron Leader, Veer, played by Shahrukh Khan. Like Asoka, the film is entirely serious in its overall tenor. Unlike Asoka, the film did quite well at the box office. The romance is destroyed by Zaara's fiancé, who keeps the two lovers apart for 22 years by framing Veer as an Indian spy. Veer spends 22 years in prison and is unwilling to speak to anyone until lawyer, Saamiya Siddiqui, takes up the case and determines to find out what happened. The lawyer succeeds and Veer and Zaara end up together.

The music for *Veer-Zaara* was just as successful as the film itself, and the music was actually released prior to the film. The main singer was Lata Mangeshkar, by far the most famous and prolific of movie score singers. In India, the singing in films is generally done by a professional singer rather than the actor, who merely lip-synchs the melody. This is true of Shahrukh Khan as well. He does not do his own singing.

*My Name is Khan* (2009) is an acting tour de force for Shahrukh, who plays an enigmatic character, Rizwan Khan, with Aspergers' Syndrome. In *My Name is Khan* the title character sets off on an unlikely quest in order to regain the woman he loves, Mandira, played by Kajol, the same actress in *Dilwale Dulhania Le Jayenge*. The whole quest, however, originates in a sarcastic remark at a moment of despair over the death of Mandira's son, Sameer, a result of post-9/11 prejudice. Mandira blames the US for the death of Sameer, but also considers Rizwan partly to blame. In the final analysis, however, Madira believes her son died ultimately because his name was Khan. Rizwan asks how he can regain her love, to which she sarcastically remarks that he must "tell the people of the United States and the President

that his name is Khan and that he is not a terrorist." Taking her request seriously, in spite of the obstacles to anyone obtaining such an audience and
overcoming the difficulties of doing so with Aspergers, Rizwan manages to
obtain an audience with the President of the United States in order to tell him
that he is not a terrorist. *My Name is Khan* is a cinematic response to the War
on Terror, specifically post-9/11 prejudice, proving that Bollywood can take
on difficult political topics with nuance and pathos.

We would be remiss to neglect to discuss at least one film dealing with the
British colonial period, and so we will leave our treatment of Shahrukh Khan
and look at a film that tells us something about Bollywood and Indian popular culture in general. *Lagaan* is a 2001 film dealing with taxation under the
British Empire. *Lagaan* is also a sports film because the central event of the
film is a game of cricket between the British and the Indians over three year's
taxation. Cricket is by far India's favorite sport, and so the film had a double
appeal. One of the other "Khans," Aamir Khan both acted in and produced
the film. The experience of British rule in India was so important to the national consciousness that it is a recurring theme in Indian culture, and in film
specifically. In Lagaan, a subplot concerns prejudice against untouchables.
The leader of the team, Bhuvan (Aamir Khan) wants to use an untouchable
as a player because he has a useful set of skills. The other players rebel, but
Bhuvan eventually gets them to accept the untouchable, which, in turn, helps
lead to the success of the Indians in the game. The point is therefore that India
will prevail if the various groups learn to work together. Unfortunately, the
tragic history of India has been precisely the result of difficulties between
contending groups. On the other hand, Bollywood functions like glue among
Indians. Hindus have no problem accepting Muslim actors like Shahrukh
Khan, who even married a Hindu woman.

As good a businessman as Shahrukh Khan has been throughout his
career, he did make the mistake in taking a pass on the worldwide hit, *Slumdog Millionaire*. The British-made film, set and filmed in India, is a good
example of Indian culture embraced by India's former colonial masters and
of a multi-directional globalization. Culture is not simply moving West to
East. There is now a multi-directional structure to world cultural interaction. Even the biography of the participants speaks to the internationaliza-
tion of Indian culture. Slumdog was directed and written by Britons, but it
was based on a novel, *Q & A*, by Vikas Swarup. The lead role was played by

Dev Patel, a Briton of Indian descent. Patel's parents had immigrated into England, not from India, but from Kenya, although they were of Indian descent. The composer of the film score, A.R. Rahman, is the son of an Indian film composer, but he incorporates musical influences from all over the world and has a university degree in Western music. Boyle, the British director, drew on his knowledge of Bollywood films to give it an Indian flavor, but he was not slavish in his fidelity to Bollywood conventions. For example, although there are no dance scenes in the body of the film, *Slumdog* finally does break out a dance number at the end of the film. The diverse and global production of the film was apparently successful because it won eight 2008 Oscars, including Best Picture, Best Director and Best Adapted Screenplay. With its stark contrast of rich and poor, modern and traditional, pure and corrupt, *Slumdog Millionaire* spoke to a worldwide audience. The film posits an implausible run of correct answers by an improbable character, a "slumdog" named Jamal Malik, played by Dev Patel. The key to the film's structure are the flashbacks to key points in Jamal's life that give us the explanation for each of his correct answers. The puzzle of the film thus provides its structure. The result is a captivating film that entertained audiences, Indian and non-Indian, world wide. But in India itself, *Slumdog* was not so popular, and opened to half-full theatres. The reasons are illuminating. For most Indians, images of the poor, crime and corruption are banal. Indians are intimately aware of these negative aspects of Indian life, but they would prefer not to watch portrayals of poverty on Saturday night. Indeed, some have characterized Slumdog as "Poverty Porn." Indian critics were more impressed with the film even though Indian audiences had their reservations.

Even though the Indian film market is dominated by relative fluff, some Indian filmmakers have nevertheless managed to buck the system and dispense with the accepted formulas of Bollywood. There is a cultural logic to the mass market that eventually produces art of a higher order in spite of itself. Once a mass market reaches a certain threshold of size, then room opens up for more sophisticated kinds of art, if only at the margins. The Indian film industry is no different. Although most producers adhere relentlessly to the dictates of the market, the market leaves openings for filmmakers such as Santijat Ray. Ray persisted and managed to get a songless film produced over the objections of Indian film financiers. Once Ray had broken through, other directors joined the effort to produce non-formulaic artistic films. The Indian film industry, like Hollywood, manages to produce a fair number of high quality films in spite of the majority of the industry aimed more at profit than artistic success.

## Music In India

Indian music today can be divided into two broad categories: traditional Indian music and popular music. Popular music outsells traditional music by a wide margin. Indian popular music has been deeply affected by Western music, both Western classical music and Western rock music. Indian popular music is now so Westernized that Western audiences have no trouble appreciating Indian popular music, which was not the case for Western audiences and Indian classical music, although there has always been a certain number of Western aficionados of Indian classical music. We cannot understand Indian contemporary music unless we understand its tradition. (It would do the student good at this point to go to Youtube and watch and listen to both Indian classical and popular music.)

Traditional music in India has a venerable tradition. It has an advanced music theory, and a history of virtuoso musicianship. India's popular music draws on this tradition, but Western musical forms, harmonies, scales, and rhythms are often mixed in with Indian forms, harmonies, scales and rhythms in India's popular music. India is quite happy to borrow from everywhere, and we see this with its incorporation of Latin and African rhythms. The mix between Indian, Western and other styles varies widely from very little Western, Latin or African mixture to a generally western song with just a little Indian affectation.

A proper appreciation of Indian music begins with music theory. Indian music is very different from Western music and correspondingly has a different music theory. Indian music has different scales and does not have harmony in the Western sense. In Western music, harmony is derived from tempered scales. Tempering evens out the distances between intervals, so that when you play more than two notes in harmony, the 3 or more notes will still be in tune with each other. The spacing of Indian scales does not allow for much harmony, and certainly no complex harmonies.

India didn't adopt tempered tuning (Indian classical musicians sometimes still eschew it on occasion) until late in its music history. Western music therefore maximizes the sonority of simultaneous notes. Because of this sonority Western music can create chords, which are usually stacked notes that are spaced by 3rds apart. Chords must have at least three notes, but there can be more. Chords are typically created by picking out every other note of a scale. For example, a C scale is cdefgabc (the musical alphabet only goes to g, but otherwise it is the same as the alphabet). From those notes we can stack c, e and g since they are far enough apart to create pleasing harmony. Music theory names these notes the root (c), the third (e) and the fifth (g) because they are a third and $5^{th}$ interval away from the root. We can stack this way on every note of the scale to get ceg, dfa, egb, fac, gbd, ace and bdf. That gives us the set of triads the form the foundation of Western music. Notes have meaning in relation to the notes of the chords played behind them, thus melodies get their meaning in Western music in relation to harmony. The same melody has a different meaning with different harmony. The note "C" has different meanings depending on whether it is surrounded by, say, a and e (ace), e and g (ceg) or f and a (fac). Notice the c can function as the root, third or fifth of the chord. Or it may be a further stacked $3^{rd}$, such as a $7^{th}$, $9^{th}$ or $11^{th}$ or $13^{th}$. It may also be an alteration of one of these notes. In any case, a note sounds different depending on which role it plays in relation to the chord.

Western music theory also structures how each chord moves to another. Much of the interest in Western music comes from the harmonic progression, the movement from one chord to the next. There are standardized progressions in Western music. The root chord of a key (in Western music theory this is called the tonic chord) can move to any other chord. The chord based on the $5^{th}$ step, however, typically goes back to the root chord. So in the key of C, the G major triad (gbd) will typically go next to the root chord, C major (ceg), with the exception of instances when it goes to the chord based on the $6^{th}$ step of the scale, A minor (ace) in this case. So Western music is able to explore *changing harmonies within a single song.* There is much more to Western harmony, but the key points we need for our comparison of Indian music are that (1) in Western music, notes have meaning in relation to triadic harmony and (2) harmonies change in Western music.

First, Indian music does not use triadic harmony (chords) as the basis of its harmonies. Indian music uses drones of fourths and fifths (C-F or C-G). Secondly, in Western music it is common for the background harmonies to change. As we have seen, there is a logic to how chords are supposed to move from one to another. Indian music, on the other hand, maintains a static drone. The meaning of the melodies is therefore in terms of these drones. This is a key aspect of Indian music and gives it much of its distinctive meditative character.

Melodies are also different from those in Western music. Melodies are created out of ragas, which are something like scales but with significant differences. We have already seen how Indian scales are different from Western scales in their frequency spacing (how they are tuned). Ragas build melodies on the basis of arrangements of subsets of the scales. Ragas are often different going up and down. It is important to realize that Ragas are not themselves melodies, but more like the framework for melodies that will arise spontaneously out of improvisation on the ragas. This points to another important difference with Western music. Indian traditional music is highly improvisatory, probably even more than Western jazz, which is known for its use of improvisation. It is therefore unsurprising that it has been primarily Western jazz musicians that have made the musical journey into Indian music.

A typical Indian music performance is a small group affair. Indian music never developed the orchestra with a large number of musicians. The performance will begin with a drone and then bring in a melody without much, if any, rhythm. Eventually, the percussion (played most of the time on tablas) enters and the melody player (sarod, sitar and violin are the most common melody instruments) interacts with the percussionist as they improvise their way together through a performance.

Indian rhythms are also organized differently. Western music usually uses measures of equal length and creates rhythms by subdividing the measure in a variety of ways. Western music is typically organized into four or three beat (waltz) measures. Indian music involves more complex rhythmic sequences. Indian music, for example, might work within a five, seven, nine or even more beat frameworks, which is very unusual for Western ears. Western rhythms are much more repetitive, which gives Western music an easy "groove" to follow. Indian music requires more close attention to follow the rhythmic pulse. Rhythm is more creatively subordinate in Western music because of the need to establish a repetitive groove, while rhythm plays a large role in the creativity of Indian music.

The foremost practitioner of jazz-Indian fusion is John McGlaughlin, the British guitarist who is one of the most highly regarded guitarists in the world.

His group, Shakti, represents an historical highpoint for the fusion of jazz and Indian music. Oddly enough, most people would consider the group to sound more Indian than Western. The interplay between the virtuoso guitarist and equally transcendent Indian musicians is truly something to behold. The student should search video clips of Shakti on Youtube.

Contemporary Indian music is a synthesis of Western and traditional Indian music. Indian popular music draws on its past, but it makes use of Western harmonies. Rarely do we hear Indian

British guitarist John McGlaughlin with his group, *Shakti*

© Sergio Perez/Reuters/Corbis

with a single harmonic center as we hear in traditional Indian music. While Indian popular music may begin with a section with a raga played over a drone, most often it gives way to the more complex harmonies borrowed from the West. And as we mentioned earlier, a good majority of popular Indian music comes from Bollywood films.

The music industry in India began in the early part of the century dominated by foreign companies. The English company, Gramophone Company of India (known as HMV, "His Master's Voice"), dominated early on. It was at this early point in India's pop music history that the short, three and one half minute song became standard. The songs were limited in length by the technology, the 78 rpm. It is interesting to note that this technical limitation has turned out to match contemporary limits on the length of songs, but the contemporary limits have more to do with marketing decision based on listener attention spans. Film music had already become the dominant source of popular music, beginning with the popularity of the first talkie, Alam Ara, which was based on a Parsi musical production. Eventually another company, Polydor, entered the market, and the two giants HMV and Polydor carved up the market between the two of them.

Peter Manuel has detailed what he terms "the Cassette Revolution" in Indian popular music. Once cassettes became available in the 1970s, they changed the face of Indian music forever and by 1990, India was the second largest consumer of cassettes in the world. Cassette players were cheap and portable, and thus they were available to large numbers of the Indian people. They also allowed for the re-copying of cassettes and even production of original cassettes, which led to the democratization of music. No longer were HMV and Polydor able to dominate the way they once were. Hundreds of new companies entered the field on the 1990s and HMV's share of the market had dropped to 15 percent by 2002.

Satellite television brought with it foreign influences, particularly American, with the introduction of music channels such as MTV. India quickly responded and even outperformed MTV by localizing its programming to Indian tastes. The result of this foreign music coming from American and elsewhere combining with Indian traditional music was the development of "Indipop," a highly distinctive music that has become internationally popular. Indipop has come to dominate both film and non-film music in India. There are musicians who are independent of Bollywood, and they are doing very interesting music. Freed from the requirements of film music, non-film popular music is often rather more interesting musically than the traditional film song. And we cannot discount the influence of Indian musicians based outside India. The singer, Najma, for example, has made several albums that are very listenable to both Indian and Western audiences.

India, a long-time world cultural powerhouse, is a major contributor to the world's popular music. Its influence is likely to continue and even increase. After the United States it is the most important generator of popular music in the world. India has been the source of wide-ranging culture with its export of religious ideas, art and literature since ancient times, and India's music industry helps India continue its role as a generator of global culture.

## ☐ JIHAD VS. MCWORLD

Although our focus in this chapter has been on China, Japan and India, it is important to make note of an important world-wide phenomenon affecting all countries of the world. We saw in Chapter One that the logic of capitalism has produced what George Ritzer called, "McDonaldization." George Ritzer argues that McDonaldization process is going on in the world today that is less connected to the particular cultures than it is to the general processes of modernization and Westernization. The process of Westernization that often comes with modernization has created a conflict with those cultures that are in danger of losing their hold on the values they hold to be central. The clearest case of this is exemplified by certain tendencies in the Islamic world. Tribal structures are threatened by modernity, which acts like an acid on traditional institutions of authority and culture. Tribal societies see their traditional values undermined and sometimes replaced by Western ideas and react with a backlash against both economic modernization and cultural globalization. Ritzer terms this sort of cultural backlash "Jihad," borrowing the Islamic term for Islamic struggle against non-believers and within the individual believer. In Ritzer's sense, however, it refers to the struggle of tribal society and indigenous traditions against the inroads on non-indigenous culture, particularly Western culture, and modernization.

The classic case of this backlash occurred in Iran. An ally of the US during the Cold War, the Shah of Iran tried to modernize his country both economically and culturally. A proponent of market capitalism and cultural modernization, the Shah brought new prosperity to Iran, but he also overstepped. One significant action he took is representative of the conflict we are

© Danny Lehman/Corbis

McDonald's in China

describing: outlawing the burkha. The Shah was in favor of greater rights for women, and so he attempted to impose freedom for (on?) them. With these sorts of actions it appears that the Shah modernized Iran so quickly that he created what Alvin Toffler called "Future Shock." The liberalization of the marketplace came to be associated with declining Islamic values and created an intense hatred of Western culture. In the case of Iran, Iran's history was replete with examples of Western interference by the West, and the Shah's methods for maintaining his power provided clear political reasons for hostility to the West, at least for the Mullahs and their conservative allies who took over the Iranian Revolution and put Ayatollah Khomeni in power. Khomeni and his allies instituted an Islamic Republic that to this day inspires anti-Westernism around the world. Even in Iran, however, there is still an ongoing conflict between modernists and traditionalists as the conservative's power waxes and wanes. This tension between Jihad and McWorld will be with us as long as there remain any enclaves of tradition resistant to modernization, and this resistance is likely to continue for a very long time.

The picture that emerges at the end of this chapter is a world in which Indian, Chinese and Japanese cultures are intermixing with Western influences and producing a Postmodern quilt of culture. Against this tendency is the logic of Jihad, which in Ritzer's terminology means the tribal orientation opposed to market rationalization of social systems and the weakening of traditional values. This is the world we will be living in for the near future, and for that reason it is important to understand the basic foundations of Chinese, Indian and Japanese culture, and to understand the broader conflict of Jihad and McWorld over time.

## BIBLIOGRAPHY AND FURTHER READING

*China Pop*, Jianying Zha, New Press, 1996.

*The Worlds of Japanese Popular Culture*, D.P. Martinez, Cambridge, 1998.

*Pop Culture India*, Asha Kasbekar, ABC-CLIO, Santa Barbara, 2006.

*Pop Culture: China*, Kevin Latham, ABC-CLIO, 2007.

# GLOSSARY

**Aesthetics:** the philosophy of art. The central question of aesthetics concerns the *quality* of an artwork.

**Alienation:** the separation of one's labor from the product of one's labor. People are alienated when they work at dissatisfying jobs that hinder them from achieving self-realization.

**Anal stage:** the anal stage works through the problem of toilet training and determines whether a person might be anal retentive (meticulous, careful, and stingy) or anal expulsive (messy, reckless, and defiant).

**Base and superstructure:** Marx divides society into its base: the economy and state of technology, and its superstructure: culture and belief systems. Marx argues that the base determines the superstructure.

**Black feminism:** the view that the combination of the racial and feminist perspective yields insights that each separately might miss.

**Camp:** art that is self-consciously derivative. Camp art recognizes the kitsch elements in art, but embraces them in the ironic or simply playful mode.

**Catharsis:** the moment of realization one comes to when learning something important from a text, particularly a tragic text, but catharsis can occur from any text that is sufficiently deep and moving.

**Class consciousness:** the set of beliefs in common among members of an economic class. Marx believes that actions and beliefs that develop among the laboring classes produce an understanding of the common plight of workers (or any underclass) and a feeling of solidarity.

**Collective unconscious:** Jung's belief that we all share access to a set of ideas, symbols, and the like and that this common access explains the commonalities in the world's cultures.

**Computer-mediated communication (CMC):** communication that occurs through some computer process, such as Facebook, e-mail, etc.

**Conservative feminism:** an argument that while equality is a necessary part of women's liberation, new thinking about women must remember their traditional and biological roles in human life.

**Contextualism:** the view that art is to be evaluated in its social, psychological, economic, or other context. Contextualist theories are defined in Chapter 2, and a treatment of several of them is given in Chapter 1.

**Critical comedy:** the use of humor to make political criticism for the purpose of social correction.

**Critical race theory:** the view that there is a deep structure to race in society that has explanatory power. In the theory of interpretation it suggests the construction of counternarratives to interpret texts.

**Cultural studies:** the study of texts.

**Dark comedy:** laughs at what are generally considered bad occurrences.

**Dedifferentiation of consumption:** the practice of corporations that order your experience so you encounter multiple opportunities to purchase different items sold by the corporation.

**Deep attention:** *see* Hyper attention.

**Disneyization:** the rationalization process by which organizations mimic the business model of the Disney Corporation. The key elements of Disneyization are theming, emotional labor, dedifferentiation of consumption, and merchandizing.

**Ecofeminism:** the view that the domination of women is part of a larger problem of the domination of nature. In the theory of interpretation, it is the view that women's place in nature can help us understand texts that treat women in certain ways. The femme fatale, for example, is a woman who uses her sexuality (her natural attributes) to ensnare men in schemes that end badly for the men.

**Emotional labor:** corporations sometimes require certain emotional states and responses in the workplace (smiling, friendliness). The attempt by the employee to display these emotions is called emotional labor.

**Eros:** (from Freud): the life instinct. Freud believes civilization is a result of the conflict of Eros and Thanatos (the death instinct).

**Existential feminism:** the view that there is no essence to womanhood. What it means to be a woman will be decided by each individual woman.

**Expressionism:** the view that the purpose of art is to express the inner life, particularly the emotions, of the artist.

**Formalism:** the view that the best way to interpret an artwork is by evaluating its formal structure and technical expertise in order to arrive at the artwork's overall structure and meaning, its "significant form."

**Genre:** a category of stories. The Western, the romance, film noir, and horror are all genres. There are also subgenres. Within the horror genre we have the vampire as subgenre. Genres have their own logic, standard themes, symbolism, and plot types according to which they should be evaluated.

**Hegemony:** Gramschi argued that popular culture is a function of competing interpretations. The lower classes do not accept popular culture uncritically; they bring their own views to the interpretive table as well. What results is a mediation of the interests of the different classes.

**Homelessness:** a condition of modern life in which we live inauthentically and in forgetfulness of the real experience of human existence.

**Hyper attention:** the type of attention displayed when moving quickly between several sources of information. Contrasted with "deep attention," which is a slower, more concentrated focus on a single source of information.

**Hyperreal:** a characteristic of Japanese animation in which actions are portrayed in a frenetic and exaggerated fashion in order to call attention to the excitement or horror of the action.

**Id:** a Freudian term to describe one of three parts of the mind. The Id operates according to the *pleasure principle*, which seeks pleasure and avoids pain.

**Ideology:** a set of beliefs that support a political position.

**Imaginary ("the Imaginary"):** (from Lacan) the state of mental development in which the self and other objects are differentiated by language from a unity known as "the Real."

**Incongruous theory of humor:** the theory that sees humor as ironic or absurd, or more simply, as the bringing together of incongruous events or things.

**Invisible hand:** Adam Smith's metaphor for the economic process in which supply and demand interact to produce a self-regulating market, which produces the lowest prices, the best products, and a stable economy. The idea behind the invisible is that the selfish actions of individuals can produce a collectively beneficial result.

**Irony:** the purposeful imparting of an idea that is the opposite of what is literally expressed.

**Kami:** Japanese god or spirit.

**Kitsch:** the type of text that attempts to match the aesthetic quality of good art by imitating significant forms that did achieve the status of good art, but ultimately failed because of the market imperatives that dictated the imitation of formerly successful artworks instead of a creative a new work.

**Lack:** (from Lacan) the basic sense of deprivation that comes from separation from the mother.

**Lesbian feminism:** the view that attempts to undermine "compulsory heterosexuality" in our ways of looking at feminist issues.

**Liberal feminism:** the view that feminists should work to achieve equality in all aspects of life. Thus, women should be paid the same as men for equal work.

**Liberal race theory:** the view that the key critical concepts to be used for understanding race are equality and color-blindness.

**Lifeworld:** those aspects of life that make up the traditional background of human existence that have yet to be completely rationalized.

**Manga:** Japanese comic book.

**Marxist feminism:** the view that the oppression of women is either caused by or made more severe by capitalism.

**McDonaldization:** the rationalization process by which businesses borrow the practices of the McDonald's Corporation. The elements of McDonaldization are efficiency, calculability, control (they really mean using technology to replace humans in as many tasks as possible), and predictability.

**McWorld:** a term meant to denote the rationalization of all cultures on the model of contemporary capitalism. It is used by George Ritzer in contrast with the concept of Jihad, or tribalism. McWorld reorders traditional culture the same way McDonald's reordered the restaurant business. "Jihad" in Ritzer's sense refers to the resistance of traditional culture to modernization. (This is not to be confused with the Islamic conception of Jihad, which means "holy struggle.")

**Macrocultural analysis:** the analysis of culture or cultures as a whole. Freud's work on civilization, the issue of globalization, the role of economics in determining culture are some examples of macrocultural analysis. Macrocultural analysis is contrasted with "microcultural analysis," which examines particular texts, such as interpreting a particular film, story, or advertisement.

**Mass civilization:** the type of civilization that develops with the rise of industrialization and the expansion of a popular culture consuming middle class.

**Meditative thought:** the type of thought that requires silent concentration and introspectively reflects on the nature of the meaning of existence (from Heidegger). Meditative though contrasts with calculative thought, which is results oriented and involves the manipulation of nature.

**Memetics:** the view that ideas, sounds and images can be profitably studied as simple or complex replicators. The quality or truth of the idea, sound, or image is provisionally set aside in order to isolate the purely replicatory power it has. Memetics is used to explain the popularity of texts aside from qualitative questions.

**Microcultural analysis:** the examination of particular texts. Interpreting a particular film, story, or advertisement counts as microcultural analysis, which is contrasted with macrocultural analysis, which is the analysis of culture or cultures as a whole.

**Mockumentary:** a humorous documentary.

**Neuroplasticity:** the view that the brain is continually changing, and with every sensory input we provide it, reprogramming itself along the way.

**Oedipus complex:** the teaching that in the phallic stage a person wants to possess the opposite-sex parent and expel the same-sex parent. For the boy, the father stands in the way of the boy's desire for his mother, but he fears his father's power, which is manifested in the castration complex (fear of castration). Eventually this fear overcomes the desire for the mother, and the boy takes to identifying with his father instead, and in the process internalizes the father figure so that a superego is formed. For girls, they notice that they do not have penises and blame their mother for their apparent castration. Girls begin to have penis envy, which only abates, to the extent that it does, by identifying with the mother, and having a child to replace the missing penis. Just as with the other stages, fixation at this stage causes various personality characteristics. A phallic fixation can lead to narcissism, the failure to be able to love.

**One-dimensionality:** the term Herbert Marcuse uses to describe the tendency toward a false consensus of support for the social and political systems.

**Oral fixation:** a fixation with putting things in one's mouth. Oral fixation occurs when a person is unsuccessful in his or her psychosexual development through the oral stage.

**Oral stage:** the stage of psychosexual development in which all consciousness is focused on the mouth. There are personality characteristics associated with this stage, depending on how one handles the frustration from the end of nursing. If one is nursed too long one becomes optimistic, but gullible. If not nursed long enough, then one becomes pessimistic and envious.

**Overreaching:** the act of overstepping natural or religious boundaries. The Frankenstein character is an overreacher because he does not recognize any limits to scientific progress.

**Pastiche:** the imitation of the significant form of art without the quality of comedy or travesty. A weak imitation of art.

**Phallic stage:** see Oedipus Complex.

**Pleasure principle:** (from Freud) describes the tendency part of the mind (the Id) to seek out pleasure.

**Posthumanism:** the view that humanity will eventually be superseded by a different sort of being or even sorts of beings. Texts that appear to show anything that suggests something about the altering of the human body or mind via technology can be interpreted from a posthumanist perspective.

**Postmodernism:** the view that we are in an era in which metanarratives are rejected. It is sometimes appropriate to see inconsistency of style, radical narrative displacements, and self-reflectivity as indicating a postmodern perspective in a text.

**Postmodern feminism:** the view that women can choose multiple and contradictory identities.

**Poststructuralism:** the view that texts not only display structure, they simultaneously undermine it with contradiction so that interpretation must discern the discontinuities as well as the continuities in texts.

**Psychoanalysis:** the interpretive theory of mental life developed by Freud, Jung, and others. It is used to interpret texts that have a significant psychological dimension.

**Psychoanalytic feminism:** the rethinking of Freudian psychosexual dynamics that elevates the role of the mother in interpretation.

**Psychological theory of humor:** the view that humor is the result of a release of tension built up from mental and emotional struggles.

**Queer theory:** the view that attempts to undermine "compulsory heterosexuality" in our ways of looking at the world. In the interpretation of texts, it is used to understand how a text constructs gender.

**Radical feminism:** the view that women's oppression is not simply a matter of inequality; rather, the structures of male domination (patriarchy) go much deeper into the order of society, so deep that they may be initially invisible and need to be rooted out. Radical feminism is sometimes associated with radical action, such as separation from men and a rejection of traditional understandings of sex roles, so the display of such action in a text can be interpreted in the terms of radical feminism.

**Rationalization:** Max Weber argued that rationalization was a force in history that tended to order aspects of reality according to a logic of development. Ideas and social structures get incrementally more rational over time. The factory system was a rationalization of work. Bureaucracy is a rationalization of governmental practices. Religion gets rationalized when it develops a sophisticated theology.

**Real ("the Real"):** (from Lacan) the perception of the world we have early in life when people feel at one with the mother. (*Note:* This is not the same as common usage in which tables and chairs are real.)

**Realism:** the view that qualitative judgments about artworks are ultimately a matter of how well the work recreates an accurate depiction of the physical world.

**Reality principle:** (from Freud) the Reality principle describes the tendency of part of the mind (the ego) to delay gratification to better accommodate itself to the reality of scarce resources.

**Renaissance space:** the type of visual image that utilizes mathematical perspective to portray what is represented with the illusion of depth.

**Repression:** the complete suppression of one's desires without sublimating them into other activities.

**Satire:** the ridicule of something by giving an exaggerated version of it. *Saturday Night Live*, for example, satirizes political leaders such as President Obama and Sarah Palin by exaggerating their particular patterns of speaking and acting.

**Schadenfreude:** the enjoyment of pain and suffering in others.

**Significant form:** the overall form, structure, and meaning of an artwork.

**Sitcom:** situational comedy, typically a television series.

**Structuralism:** as an interpretive theory, the view that to understand a text one must discern the deep structures of the text, particularly by finding identities and oppositions.

**Sublimation:** the act of subduing one's baser impulses and redirecting of the energy of those impulses to productive activities.

**Sublime:** refers to those aspects of an artwork that take us beyond the beautiful. Generally associated with an aesthetic appreciation of the awesome or horrific, the sublime is something that begs for our attention in spite of the fact that it might not be beautiful in the traditional sense. The Grand Canyon is thought to be sublime. A painting of a terrible storm, such as we see in Turner, is considered sublime.

**Superego:** that part of the mind that governs the moral life of people. It is formed in the process of psychosexual development. It is ultimately the result of internalizing the father figure in one's life into the unconscious where it works to discipline the Ego by making it feel guilt or shame in a way similar to the way an actual father disciplines a child.

**Superiority theory:** the theory of humor that says humor results from the feeling of superiority the viewer feels in relationship to bad or stupid behavior.

**Superstructure:** (*see* Base and superstructure).

**Suspension of disbelief:** the principle of charity in interpretation dictates that we suspend our disbelief concerning the plausibility of one or more premises of a text. The suspension of disbelief primarily applies to the key idea or "conceit" of the text. Once granted, the rest of the text is expected to adhere to the normal canons of reason.

**Taste:** one's ability to appreciate the aesthetic quality of a text.

**Text:** any artifact that can be interpreted, such as films, books, TV shows, artworks, music, myths, advertising etc.

**Thanatos:** (from Freud) the death instinct. Freud believes civilization is the result of the conflict between Thanatos and Eros (the life instinct).

**Tongsu:** propagandist popular music in contemporary China.

**Womanism:** the view that most feminism is insensitive to the life experience and perspective of black, Chicana, Asian, or other nonwhite, non-middle-class or differently abled women.

**Yaogun:** authentic contemporary Chinese popular music. (In contrast to Tongsu, which is propagandistic and inauthentic).

# INDEX